A Yorkshire Lad

A Yorkshire Lad

my life with recipes

Brian Turner

with Susan Fleming

HEADLINE

To my Mum and Dad

First published in 2000
by HEADLINE BOOK PUBLISHING

First published in paperback in 2001
by HEADLINE BOOK PUBLISHING

10 9 8 7 6 5 4 3 2 1

ISBN 0 7472 7367 7

Edited by Susan Fleming
Food photography by Juliet Piddington
Home economy by Louise Pickford
Food styling by Helen Trent
Typeset by Letterpart Limited, Reigate, Surrey
Design by designsection, Frome, Somerset
Colour reproduction by Radstock Repro, Bath
Printed and bound by Rotolitho Lombarda, Italy

HEADLINE BOOK PUBLISHING
A division of Hodder Headline
338 Euston Road
London NW1 3BH

www.headline.co.uk
www.hodderheadline.com

contents

acknowledgements

Labours of love, as this book has become, cannot be achieved by oneself alone.

I have been so lucky over the years at Turner's to have the support of a loyal, friendly and dedicated staff. Everyone needs a mention, but that would be impossible, so can I just say a big thank-you to Jon Jon Lucas, the present head chef, to Charlie, John and Vince in the past, to Louise, my miracle-performing PA and manageress, not forgetting Paula and the loveable Sheila who were with me at the beginning of the book project. Also to Val Brown and Nicolas, for my continuing wine education, and to my gastronomic friends, Michael Mills, my chairman, Stuart Courtney, Tim Etchells and Michael Proudlock.

Thanks to Heather Holden-Brown for talking me into writing the book, to Lorraine Jerram for holding my hand, to Bryone Picton and all the rest of the friendly staff at Headline, who have been so encouraging. And to Juliet Piddington for the wonderful food photography and Helen Trent, the stylist.

I owe appreciation to all those people already mentioned in the book whose patience I often stretched while trying to ensure that facts, figures and dates were as near reality as humanly possible.

And of course thanks to my mentors in my second career: Paula Trafford, Richard and Judy, and the team at *This Morning*, Peter Bazalgette and Linda Clifford at *Ready Steady Cook* for the great times; and Paul Freeman and Anne Stirk for the Anglia series.

And nearly last, but certainly not least, thanks to my family – Denise, Simeon and Ben – who never see me, but who have always supported me through thick and thin, through everything I've attempted to do.

Finally, thanks to Susan Fleming for the great fun, the wine drunk, the memories revived and the plotting of the future. She took all the ingredients, stirred the pot, and made what we consider to be a fantastic dish. *Bon appétit.*

picture credits

Many people have kindly sent me photographs over the years, some of which may appear in this book; in which case: thank you. Thanks also to the following for supplying pictures: David Anderson, Chalk Farm Salvation Army: 59, 79; Anglia TV: v (bottom), 218; Anthony Blake: 135, 171; Brass Band World: 219; The Capital Hotel: 105; Ian Cartwright FBIPP (www.avalonphoto.co.uk): 11, 22, 177, 189; Steve Frak: 207; Morley High School: 30, 31; Dominic O'Neill: 106; PA: 216, 230, 237; Ross-Parry Picture Agency: 227; The Savoy Group: 45, 48, 54 (bottom), 69; Marc Stanes, Academy of Culinary Arts: 160, 231; David Steen: 181; Brooke Webb/Times Newspapers Ltd: 25

preface

Richard A. Shepherd CBE

Having known and worked with Brian since 1964, I think I am more than adequately qualified to comment on his contribution to the catering industry. We have shared a great deal of life's emotions together, both the highs and the lows, and reading his story made me realise just how close both of our experiences have been. Neither of us was treated particularly well during our training years, and we always vowed that, when we were in a position to change things, we would. Brian indeed has played a significant part in helping to clean up the image of our industry with regard to conditions and attitude, especially over the last twenty years.

Brian's achievements, as outlined in this book, demonstrate how any young person with a love of food, who is prepared to work hard, can and will succeed. We have never looked upon our work as being a job, but as a way of life, and one thing that can safely be said is that no one should go into the business looking for a soft option. You also need drive, dedication and, above all, pride.

Brian has always been a great team leader and motivator, not forgetting his most important asset, being an excellent cook. That, I believe, is the highest accolade to pay any chef. He has also become a household name recently, with the increased popularity of cookery programmes on television and in the media – and rightly so. He knows his subject thoroughly, and hopes this exposure will encourage youngsters to come into the industry. And in his role as chairman of the Academy of Culinary Arts, he works tirelessly to bring real food back into homes and schools. How can you teach somebody to cook if they do not know how to eat?

I enjoyed reading Brian's story, and at the end could only conclude that I will always be 'the little fat kid from Weston-super-Mare' and Brian will always be 'the lad from Yorkshire'…

introduction

I am told, quite reliably, that we sell more cookery books in this country *per capita* than any other country in the world. At the same time, however, the word is that people don't cook as much at home as they should and used to. This poses a great dilemma for me. Although I'm very eager to promote home cooking and families eating together, I'm also a chef and restaurateur, and it's in my professional (and financial) interest to encourage the spread of the eating-out culture. So why do chefs write books, then? I think they are trying to encourage people to be more discerning when they eat out – introducing them to new tastes, whilst not forgetting old ones – which might thereafter make them more adventurous when cooking at home.

However, it's difficult these days to publish a cookery book that is different. And why then am I entering the arena at this late stage? I have been persuaded, is the answer, despite thinking I hadn't much new to say, but I must admit I've enjoyed casting my mind back over the years, remembering people, places, stories, dishes and recipes. What this book will do, I hope, is communicate to those who are interested the possibilities there are in this industry I've loved and worked in for nearly four decades. It may be hard work and full of stress, but it's great fun as well. The book also offers an opportunity to see and appreciate – and perhaps understand a little better – the changing face of food, cooking and gastronomy in this country over those same years, which have seen more growth in style and quality than we shall ever experience again.

To be honest, I haven't written a big book before because of the fear of no one wanting to buy it. I have a nightmare vision of self-consciously presiding over a pile of pristine Brian Turner books in a bookshop, and no one but my Auntie Kathleen coming in...

part one
IN THE BEGINNING

Early Memories of Food and Other Things

When my father came back from the war in 1945, my mother and he lived with my maternal grandmother in Elland, on the outskirts of Bradford and Leeds. A year later I was born, on 7 May. I was eighteen months old when we moved to Morley, a good few miles east, on the busy road between Bradford and Leeds. This was where my father had been brought up, where his family still lived, and where he'd worked before going off to Europe, so I expect he felt he was properly coming home at last.

Yours truly, looking jolly, aged about one year.

We lived on Denshaw Drive in Morley, in a prefab, those small houses that were built after the war to boost the housing stock. Although they are roomier than the façade suggests, we were soon a bit cramped as my brother Robert was born a few months after we'd moved in. And when the twins, Gillian and Philip, arrived about three years later, we were forced to move again – but only about 800 yards down the road, to Denshaw Grove. That semi-detached house is the one I remember the best: I started school when we lived there, and I associate it with my earliest memories of food.

A Rayburn stove, a smaller version of the Aga, cooked the food and warmed the kitchen. No one in Yorkshire had central heating then unless they were very rich (I'm sure we weren't), and it was always freezing in winter. I remember coming down for breakfast in the morning: you had to summon up all your courage to get out of bed in the first place, then you raced downstairs to stand half-dressed in front of the open Rayburn while eating dripping on toast. I still enjoy that classic northern treat today, I must admit, and I think I'm quite healthy on it! We used to have 'eggy bread' (French toast) as well – slightly stale

On the beach at Hornsea in 1947, aged about eighteen months, shoes, knitted suit and all.

bread slices dipped in beaten egg and fried. The posh French name is *pain perdu*, 'lost bread', which is what you're doing, salvaging bread that might have been 'lost'. The idea still comes in handy, and I've done some great dishes over the years with a little round of French toast underneath and some caramelised fruit on top (see page 85). We even have such a dish on the menu at Turner's today. Some dishes last for ever.

My mother did most of the cooking at home, although by this time my dad was earning a living by cooking, in a local transport café. I suppose when he'd been frying-up all day, he couldn't face more of the same at home. Mum used to cook long, slow dishes in the constant heat of the Rayburn, and I remember lots of meat stews and baked vegetable meals. Meat was still fairly scarce in the early 1950s, because of course food rationing didn't end until 1954. We certainly couldn't afford prime cuts of meat, but then, as now, I truly believe that some of the cuts that are valued least today are the most delicious. Beef shin, ox cheek, many items of offal and oxtail all need long, slow cooking, but are bursting with rich meaty flavour. Mum used to put cobbler-type dumplings on top of stews, which we used to call biscuit rings. She would roll out the dumpling mixture and cut it into doughnut shapes with a hole in the centre. These would be arranged on top of the meat and baked. They didn't rise much, but were deliciously crisp on top, soft underneath. She used to cook pork chops in the oven too, the fat melting and disappearing, flavouring and moisturising the flesh. When you picked the chops up, the bones came out clean as a whistle. The meat was so tender that it ate like rillettes, but I wasn't to find that out until much later in life.

Other family favourites at the time included cheese and potato pie – just mashed potato, butter and cheese. My dad loved cheese, so he would use it a lot – and it was fairly cheap, less expensive than meat. One of his specialities, when he did cook at home, was what we called cheese and onion stew. It's a simple title, isn't it, but that's what it was. He would slice an onion, and boil it in milk, usually the top of the milk. When it was reduced and creamy, he'd add the

Pork Chop, Garlic and Apple Casserole
SERVES 4

One-pot dishes that looked after themselves in the oven were the norm, and probably still are, for people with families to cook for. This is slightly more refined, using apple and garlic. I don't think my mum had ever seen garlic...

2 tablespoons olive oil

4 x 175g (6 oz) pork loin chops

10 garlic cloves, peeled

1 large onion, peeled and finely chopped

12 plum tomatoes, skinned, seeded and chopped

300ml (½ pint) *Pork Stock* or *Vegetable Stock* (see pages 240 and 243)

6 tablespoons red wine

4 dessert apples, peeled and cored

juice of ½ lemon

25g (1 oz) unsalted butter

2 tablespoons chopped fresh parsley

Preheat the oven to 180°C/350°F/Gas 4. Heat the oil in a flameproof casserole and sauté the pork chops for 2–3 minutes on each side until browned. Remove from the casserole and set aside. Crush 2 of the garlic cloves, add to the fat in the casserole with the onion, and cook for 3–4 minutes until softened. Add the tomatoes and cook for a further 2 minutes. Return the chops to the casserole, pour in the stock and wine, and bring to the boil. Cover and place in the preheated oven for 30 minutes.

Meanwhile, put the remaining garlic cloves in a pan of cold water, bring to the boil, and simmer for 5 minutes. Refresh in cold water and drain. Use a melon baller to scoop balls from 3 of the apples. Sprinkle with lemon juice. Melt the butter in a frying pan and fry the apple balls and whole garlic cloves for 4–5 minutes. Set aside.

Finely chop the remaining apple and add to the casserole. Cook for a further 30 minutes.

Remove the casserole from the oven, and the chops from their sauce. Blend the sauce in a food processor. Return the chops to the casserole, pour over the sauce, and add the apple balls and garlic cloves. Simmer on the hob for 10 minutes until the apple is just tender. Sprinkle with parsley, then divide between 4 plates. Serve with seasonal vegetables – cauliflower in a cheese sauce would be good.

Sage Lamb Cobbler
SERVES 4

I've always loved cheese, and it must be because of the way my dad and Grandad Riley used to cook it. So I'm always looking for a way to sneak cheese into a dish. This recipe works perfectly well with or without the cheese – go on, try it!

900g (2 lb) boned neck of lamb

25g (1 oz) plain flour

2 tablespoons groundnut oil

225g (8 oz) onions, peeled and chopped

55g (2 oz) dried peas, soaked overnight (my mother would have used marrowfat)

225g (8 oz) each of carrot and swede, peeled and diced

salt and freshly ground black pepper

paprika

600ml (1 pint) *Lamb Stock (see page 240)*

Scone cobbler mixture

225g (8 oz) plain flour

1½ teaspoons baking powder

½ teaspoon chopped fresh sage (or tarragon or dill)

55g (2 oz) unsalted butter, softened

85g (3 oz) Wensleydale cheese, grated

1 medium egg, beaten

2 tablespoons milk

Preheat the oven to 160°C/325°F/Gas 3. Cut the meat into 2.5cm (1 in) pieces, dust in flour, and fry in the oil in a casserole until coloured.

Add the onion to the casserole, and fry to lightly colour, then add the soaked drained peas, diced carrot and swede. Season with salt, pepper and a pinch of paprika, then add the stock. Bring to the boil, stir, cover with a lid, and bake in the preheated oven for 2 hours. Turn the oven up to 200–220°C/400–425°F/Gas 6–7.

To make the scone cobbler, sift the flour, baking powder and a pinch of salt into a bowl. Add the sage, and rub in the butter. Mix in the grated cheese, then the beaten egg and milk until you have a soft dough. Knead, but not too much, then roll out to 1cm (½ in) thickness. Cut out into 3–4cm (1½ in) rounds. Arrange these on top of the meat in the casserole, overlapping slightly, and brush with a little more milk. Put in the hot oven, uncovered, and bake until the scone topping is cooked, about 20 minutes.

cheese off the heat and lots of pepper (it was always ready-ground pepper, as in those days in our house we didn't know about peppercorns and pepper grinders). He'd then pour it on to a piece of bread and butter, which would soak it up like a sponge. I used to make this for my supper at the Capital many years later, with the boys in the brigade looking on in horrified astonishment! (In fact I've only just heard that the Rileys were also such simple cheese cooks. Would you believe that Grandad Riley, my mother's father, had an enamel plate which he would put directly on the gas, add some milk, some cheese, and then, great horrors, some sugar? I'm told he lapped it up.) Dad would also cook potatoes and onions together. He'd sauté the onions in dripping, then put sliced potatoes in with a drop of water. A Pyrex dish would then go on top, so that the potatoes steamed. When the water evaporated, they would start to fry again, and that's when he would stick them in a hot oven to get crisp on top. Fantastic tastes, and it was probably my first experience of *pommes boulangère*, which it basically is. Fancy that, a classical French dish turns up in 1950s Yorkshire! I still make the dish at home, good with bread and butter and brown sauce.

Auntie Kathleen, my father's sister, was important in my childhood as well, and not just in a culinary sense. When Gillian and Philip were born, my mother, who had always ailed slightly, became very tired. Twin babies and two toddlers – both boys! – must have been quite a handful, so Kathleen looked after Robert and me when she could, particularly at weekends. She didn't get married until later in life, but was (and is) a true Yorkshirewoman in her warmth and generous affection – and in her baking skills. She was famous for her fairy cakes and scones, but her trifles were unforgettable. Robert and I used to vie to be Kathleen's 'best boy' on trifle days, because we would be allowed to lick out the trifle mixing-bowl. Once, on my birthday, I ran across the road to show my little friend Christine that I'd been good and had got the trifle bowl. Typically, I tripped, broke the bowl, and split my leg open. I remember sitting on the settee, almost comatose, as I had an inherent fear of my own blood (something that has remained with me to this day). Despite that, though, I'm still a great trifle fan, and am constantly trying to play with and improve on the basic recipe. Another memory is of pancakes, which my Mum used to make. We often had them just with sugar, but sometimes she would use them as an alternative to potatoes; she would pile them up in a stack, sandwiching a stew.

White Chocolate and Raspberry Trifle
SERVES 4

Trifle used to be the staple dessert of families in the 1940s and 1950s, and was quite simple. When I went to college, I encountered the addition of sherry. Now we've moved on again, and here we have the richness of white chocolate, unheard of forty years ago. This is the one where everyone cleans the plate.

175g (6 oz) white chocolate

2 medium egg yolks

25g (1 oz) caster sugar

150ml (¼ pint) milk

85ml (3 fl oz) double cream

2½ tablespoons icing sugar

4 x 4cm (1½ in) slices Swiss roll (bought or home-made)

2 tablespoons Kirsch liqueur

225g (8 oz) fresh raspberries

a few fresh mint sprigs

Put a 55g (2 oz) piece of the white chocolate in the fridge; this will make it easier to grate later. Break the remainder into small pieces.

Cream the egg yolks and caster sugar together in a large bowl. Whisk for about 2–3 minutes until the mixture is pale, thick, creamy and leaves a trail.

Pour the milk and cream into a small, heavy-based saucepan and bring to the boil. Pour on to the egg yolk mixture, whisking all the time. Pour back into the pan and place over a moderate heat. Stir the mixture with a wooden spoon until it starts to thicken and coats the back of the spoon. Add the broken-up pieces of chocolate and stir in until completely incorporated. Remove the pan from the heat and allow to cool slightly. Cover the custard with a little icing sugar and a piece of clingfilm to prevent a skin forming.

Place the Swiss roll slices in a large glass bowl and sprinkle with the Kirsch. Scatter with fresh raspberries, reserving a few for decoration. Pour the white chocolate custard over the Swiss roll and leave to set in the fridge, preferably overnight.

To serve, decorate the trifle with the reserved raspberries. Take the piece of white chocolate from the fridge and finely grate over the trifle. Finally, dust with a little icing sugar and place the mint sprigs on top. You could make individual trifles: martini glasses are good.

Pancake Stack
SERVES 4

I hope my mum forgives me, but I've updated her traditional recipe which, I have to say, stood me in good stead throughout my childhood.

Pancakes

115g (4 oz) plain flour

a pinch of salt

2 medium eggs, beaten

300ml (½ pint) milk

1 tablespoon melted unsalted butter

2 tablespoons groundnut oil for frying

Filling

450g (1 lb) stewing steak

1 tablespoon beef dripping

2 medium onions, peeled and chopped

1 garlic clove, peeled and chopped

25g (1 oz) plain flour

425ml (¾ pint) *Beef Stock* (see page 240) or 300ml (½ pint) *Beef Stock* and 125ml (4 fl oz) white wine

½ teaspoon chopped fresh thyme

2 large carrots

1 small swede

2 large potatoes

4 plum tomatoes

To serve

1 tablespoon chopped fresh parsley

2 hard-boiled medium eggs, shelled and sieved

For the filling, cut the meat into strips, like a little finger. Heat the dripping well in a saucepan. Sprinkle the meat carefully into the fat and fry to a brown colour. Do not stir or move the meat at this time. Add the chopped onion and colour golden with the meat. Add the chopped garlic, then the flour, and stir. Allow to colour slightly, stirring well. Add the stock slowly, stirring, and bring to the boil. Skim the scum from the top. Add the thyme, cover with a lid, and cook gently for 1 hour on top of the stove.

Peel and wash the other vegetables, except for the tomatoes, and cut into 5mm (¼ in) dice. Cut the tomatoes into quarters lengthways. Take the lid off the stew and add the vegetables and tomatoes. Cover and cook slowly for a further 30 minutes until the meat and vegetables are tender. Check the seasoning.

Meanwhile, for the pancake batter, sift the flour and salt together. Add the beaten

egg, then most of the milk, and beat well to remove any lumps. Add the rest of the milk and whisk well, then leave to stand for 30 minutes. Whisk well again and add the melted butter for flavour.

To cook the pancakes, heat a pancake pan, then add the oil and heat. Pour the oil back into a heatproof container. Carefully measure the batter into the hot pancake pan from the elevated near side, tilt the pan and cover the bottom with a very thin layer. Continue to heat gently. You can tell when the batter is set and ready to turn over as the top side will start to dry out. Turn over, cook to set, and remove the pancake from the pan. Repeat with the oil in the pan, the oil out of the pan, and the batter in, until you have used up all the batter. Stack the pancakes on top of each other covered with a damp cloth to keep them fresh. You need at least 12 pancakes.

To serve, using a slotted spoon, put some stew on the bottom of a soup plate. Lay a pancake on top and then another spoonful of stew. Another pancake, more stew and then a third pancake. Pour some sauce over the top of the pancake stack, and sprinkle with a mixture of the chopped parsley and sieved hard-boiled egg.

Left: *Robert and I posing in the garden in 1951: I was about five, he about three.*
Right: *About the only photograph in existence of Grandad Riley. Note his spats and watch chain, very dapper. The other two are Grandma and me.*

We visited the rest of the family quite often, usually on Sundays. Gran, my mother's mother, lived in Elland, and we would drive across to see her. (I still remember the excitement when Dad brought home his first car in the early 1950s, a light-coloured Ford Prefect, and our first black and white television set – memories probably shared by most people the same age as myself.) She lived in Back Katherine Street, so you had to go round the back alley to get in, past the outside lavatory and the boiler room where she did the washing in a copper. Grandad Riley had died when we were quite young, in 1951, so I don't remember him much; he had been married before, to a lady called Lily, after whom my mother was named. (His name was Ben, and one of my own sons in turn is named for him.) Auntie Betty, Mum's younger sister, still lived at home with her mother, and next door but three was Mum's younger aunt, our great-aunt, whom we called Aunt Ann. It was Aunt Ann who taught me to play cards, and was famous (to us children at least) for drinking her tea noisily from the saucer – she never drank from a cup.

The Rileys were Wesleyan Methodists, so didn't drink. They weren't complete teetotallers, and I suspect they had a nip at Christmas, when we had wonderful family gatherings, days packed with eating and parlour games. Forming the core of Elland Riley parties were all the above, plus Auntie Edna and Uncle Harry and their children, Selwyn and Eileen, my cousins, Mum's brother, Donald, his wife Auntie Joan, her relations and Harry's relations. My father might go and have a few drinks with friends in Elland while the huge leg of pork was roasting. After the roast there would be a huge selection of pies, trifles and puddings, as both the Rileys and Turners loved desserts. There always seemed to be an argument about who'd had the most cream: we were all great cream lovers. Most Sundays, on the way to Elland, we'd go through Batley, across the Birstall crossroads, up the hill, and stop at a dairy attached to a dairy farm. We'd have ice cream made with full-fat milk, a taste I've rarely experienced since, sadly.

I never knew my paternal grandparents very well: the only time I saw my dad cry was the night he told me his father had died (until my mum died, years later, in 1983). The Turners weren't nearly so family orientated as the Rileys, and we saw them much less, even though they lived in Morley. Neither did we have so many family gatherings. I saw Aunt Lorna and her children occasionally, and I saw Dad's Aunt Edna quite often, as she was the dinner lady at the grammar school I went to.

We used to be mob-handed on holiday as well, taking someone with us, either Auntie Betty and Grandma, or Auntie Kathleen, to help my mother. Occasionally we went to the west coast, but mostly we'd go to the east coast. I remember Blackpool, Scarborough, Lytham St Anne's, Bridlington, but particularly Filey. I used to love Filey Brigg, a huge headland with waves lashing against the rocks, where I used to fish. We stayed in caravans or in fishermen's cottages, self-catering on the east coast, bed and breakfast in Blackpool, although don't ask me why. I can only assume it was due to connections

Paddling at Bridlington, in seaside uniform of shorts, shirt and pullover, just in case it was cold...

Above: *I've loved cricket since I was very small; here I am, anticipating the next delivery on the beach at Blackpool. Note the wicket-keeper's headgear!*

Right: *What did I say about holidays in England? Here we are enjoying the summer in Filey, hats, coats and all. From left, Mrs Gray, my mum's friend, with Gillian, Auntie Annie with Philip, Grandma Riley, me, Robert, Mum (kneeling) and Dad (fast asleep).*

of the Rileys, as Uncle Donald and Auntie Joan used to turn up every now and again. We stayed next door to the Derby Baths, where we used to swim.

I associate small steak puddings with Blackpool, and I still make individual ones today: I cut the meat a bit smaller, cook it off, then encase it in suet pastry. Fish and chips was a constant treat, at home and away, and my dad told me one or two golden rules about our British national dish that I've never forgotten. You must only buy from a shop with a queue, never one that was empty (if there was nobody there, you'd want to know why). By the time you'd reached the front of a queue, the fish and chips would have been fried fresh for you. You'd buy enough to take home, but a fish to eat on the way. The same applied to a drink in pubs. It always amazed me that my father, going into a pub to place his order for the six or seven of us, would order a pint for himself first, and then find out what all of us wanted. It seemed rather rude to me, but it meant by the time the order was filled, he'd finished that first drink and could have another. There was

a great deal of logic in my father, and there is still, in a man who reached his eightieth birthday in 1999.

It's funny how things that are going to be important in future life seem to imprint on your consciousness very early on. My memories of childhood are overlaid with the foods I ate – as well, of course, as the usual milestones such as starting school (I didn't like the school dinners, although I enjoyed the companionship), those yearly holidays, family gatherings, church-going... Smells, though, are very evocative, and I think my olfactory memory has contributed to what I do and am today. (Perhaps that's why God gave me such a large conk!) Where we lived in Morley was at the bottom end of the town, perhaps only 800 yards from open fields. Nowadays, of course, it's all built up, but Peter Lane and the Valley were

Top: *A family group taken in 1954 at Grandma Riley's house. It was cousin Christine's first birthday. At the back are Auntie Joan, Uncle Donald and Mum; Grandma Riley and Auntie Annie are sitting; and the children from the left are Robert, Christine, Gillian, Philip and me.*

Above: *Mum with Robert and me in 1951, plus the new arrivals, Gillian and Philip. Quite a handful!*

Another family group, taken in about 1955, on a visit to Elland.

wonderful for us when we were growing up. We played football, cricket, ran races, trekked across fells and dales, and my love of birdwatching dates from that time. But the smells of Morley are what remain with me. On the right-hand side of the valley there was a gasworks, which burned coal and coke to produce gas – and an awful smell. Over on the other side was Jackman's Farm, which still exists today; this area was and is the foremost rhubarb-growing centre in Europe. At certain times of the year they would heavily manure the rhubarb fields, to enrich the soil and encourage growth. And then there was the dripping works, owned by Green's, while another part of the family owned a butcher's shop in Morley. They would render beef and pork fat down for dripping and lard, but they also made sausages and raised pork pies. So, depending on the day, and which way the wind was blowing, the Morley air was imbued with rotten-eggs gas, ripe manure, or roast beef or pork! A good sense of smell is important to every cook, and my nose was trained well at a very early stage. Somehow I still miss that combination of smells, even though some were obnoxious, as all we seem to get these days, especially in London, is petrol fumes and other modern-day nasties.

Rhubarb Plate Pie
SERVES 4

It strikes me that the plate pie – made on an old enamel plate – is a phenomenon of the north of England. And as I obviously come from Yorkshire, rhubarb has to be my favourite, but all kinds of fruit work just as well.

55g (2 oz) unsalted butter, melted

450g (1 lb) young rhubarb, peeled

finely chopped peel of 1 orange, blanched for a few minutes

½ teaspoon chopped fresh root ginger

115g (4 oz) caster sugar

egg wash (2 medium egg yolks and a little water)

icing sugar

Shortcrust pastry

175g (6 oz) plain flour

a pinch of salt

85g (3 oz) unsalted butter

25g (1 oz) lard

about 2 tablespoons water

To make the pastry, put the flour in a bowl or on a work surface, and add the salt. With the fats at room temperature, rub into the flour until the consistency of breadcrumbs. Make a well in the centre, and add enough water to allow the pastry to come together. Leave to chill for at least 30 minutes.

Preheat the oven to 240°C/475°F/Gas 9. Divide the pastry in half and roll out one half into a 25cm (10 in) circle on a floured board. Brush a 25cm (10 in) pie plate with melted butter, lay the rolled pastry on it, and trim around the edges. Brush with more melted butter.

Cut the rhubarb into 2.5–5cm (1–2 in) sticks, wash and shake nearly dry, then put into the middle of the plate. Sprinkle with the blanched orange peel and the ginger, then the caster sugar to taste (depending on the sourness of the rhubarb). Roll out the other half of the pastry to cover the top and cut a 5cm (2 in) circle out of the middle. Wet the edges of the base pastry with egg wash, then lay the second piece on top. Push the edges together to seal. Trim and decorate the edges by pinching with a thumb and finger. Brush the top with egg wash and sprinkle with icing sugar. Bake in the preheated oven for 10 minutes, then for 20 minutes at 220°C/425°F/Gas 7 to cook the fruit through completely.

When cooked, sprinkle with icing sugar and serve with clotted cream or crème Chantilly (whipped cream, with sugar and vanilla seeds).

Head Chef at the Transport Café

I became a head chef at the tender age of twelve, all due to my dad. Before he had gone off to war, he'd worked as a designer in the Co-op, in the fruit and vegetable section. He would chalk the daily signs – 'Oranges from Tangier, special today' – and draw a cartoon orange head saying 'Come in and buy me!'

He was really quite artistic, although he didn't take it any further. It may have been this food connection that led him to choose the Catering Corps during the war, and I suppose that's what drew him into the food business thereafter – and thus me, too.

He worked at first with a chap called Tim who had a transport café in Hunslet, opposite the Regal Cinema in Low Road. I was too young to help much then, apart from cleaning, but we kids had some good times playing in the backyard or, when the weather was bad, going to the Priestleys' house up the way, to keep warm in front of their huge coal fire. They looked after us as if we were family, which is one of my abiding memories of that Yorkshire childhood. Family was everything in those days, everyone was your aunt or uncle, and there was a link of affection, of shared hardship, however tenuous that link actually was. You could walk around safely, leave your doors open, and we kids were never under threat with so many 'relations' to look out for us.

With Grandma Riley in Scarborough, shortly before I became head chef of my dad's transport café.

Although it was a poor area, people used to love to walk, talk and eat together. I grew up saying 'Hello' to everyone I met – something that was looked on as a bit odd when I later went to London! But I still do it today in the early mornings while waiting for deliveries, greeting passers-by and neighbours in Chelsea which, after all, is really just like a village.

Dad eventually bought the café from Tim, but he could only afford it because it was in such a rundown area. In fact, the site was compulsorily purchased after a few years. The Government said, 'Sorry, we're going to give you 2/6d and you're going to have to like it or lump it.' It was on the main road between Wakefield and Leeds, on the Wakefield Prison side. People used to regularly escape from the prison in the local smog which, in the 1950s, had the reputation of being the densest and most regular in Europe. It was as bad as a London pea-souper. When the smog came down, convicts would come over the top, go to the main road, or just off it, and they'd break into the café to try and find some cigarettes or cash, or to get something to eat. We didn't have a telephone at home in those days, but we'd often get a knock on the door – 'There's been a call from the police in Leeds. The café has been broken into.' One of my earliest memories is of walking through that wall of smog with a torch, the full eight miles to the café, while my Dad drove at a snail's pace behind. The damage was usually minor, but it was irritating, and of course I found it all quite exciting!

We had a few happy years there, then Dad bought a café in the Swan Buildings, next to The Swan public house in Hunslet. It was a bit nearer home and, although still in an area ripe for reclamation, he made a success of it. It was there on Saturdays that I used to cook. The four of us would go in with Dad at about seven in the morning, which would give Mum a chance to clean the house and relax. We'd all have jobs to do: the twins would help clear the tables and wash up, I cooked, and Robert would cut the bread and breadcakes (large sweetened baps, also known as Yorkshire teacakes). Annie Denton, Dad's right-hand woman, would be there to take the orders and serve, while the other four ladies, including Mary Baxter, would have the day off. Dad was the general supervisor, checking that all was well in every area, and he also answered the phones. We used to do a lot of takeaways for the local factories and mills; people who had been working since about six in the morning used to want their 'breakfast' at about half-past ten or eleven. Dad had to ask whether they wanted fried breadcake, plain breadcake, buttered breadcake, or white bread (no brown in those days), and then the filling required. Robert was in charge of wrapping the breadcake sandwiches in paper bags torn from a hook on the wall, and was a dab hand at twisting the bags closed at the corners. The bags then went into a box, and were ready when someone came in. 'Order for Jackson's Mill.' Woe betide Dad or me, or the hapless delivery person, if the order was wrong.

Saturdays were always very busy. It was so cold when we first opened up, we'd have to park our bums on the storage heaters to get warm. But once we started working, particularly at the old blue-enamelled Benham stove, the whole place

Turner's English Breakfast
SERVES 4

Thanks to my dad, if anyone can cook breakfast, I can. I'm old enough to remember the days when possibly the only claim to fame we had gastronomically in this country was the good old English breakfast. And the great thing about a breakfast is, it's wonderful at breakfast time, satisfying at lunch time, and if you're in the mood, a rarity, it works well at night.

1 x 420g (15 oz) tin plum tomatoes, or 4 fresh tomatoes, halved

1 x 420g (15 oz) tin baked beans

salt and freshly ground black pepper

8 good pork sausages

8 good back bacon rashers

lard and bacon fat for frying

2 large potatoes, boiled and skinned

4 medium open-cap field mushrooms

4 slices medium-sliced white bread

8 medium eggs

Make sure you have enough pots and pans and stove-top space. Put the tinned tomatoes and beans in small pans, and heat gently. Add some salt and pepper to the tomatoes, and let their juices gently reduce. Start the sausages and bacon frying in fat in separate pans – or grill them if you prefer a slightly healthier option. Slice the potatoes and fry until golden and crisp in a little more fat, preferably using that rendered out of the bacon (always keep bacon fat, strained, in a little pot by the cooker – the flavour is wonderful in so much cooking). Fry the mushrooms and the bread in very hot bacon fat, but on one side only: that way neither of them will absorb too much fat. Grill the fresh tomatoes if using, just enough to heat them through. Finally, when everything is nearly ready (keep warm in a low oven if necessary), fry the eggs. My dad used to spend a lot of time with a spatula, flicking fat over the egg because he, like me, thought there was nothing worse than a cold yolk.

To serve, arrange the breakfast components on hot plates, with the eggs on top of triangles of fried bread. Lift the plum tomatoes carefully out of the reduced juices with a slotted spoon. Have toast handy, and some brown sauce (tomato sauce if you must) is essential.

Tomato Ketchup

This is an up-market version of my dad's tomato dip. And why make your own tomato ketchup, you may ask? Well, I promise you, once you've got the hang of this, and realise how simple and tasty it is, you'll know the answer.

12 large ripe plum tomatoes
6 tablespoons red wine vinegar
4 tablespoons unrefined caster sugar
a dash each of Tabasco and Worcestershire sauces

Immerse the tomatoes in boiling water for a minute, then remove from the water and take off the skin. It should slip off easily. Remove and discard the seeds, and finely chop the tomato flesh.

Bring the red wine vinegar and sugar to the boil, stirring until the sugar has dissolved. Add the tomato flesh to the vinegar and boil quickly until the sauce becomes smooth. Remove from the heat, and add the Tabasco and Worcestershire sauces. Leave to cool.

Sausage Stew
SERVES 4–6

Sausages have always appeared regularly in my life – those wonderful sausage sandwiches Dad used to make, Ernie Ward showing me how to make them when I was a young lad. And just recently, along with Derek Thompson, I barbecued some sausages at Newmarket for Channel Four racing – the 'sport of kings' (and Yorkshiremen). At the end of the day, this is one of the simplest and best recipes – and what's more it's great for using up leftover sausages.

900g (2 lb) best pork and leek sausages

2 tablespoons groundnut oil

1 medium onion, peeled and sliced

1 medium red pepper, seeded and cut into thin strips

1 medium green pepper, seeded and cut into thin strips

1 tablespoon harissa (a hot mixed spice powder or paste)

600ml (1 pint) *Brown Chicken Stock* (see page 243)

1 x 400g (14 oz) tin chickpeas, drained and rinsed

4 plum tomatoes, quartered

4 slices white bread, made into breadcrumbs

55g (2 oz) Parmesan, freshly grated

Preheat the oven to 180°C/350°F/Gas 4.

Slowly colour the sausages in half the oil in an ovenproof frying pan. Put into the preheated oven and cook slowly for 20 minutes. Take out and leave to cool.

Meanwhile, prepare the vegetables. Sauté the onion and red and green pepper in the remaining oil, allowing to colour slightly. Add the harissa and stir in well, then add the stock, bring up to the boil and cook for 20 minutes on top of the stove.

Meanwhile, preheat the oven to 200°C/400°F/Gas 6.

Cut the cooled sausages into 3 pieces each. Add these to the stock and vegetables, and bring to the boil. Add the drained chickpeas and tomato quarters to the stew, and bring back to the boil again. Pour into an ovenproof serving dish. Mix the breadcrumbs with the grated cheese, and sprinkle well over the top of the stew. Bake in the preheated oven for 15 minutes or until well coloured on top. Serve with mashed potatoes and green vegetables.

steamed up with the production-line cooking (were we the inventors of what I imagine it must be like cooking in the McDonald's of today?). It was the classic English breakfast, consisting of fried bacon, pork sausages, baked beans, tomatoes (always tinned in those days), fried mushrooms, fried potatoes, fried bread and a couple of fried eggs – all cooked in bacon fat mixed with a little lard. The customers would come in, and Annie would take the order and shout it back. I always had to make sure there was enough bacon and sausage cooked in advance to cope, and that the beans and tomatoes were warm, but it was all very fresh, and the eggs were done to individual order. Sometimes it was so hectic, I just fried eggs for all I was worth, flipping them out of the pan and on to a plate (a skill I was to repeat several years later when I was 'egg chef' at Butlins!).

On the tables there were bottles of brown sauce and tomato ketchup. Dad used to make his own equivalent of ketchup, handy on breadcake breakfast bacon or sausage sandwiches, by reducing chopped tinned tomatoes (yet again) with salt and pepper only – there was no garlic in those days! – until they were quite syrupy. He would take a breadcake, cut it in half horizontally and fry the cut side as he would for fried bread in bacon-flavoured fat. He'd then dip it in his tomato sauce and add the chosen topping, for bacon and tomato dip sandwich, sausage and tomato dip sandwich. He used to fry the sausages in advance, cool them and then cut them in half and fry them again when he got an order. I quite often went to Ernie Ward's, which was just across from the café, and watch them making sausages – mincing the meats in an old-fashioned chopper-mincer, and linking them in natural skins – then I'd take them back to the café. Another Dad speciality was releasing the sausagemeat from the skins and making cakes with them, with mashed potato, something I still do today – and that home-made tomato ketchup is an absolutely *essential* accompaniment!

During the week, Dad would serve much the same, but would offer a roast or other daily special as well. Inevitably, roast beef and Yorkshire pudding would appear, but he had an odd way of cooking the beef. Each day he would boil a piece of topside until cooked through, then leave it to cool. The day after, he would put the cooked meat in the oven with some fat to roast through until hot. It had a nice flavour, but it was more like rillettes in texture, and always looked grey because it had been boiled. But the boys in the transport café liked it, with a good brown gravy on top, and accompanied by Yorkshire pudding,

In March 1999, I proved that my early breakfast training at Dad's transport café was invaluable. A few other top chefs and I competed to feed four builders (rather than lorry-drivers), and my traditional English breakfast was voted the best!

vegetables and potatoes. I grew up thinking that roast beef was boiled beef that was then roasted. The cold roast beef was used in sandwiches, or in a beef and potato plate pie, another of Dad's specialities. Nothing was wasted. All the food that Dad served was plain, humble even, but it was *good* food. The fish was always fresh and was freshly cooked to order; he would not tolerate poor quality. As he wouldn't in his 'workers': I once burned myself quite badly, and he smacked my head rather than sympathise, because I had been so careless. The only thing I didn't like on the café menu was mushy peas. Sorry, but this Yorkshireman doesn't care for them, and never has.

On those hard-working Saturday mornings, we'd close at about eleven. Annie would go home, and Dad would leave the cleaning up to us four. He'd close the door behind him, locking us inside, and go off to the pub next door for half an hour. We had to wash and dry the dishes, mop the floor, clean the tables, put the chairs up. Hard labour perhaps – and we were all under twelve! – but we got our pocket money out of it (and it was more than I would have got delivering papers). In the afternoons, Robert and I might go to football

Fish and Chips
SERVES 4

My dad's fish and chips were adequate, but as life's gone on, I've had some fantastic fish and chips. It may seem strange that a man who's experienced all that I've experienced gastronomically can eulogise about fish and chips more than anything, but they're part of that eating past that always stays with you. I love finger food, and I'm more than happy to eat fish and chips without a knife and fork. Some of the best fish and chips I've ever had have come from back-street shops in villages and towns in Yorkshire; they simply offered 'fish and chips', not even specifying whether cod or haddock. But, consistently, my dear friend Norman Lodge, who runs the Mermaid in Morley, supplies the best for me. I'm fairly certain the trick is in the batter (he won't give me the recipe), and the dripping he uses.

675g (1½ lb) King Edward potatoes

sunflower oil for frying

4 x 225g (8 oz) boned and skinned haddock fillets

Batter

115g (4 oz) plain flour

2 teaspoons salt

125ml (4 fl oz) malt vinegar

85ml (3 fl oz) water

To make the batter, put the flour in a bowl with the salt. Whisk in the vinegar and water and leave to rest.

Peel and cut the potatoes evenly into long chip shapes, 5mm (¼ in) square in thickness. Dry them well. Meanwhile gently heat the oil in a heavy-based frying pan to 185°C/365°F. Slowly cook the chips in the oil to allow them to cook through but not colour as yet. Take out and drain. Increase the heat of the oil to 200°C/400°F, and remove the wire basket from the hot oil if you used one; this is not necessary for the fish.

Dip the fish fillets in the batter, allowing excess to drip off quickly, then drop into the pan of hot oil. Allow the fish to sink to the bottom; it will start to float as it sets and cooks. When it is a deep golden brown, take out, drain and keep hot.

Keep the fat hot, and put the chips into the wire basket and into the oil. Cook until crisp and golden brown. Take out, drain, and serve immediately with the fish.

with Dad to watch Leeds United, of course, whom I still enthusiastically support. (At one point a few years ago, when the future of Leeds was in the balance, it was mooted by one in the inner sanctum that I might be asked to become a director. Every boy's dream. I held my breath for three months, but sadly it never happened. However, you never know...) In the evenings at home, there always seemed to be an episode of *Quatermass* on television. We children weren't allowed to watch it, sent out into the kitchen, but 'He's got the mark!' is a phrase still guaranteed to send a shiver up the spine of anyone approximately the same age as me.

Those early stints in the café taught me an incredible amount that has stood me in good stead throughout the years. It was the first time I realised how important it was to give customers what they wanted. Sometimes it can still be difficult: how do you define exactly what someone means when they say they want their steak 'medium'? (a paint colour chart might be useful!) But when a couple of six-foot lorry drivers demanded to be fed, you soon learned to get their order right, to serve it to them hot, and to serve it to them fast. That sense of timing has been an essential part of my training, but it was the heat, the excitement, the pace that really attracted me. They say, 'If you can't stand the heat, get out of the kitchen.' Well, I was enticed, excited and enchanted by that hot, smelly, sweaty environment, and I remain so to this day.

School and Other Influences

I joined the Salvation Army when I was at junior school. I have to admit that it wasn't actually because of religious conviction, but because I was in pursuit of a girl (and I was still under twelve)! Tony Aveyard was my best mate in those days, and he and his sister Pat, who was three years older, belonged to the Salvationists. It seemed to me the only way to get to see her. We children attended church already, with Auntie Kathleen, who was a Zion Methodist (my parents and paternal grandparents had stopped going). When I announced my intention of leaving the Methodist Church and joining the Salvation Army, Mum insisted that all four of us join at the same time, and so we did. Throughout my entire teens and early twenties I was a member, and

In my Morley Grammar School uniform in about 1958. I look happy enough, don't I?

I support them today, although I have no time to attend meetings regularly. (The 'intemperance' of my job sits awkwardly with the Army but, because of its influence, I didn't drink in any serious way until at least my late twenties.) My brother Robert in Australia is still actively involved, though, some thirty-odd years later. And all this came about because of Pat Aveyard. When I did a 'first kiss/love' type of programme with James Whale a few years ago, Pat's aunt heard it and phoned Pat, now in Canada, to tell her. We're planning to meet again some time in the year 2000.

They were a good bunch of mates in the Salvation Army. We used to go to the youth club on a Friday night where I remember very competitive table tennis championships, and for pie and pea dinners on a Saturday night after band practice. I still hanker after those pies, some of them raised pork pies, some plate pies – mincemeat, onion and potatoes on an enamel plate with pastry on top. I also remember experimenting with smoking when I was eleven: on the way to Salvation Army meetings, I would buy two Woodbines and a packet of mints, have the smoke first, then the mint to kill the smell and taste! Robert and I were members of the Salvation Army junior band. I played the tenor horn, and occasionally the bass drum on the march. I was keen, but not particularly talented; Robert was always the better musician. We also went on lots of Sunday School trips. I remember once going to Morecambe, which has a very long beach and lots of mud flats. It's actually rather dangerous, with sinking sands and a tide which comes racing in at high speed. My brother Philip's foot got stuck in the mud, and when he pulled it out, he'd lost his sandal. We cried all the way back in the coach because we were so scared of what Mum would say. I don't quite know why, as Mum wasn't that kind of person, she was very kind and gentle, but we Turners have a habit of displaying our emotions in tears. *Bambi* still gets to me!

Brian Turner's Pork Pie

MAKES 2 x 10CM (4 IN) PIES

Pork pies for me, along with fish and chips and roast beef and Yorkshire pudding, are stalwarts of home comfort food. I love to eat them hot, dipped in HP sauce.

Filling

350g (12 oz) pork with some fat, minced

115g (4 oz) smoked streaky bacon, finely chopped

½–1 teaspoon chopped fresh sage, to taste

½–1 teaspoon freshly grated nutmeg, to taste

½–1 teaspoon Worcestershire sauce, to taste

salt and freshly ground black pepper

Pastry

280g (10 oz) plain flour

½ teaspoon salt

115g (4 oz) lard

75ml (2½ fl oz) boiling water

To finish

2 gelatine leaves, soaked in water to soften

150ml (¼ pint) *Pork Stock* (see page 240)

Preheat the oven to 200°C/400°F/Gas 6. To make the filling, simply mix all the ingredients together. Season well.

To make the hot water crust pastry, sift the flour and salt into a bowl. Add the lard to the boiling water and allow to melt. Add the flour to the lard and water, and beat with a wooden spoon until the dough comes together. This must be used whilst hot, so work quickly. Cut a piece of about 55g (2 oz) from the dough, and keep warm. Cut the remainder of the dough in half. Roll these pieces into balls, and shape into pie cases using something like the base of a 10cm (4 in) ramekin. Press this into the ball of dough, and mould the dough evenly up the sides. Allow to set and then remove the ramekin.

Fill the two pie cases with filling. Cut the remaining dough in two, and roll each out to a circle for the top of the pies. Brush the edges with water, lay the lids on top, then seal and crimp the edges using your fingers. Make a small hole in the middle of the pastry lids. Bake the pies in the preheated oven for 20 minutes, then reduce the oven heat to 180°C/350°F/Gas 4 and bake for about another hour. Remove from the oven. Melt the gelatine in the hot stock. Pour this mixture carefully through the holes in the centre of the pie tops (you may not need it all). Leave to cool and set overnight.

Morley Grammar School in about 1960. It's now known as Morley High School.

I wasn't a very successful sportsman – our junior soccer team once lost ten nil when I was the goalkeeper – but throughout the years I used to cycle a lot at the weekends, up to East Ardsley, just past the gasworks and the rhubarb centre. On summer evenings I used to trainspot as well, cycling some thirty-odd miles to Doncaster just to see the trains. Fancy me, a 'trainspotter'! Grammar school was fairly mundane (certainly in a food sense), but it was good to be part of one of the many gangs. A crucial turning-point in my life came in the third year. You had to make a choice: to take woodwork or metalwork if you were a boy, needlework or domestic science if you were a girl. Three of us boys decided to take what was then a very revolutionary step, and opted for domestic science. We were teased mercilessly about our sexual inclinations – cooking wasn't considered a very masculine thing to do – until the other lads realised that we had stolen a march on them, as we were working alongside the girls all the time! The other two, Eddie Hughes and John Shooter, dropped out after a year to concentrate on their GCEs; I persevered, and passed my GCE O-level with flying colours. (I'm ashamed to say I failed the only two my mother cared about, English Language and English Literature.)

The main inspiration behind that success was my domestic science teacher, a thin, committed, enthusiastic, bespectacled spinster called Elsie Bibby. She had taught a few boys before, and one in particular was her hero. The late great Michael Smith, an inspiration in his turn to a whole generation of food writers and cooks, had learned much of his business from Elsie Bibby, and he was held up as an example of what could be achieved to all who came after him in her class. When I arrived on the scene, Michael Smith was writing a cookery column for the *Yorkshire Post*, and also ran a small restaurant/demonstration kitchen called, appropriately enough, The Kitchen, in Leeds. Miss Bibby took the class to see Michael demonstrate once, and he killed and cooked a live lobster in front of us. The girls thought it barbaric, but I thought it gastronomically fantastic: a whole new world was opening up in front of me.

Anyway, for that whole first year, Elsie Bibby would talk about nothing else but Michael Smith, but then in the second year I took his place. In other cooking classes, the teacher would wander around to see who had produced the best result for the others to look at, but I'm afraid Elsie Bibby always said without hesitation, 'Let's look at Brian's, it's bound to be the best.' This didn't do me much good with the girls, but convinced me of where my future lay. My dad was in catering, Miss Bibby was all for it, so I elected, when I left school at sixteen, to go to the Leeds College of Food Technology.

The staff at Morley Grammar School in April 1959, the year I took up cooking. My first mentor, Miss Elsie Bibby, is in the front row, fourth from the right.

Catering College

I was in the forefront of fashion when I was at college. Note the quiff, the thin tie and the winkle-pickers…I don't think so!

The Leeds College of Food Technology is in Calverley Street, just below the university and opposite Leeds Infirmary. There was an annexe in Gower Street, an old Victorian school which the college had taken over. (I hear it's a Chinese restaurant now.) I started in September 1962, taking a basic catering course, two years of City and Guilds 150 and 151 (as they were then). On reflection, it was an interesting time to be embarking on a cooking career. The first edition of what was to become the *Gault et Millau* guide appeared in France in 1962, and the *Sunday Times* started publishing its colour magazine, which was so influential about food, then and over the years since.

I used to drive with Dad from home to the café in the Swan Buildings, up at about six, there by about seven. I'd make myself some breakfast. Every morning I had fried bacon, egg, sausage, baked beans and so on, whatever I fancied, and a cup of tea and a look at the paper, and then I'd catch a bus from Hunslet into Leeds, to be in college by about nine. That hearty breakfast was a good start to the day, primarily because it meant I didn't really need to eat at lunchtime. They did have a refectory at college, and I was given some money for meals, but I tended to save it for other things (of that, more below). Once I got to know my way around, I just used to go into the centre of Leeds and eat fruit in a park in the summer, or wander in winter through the centrally heated rooms of Schofield's, the up-market departmental store (which had an *à la carte* restaurant, noted in the *Good Food Guide* in 1963). I always remember, with the arrogance of youth, how I used to look askance at the ladies demonstrating Morphy Richards and

Kenwood machines in the kitchen appliance department. How embarrassing, I thought, I'm a *real* cook, but they've got to stand there and sell machines to make a living. How are the mighty fallen, and made to eat their words! Now, some forty odd years later, I'm doing much the same things, demonstrating and, if not selling, *encouraging* the selling of pots and pans! But I love it, it's a great way of meeting the public, and Meyer products are such good quality.

Mum and Dad were very proud of the fact that I was at college, particularly Mum, for being at college then was like attending university today. But when asked what I was studying, Mum would be less forthcoming, glossing over the facts. Although Dad was a cook, I don't think that she really liked the idea of me wanting to be a chef. It's actually, of course, only in the last twenty or so years, that 'chef' has become a profession that lots of kids aspire to. In the early 1960s, there were no such things as 'celebrity chefs'. Going to catering college at that time taught you the ground rules which you could then base a career on as you chose: go to a typical British restaurant or hotel restaurant and stick, or move onwards and upwards, in the French system, aiming for all-round expertise and the chef's toque. The latter was for me. And, as the years passed, I think Mum began to appreciate what I was achieving and was happier about it. Sadly, she died before she could share in the fun and successes of the last few years. She looked after us so unselfishly during our childhood; I would have loved to have had time to treat her to a few more pleasures in return.

The course was fairly straightforward. I don't have very clear recollections of my first day, but I do remember my amazement at the sheer size of everything. I'd been used to domestic ovens only, and the enormity of the commercial ovens at college was awe-inspiring. In the first year I took several beginners' classes – in baking, general cooking, hygiene, waiting on table, management and accounting. There was a demonstration theatre, where they would show us how to prepare a joint of meat, for instance. This class would be followed by another in which we would work with an individual piece of meat to reproduce the process. There was enough money around then to enable us to do that; nowadays, I'm afraid, catering students have to share pieces of meat, or they have to pretend, as the money available to colleges is so tight – and this despite the current popularity of cooking as a profession! I wasn't very interested in the management and theory sides, but it was lovely to get into a kitchen and cook, and to be able to order the ingredients. It gave me a great sense of satisfaction, too, to wear my hat and whites. Baking was my favourite in the early days (though not today!), and we had to do a separate baking and pastry course. The bakery suite was on the next floor up, and we made fruit and cream tarts and pies, which were put on sale downstairs. You could actually mark your own box, and buy it to take home, which I quite often used to do (I mentioned my family's love of cream, didn't I?). I'm not so skilled at pastry these days, but I still like to make tarts which are heavily influenced by the basics I learned then.

In the second year, these same subjects were taken to the intermediate stage, and you actually took part in a production kitchen. I loved this, as it was my first experience, after the transport café, of cooking for the public. In a production kitchen, the group of students is split into two parts, waiting and cooking, and you would alternate weekly. In the theory lessons on the morning before, you would plan the menu, the order of work, the individual duties, and then do the buying. The next morning, half of us would cook the meal and half would serve it. The production kitchen was open to the public, which helped finance the college, and gave lots of people a jolly good, cheap meal. This happens in all colleges these days, but wasn't common in the early 1960s, and Leeds was quite advanced in that respect. (Interestingly, the College of Technology restaurant in Portsmouth, doing much the same as Leeds, was mentioned several times in no less a publication than the *Good Food Guide* in the late 1950s, early 1960s.)

I met a good team of people at college, including my wife, Denise, and many of us are still in touch today. John White was a little older, as he had been working before coming to college, so he was a sort of natural leader and we all gravitated to him. He was actually going out with Denise in that first year, although he switched to Margaret Adamson in the second, leaving the field a little clearer for me. I, meanwhile, remained besotted with Geraldine Lees, a tall, rather posh blonde from Acomb, by York, until she met someone five years older, and far more intellectually sound. (A few years ago, she reintroduced herself to me after a demo; she's running a family hotel in Scotland.) Denise and I still see Barbara and Joan, my cohorts in a singing group called the BJs (after Barbara, Brian and Joan). Ruthie Wainwright we still see, who married Martin Wray; he was the son of a vicar, became an ardent communist at college, then reverted to the church. There was also Neil Mathieson, whom I have lost

Yorkshire Curd Tartlets
MAKES 8 x 5CM (2 IN) TARTLETS

When we did our pastry classes at college, we always seemed to be making tarts of one kind or another. Yorkshire curd tart – which is very like a cheesecake – is traditionally made into an actual tart, not tartlets as here, and the recipe usually includes currants, not sultanas.

Pastry	Filling
225g (8 oz) plain flour	225g (8 oz) curd cheese
a pinch of salt	55g (2 oz) unrefined caster sugar
1 tablespoon unrefined caster sugar	1 teaspoon grated lemon rind
115g (4 oz) unsalted butter, diced	2 medium eggs, separated
1 tablespoon water	2 tablespoons sultanas
1 medium egg yolk	1 tablespoon melted unsalted butter
	a pinch of freshly grated nutmeg
	icing sugar for sifting

Preheat the oven to 220°C/425°F/Gas 7.

For the pastry, mix the flour, salt and sugar in a bowl, then rub in the diced butter until the texture of breadcrumbs. Make a well in the centre, and add the water and egg yolk. Mix to a smooth pastry consistency, and leave to rest for half an hour. When rested, roll out and use to line 8 x 5cm (2 in) tart tins.

For the filling, mix the cheese, sugar, lemon rind and egg yolks together. Stir in the sultanas, melted butter and nutmeg. Whisk the egg whites until stiff, and fold carefully into the filling mixture.

Prick the pastry in the tart tins, using a fork, then fill with the mixture. Smooth the tops. Bake in the preheated oven for 10 minutes, then reduce the temperature to 180°C/350°F/Gas 4 and continue to bake for another 25 minutes. Remove from the oven, and leave to cool. Take out of the tart tins. Sift some icing sugar over the top to serve.

Fruity Bread Pudding with Rum Sauce
SERVES 6

Bread pudding was another of those northern 'delicacies' that I grew up with, but didn't learn how to make until at catering college. I think I was seventeen before I realised, thanks to my mum, that rum sauce didn't have to have lumps in it. So now, combining the two, and adapting a classic Norfolk recipe given to me by cookery writer Mary Norwak, this is the ultimate.

8 slices medium white bread

300ml (½ pint) milk

350g (12 oz) mixed dried fruit

55g (2 oz) mixed chopped peel

1 eating apple, peeled and grated

3 tablespoons soft dark brown sugar

2 tablespoons dark marmalade

40g (1½ oz) self-raising flour

2 medium eggs, beaten

juice of 1 lemon

1 teaspoon powdered cinnamon

115g (4 oz) unsalted butter, plus a little extra for greasing

icing sugar

Rum sauce

25g (1 oz) unsalted butter

25g (1 oz) plain flour

150ml (¼ pint) milk

300ml (½ pint) double cream

½ vanilla pod, split open

25g (1 oz) caster sugar

a good slug of dark rum to taste

Preheat the oven to 150°C/300°F/Gas 2. Grease a 28 x 20cm (11 x 8 in) roasting tin.

Break the bread up into pieces, including the crusts, and soak in the milk until soft. Beat well until the mixture is like soft cream. Add the dried fruit, peel and grated apple, then stir in the sugar, marmalade, flour, eggs, lemon juice and cinnamon.

Melt the butter and pour half into the mixture. Beat well and pour into the greased tin. Pour the remaining melted butter in a thin stream over the surface. Bake in the preheated oven for 1½ hours, and then for 30 minutes at 180°C/350°F/Gas 4.

Meanwhile, make the rum sauce. Melt the butter in a small pan, and add the flour, stirring together well. Cook for 1 minute, then slowly add the milk and cream, and beat until smooth. Scrape and stir in the vanilla seeds, and cook for a further 3 minutes. Add the sugar and rum, then stir together for a few minutes to melt the sugar. To serve, cut the bread pudding into squares or diamonds, and serve it hot or cold, sprinkled with icing sugar, with the hot rum sauce.

touch with. I went on holiday with him when we graduated, and then shared
digs with him when we both arrived in London. Some of these friends were at
college, I felt, just to have something to do, whereas I was very serious about
my future: after all, I'd already been a head chef for four years or so! But I really
enjoyed those two years, and have many happy memories.

One of my principal passions at college was music. I was still in the Salvation
Army band, but it was when Diana Dixon-Smith played one particular long-
playing record in the college common room that life changed for quite a few
of us. This was the early 1960s, and the Beatles had just burst upon a music
industry dominated by the Americans and at home by Cliff Richard and Tommy
Steele. We were knocked out by these Liverpool lads – northerners like us – and
we became great fans right from the beginning. Throughout those two years of
college, we went to see them perform whenever they were at Bradford, Leeds or
York. We perfected a very crafty system for buying tickets in Leeds. The Odeon
box office didn't open until ten o'clock in the morning, so, to ensure we'd get
tickets, I would forgo my cooked breakfast and come in earlier from the café.
I was in the queue by about twenty to eight, and would be relieved by one of the
girls at about quarter to nine. They'd be late for college – they never ran out of
excuses, though – but I had done the donkey work of the early shift.

I suppose I was a bit of a Beatles groupie in those days, and met and talked to
all of them several times. For instance, the bands all used to stay at the Metropole
in Leeds and, after the concerts, we'd hot-foot it down there and hang about until
they arrived. I actually had four programmes of Beatles concerts, all signed by all
four lads. Tragically, when I left home, I put them in a cupboard and my tidy
mother, thinking I was too old for that sort of thing now, threw them out. Then,
I could have sold them for at least a thousand pounds; I can't bear to think of what
they might have been worth today! I also listened to other groups, such as the
Searchers, Freddie and the Dreamers, Gerry and the Pacemakers, Wayne Fontana
and the Mindbenders, Del Shannon and Roy Orbison, all the great 1960s pop
stars. Our college dances used to feature bands such as Kenny Ball, Acker Bilk and
Alex Welsh, as we were all mad about traditional jazz, too. From a musical point
of view, it was a wonderful decade to grow up in and of course I was still playing
my semi-classical stuff for the Salvation Army every weekend. I was also very
sixties sharp in a sartorial sense: I had a brown suit, I seem to remember, and went

to college dances in a Teddy boy jacket, three-quarter length black with silver flecks in it, set off by fluorescent violent green or pink socks!

* * *

Just like any other student, I applied for holiday jobs. I did a few weeks at the Buck Inn at Buckden, in the Dales above Skipton, in the Easter holidays. Then, in that long summer vacation between first and second year, because we were good pals, John White and I both applied to go to Butlins in Bognor Regis (Butlins was where the birds were, or so we were told). But for some reason, I was accepted and John was turned down. I decided, after some heart-searching, to go by myself, which was quite brave for a guy who had never really been away from home before, and who was still only about sixteen or seventeen. I relished the challenge though, finding my way from Leeds to London, across London, then down to Bognor.

In those days the Bognor Regis Butlins actually had barbed wire round the perimeter to stop people getting in, but the campers used to joke 'to stop them getting out'! The system of contract payment for staff was quite clever in retrospect. The pay wasn't bad, but they only gave you half of it per week as you went along. The deal was that they would hold the second half, and it would be paid to you, rather like a healthy bonus, when you fulfilled your contracted term. If you ran out on your agreement, you would of course forfeit half your earnings. This guaranteed consistency for Butlins, a full staff when they needed it, and wasn't a bad arrangement for the staff, some of them students, some of them the transients you find in every commercial kitchen, who might blow a week's salary in the pub. It was almost like a short-term pension scheme, but mandatory, and I think some of our youngsters today could benefit from the same sort of financial planning.

The majority of the staff were billeted inside the camp, in rather tacky staff quarters around the perimeter fence. For reasons I didn't quite appreciate, concessions were made to university degree students; if you needed a bit of peace and quiet to study in your time off, you were put in one of a couple of houses just outside the camp. Three students from Northamptonshire and I ended up sharing one of these houses, which was very much more civilised in terms of comfort. The chaps already based in the house had evolved a ceremony to mark the passing of the days towards the end of their contracts, and the payment of their 'bonus'. On the wall there was a giant planner, and at the end of every day, someone would cross off a square, salute and raise the Union Jack... One more day completed, one day less to suffer!

And suffer we did, for we had to work extremely hard. I had foolishly mentioned that I was used to breakfast duty, and so was forced to get up early each morning. (However, that meant I had more time free during the day, a distinct advantage.) But cooking breakfast for up to 5,000 people, from seven until ten, was no picnic. I was the egg frier. I had to stand at a great metal plaque about three feet square, which was the grill. A crate of eggs stood at one side, raised on a couple of boxes so it was at hand height. I picked up an egg, and cracked it one-handed on to the grill, immediately followed by another, another and another. The idea was to go fast enough that by the time the last egg was put on the grill (about sixty at a time) the first egg was just cooked. Then I used a spatula to transfer the eggs to a tray to go on to racks and hotplates. It was a constant service, three hours of the very same thing, and eight weeks of that was a long time.

Apart from the mind-numbing boredom of the job, I had a good time. I got on well with the lads in the house, who brought a sanity to the whole experience. Ingrid, a blue-eyed blonde from Stavanger, Norway, in Bognor to learn English, brought me a great deal of a different kind of pleasure. Bill Evans, by his own admission an illiterate and occasionally drunken Welshman, became my unofficial minder, rescuing me once, in a walk-in fridge, from a butcher with a cleaver and intentions which were definitely not heterosexual. Bill was my first introduction to a type of man who was to become familiar to all of us in the catering trade. They were transients, moving from job to job, drinking too much, and possibly even getting themselves in trouble with the police every now and then. Bill was a pot-wash man at Butlins, in charge of a sink constantly full of filthy dishes, and I used to see that he had a good breakfast every day. Although I didn't properly drink in those days, I used to join him occasionally for a pint, and we became pals.

All these friendships helped me to deal with the tedium as well as the excitements. They also helped me to put a number of things in perspective. As a home-loving boy, from a sleepy backwater town, I'd not really experienced much of the 'outside world' before. Those eight weeks made me appreciate what I had at home – all those comforts, that unconditional affection – and they also made me grow up. I started my second year at Leeds knowing and understanding a lot more about life.

* * *

The production kitchen was the highlight of my second year at college. I had always liked preparing food for people, but this was a genuine taste of the reality of what you were in the business for. Here we were planning real meals, which were going out on silver flats with nice garnishes. There was a great sense of satisfaction in cooking, tasting and arranging, and it made me feel really good. I still feel the same nearly forty years later!

The production kitchen was at Gower Street, and was run by an ex-Army chef. He introduced himself to us by saying, 'My name is Richards, spelled BASTARD. You'll do what I tell you.' He ran that place with a rod of iron, and picked out John White and me straightaway as potential troublemakers. We weren't, in fact, but we were social, confident, voluble, and thus I suppose highly visible. Just as in the Army, someone had to get the blame, whether they were responsible or not. John and I suffered quite a lot at the hands of Mr Richards, but it was water off a duck's back. In fact, his principal mode of punishment, making us wash up and polish the pots and pans, actually stood me in good stead. I became quite expert at it, and in later years it made me appreciate and value a good pot-wash man, having learned at first hand what a horrendous and thankless job it is.

Once a year you were allowed to bring your parents in for lunch. It wasn't offered free, but the college acknowledged that parents might like to see how their offspring were progressing. On that day you were always on the waiter rota, because if you were cooking the meal you wouldn't be seen. The waiters would help with the *mise-en-place* in the morning, and perhaps polish the silver, then be on view during the actual service of the meal. My father had taken the lunchtime off from the café (something he never did) and was coming into Leeds with my mum. I was rather nervous. In the middle of preparation, sharpening a knife and talking (as always), I cut my thumb quite badly. Feeling faint because of the blood, I went to sit outside the kitchen, where it was just beginning to snow. The blood ran from my hand and formed a scarlet pool on the snow, and much to everyone's horror, Denise announced dramatically that I was dying! I promptly fainted. A frantic discussion ensued as to how I could be got to the infirmary. Alison's Mini was outside, but she couldn't back it out of the parking space. (She'd only passed her test the day before.) Jeff Hedley, the lecturer in charge of waiting, took charge of his bleeding pupil. An hour or so later, I was back, stitched, bandaged and subdued. Quite unable to perform as a waiter, I had to be the cashier, a very unglamorous job, and a great disappointment to my parents and myself. When I went out to tell Dad, he smacked me round the head, for the second time in my life, and said, 'You stupid boy!' And he was probably quite right!

In that second year, I took many more freelance night and weekend jobs. The college used to lend us out as extra staff at banquets, usually in Harrogate. We were waiters in the first year and, when the coffee was served, we'd be bussed back to Leeds. In the second year, when many of us had our own transport, we were allowed to be wine waiters, serving after-dinner drinks. We soon worked out a good scam for making money. As we were in Yorkshire, there were always jugs of beer on the tables. Working in pairs – John White and I were one such – we'd go round the tables while people were dancing and collect up jugs that were almost empty. Out at the back, where the bar was, we'd pour the leftover beer into another jug to fill it up and get a good head. Then we'd go back out front and sell it for cash, often to one of the tables we'd got the beer from in the first place. It was quite a lucrative little business as I remember. Sorry, everybody!

Another aspect of these banquets was the grave matter of the teaspoons. Now teaspoons in the 1960s were exactly what they are today, the commodity that disappears most frequently from hotels and restaurants. No matter how hard you try, they just disappear. At many venues the waiters were given twelve teaspoons, or the number needed at their particular table, and if they didn't hand them all in at the end of the evening, they didn't get their wages! What this meant was that as you went around and cleared throughout the evening, and saw a spare teaspoon anywhere, you'd pick it up and put it in your pocket, just to make sure. Denise found four teaspoons in her pocket the morning after a 'do' at a hotel in Ilkley, and her horrified mother made her go back to return them!

My dad was responsible for getting me a regular night and weekend job. This was obviously partly for financial reasons as I wasn't getting a grant, and he had to pay for me, but I think he knew the experience would do me good as well. He introduced me to a Mr Hayward, the general manager of Gilpin's, an outside catering company very famous locally. They owned the Guildford Hotel in Leeds, and I became general factotum or dogsbody in their busy kitchen at nights. My dad's famous logic came into play again here. As he knew my mum wouldn't want her precious baby coming home alone at night – I must have been about seventeen at this point – he suggested that he should come and fetch me. This meant that he could have a pint in The Gardeners, perhaps another in The Woodman, and then a final one in the Guildford bar while waiting for me. I think he enjoyed what could have been a tedious chauffeuring job. You owe me one, Dad...

I got myself a Saturday job as well, working at Jacomelli's, a flashy restaurant in Boar Lane in Leeds, which was very busy on Saturday nights. It had two main rooms, the Pigalle Grill and the Cheval Blanc. My job there was to 'feed' the guy cooking the main courses with whatever he needed. When the orders came down, he'd shout to me and I'd run around getting him bits and pieces from the fridge, cutting, chopping, although never actually cooking much. Despite that lack, I enjoyed myself, as it was a re-run, but magnified a hundred times, of those sensations I'd experienced on Saturday mornings at the café. It was hot, sweaty and stressful, but it reconfirmed that the ambience and atmosphere of a busy kitchen were just up my street. In fact, even in those days, I tended to go for restaurants serving good food, as Jacomelli's was listed and rated in the *Good Food Guide* of that same year: 1963.

The two years of college came eventually to an end. Despite the fact that they didn't think I was the greatest cook in the world (they actually thought I would make a better manager), I got the highest marks in the 151 practical examination. As a prize, I got two knives from Peter Maturi's, the shop where the college bought all their knives and where they had them sharpened. I kept both of them, a Granton ham slicer with a scalloped edge, and a boning knife, for over thirty years, until the latter got stolen a few years ago. In fact I did a little demonstration for Maturi's in late 1999 to help celebrate their centenary. The shop and their knives obviously share the same staying power.

Now was the time to start thinking about my future. My experience at Butlins had opened my eyes to new things, to new ways of thinking, and quite quickly I realised that I would need wider horizons than Leeds and its environs could offer. Swinging London, the big city, the magnet for everyone of my age in the

1960s, was where it was all happening, so I wrote to all the big London hotels. I got a few replies, mainly negative, but the Savoy did say that, although they didn't have anything at the moment, there was something going at Simpson's-in-the-Strand, their associate restaurant. If I wanted to start working there, they said, then I could perhaps move on to the Savoy later, when there was a vacancy. That seemed interesting to me, so I accepted.

Neil was moving to London too – he had a job working front of house at the Park Lane Hotel – but he wasn't due there until August, and I was to start in September. To celebrate our success, and to pass the summer, we went on holiday together, two weeks in the Lake District, staying in a caravan. It poured with rain the entire first week, drumming relentlessly against the thin roof and walls. We played endless games of cards and dominoes, interspersed only by the odd swift and wet foray to the pub for something to eat. Although Neil stayed on, I gave in after that week and hitched my way to Filey to meet the family on their holiday. I probably looked a little outrageous: I had an old blue coat with a corduroy collar, a flat cap with feathers sticking out, big hiking boots, a walking stick and a backpack. In Filey, I saw Mum and Dad in the distance, and as I walked towards them, all the kit on, I heard Mum say, 'Look at that tramp over there... Oh no, it's Brian!' I was stunned, as indeed was she, and I think that's the last time I ever went on holiday with my parents. I got rid of the coat soon afterwards too.

However, I did spend a few days with them, and then it was time to go to London. I was excited, of course, but also miserable. I remembered the home-sickness I'd experienced at Butlins, and knew that, despite the new life that was opening up for me, the same could happen again. My parents came to Leeds station to see me off, my mother tearful, and my dad a typical Yorkshire stoic, not showing any emotion at all. He thrust a £20 note in my hand, and said, 'Son, good luck for the future. I'm sure you'll be fine. Don't worry about the money, you can keep it for as long as you need it.' It was very obvious that it was a loan, not a gift, but that £20 made all the difference (I paid it back within the year). It was after all about two weeks' wages. I felt rich as the train steamed out of Leeds on its way south to my future, but also very frightened.

part two
STARTING OUT

Simpson's-in-the-Strand

When I arrived in London in 1964, my friend from college in Leeds, Neil Mathieson (then at the Park Lane Hotel), had already found a place for us to live, in the Caledonian Home for Christian Gentlefolk. (You were supposed to be Scottish to merit a bed, but Neil was actually of Scottish descent.) It had grey-painted walls, grey wallpaper, grey sheets, grey blankets, even the outlook and the people were grey. It was in Euston, opposite the Quakers' headquarters, and you could see King's Cross station from the window. The temptation that first week to get on a train and go straight back home was tremendous. I cried myself to sleep every night, but I had to stick it out. Yorkshire grit and all that...

When I started work at Simpson's-in-the-Strand in 1964, at the age of eighteen, as staff I wasn't allowed to go through the restaurant's imposing front door.

At Simpson's I was to get the princely sum of £9 a week, and it was within walking distance – down Gower Street and on to Holborn. I found lots of different ways of getting there. Walking to work on that first day, weaving through the large, unfamiliar buildings, fresh from college and home was fairly daunting, to say the least: I was nervous inevitably, homesick, and hated where I was living. I'd planned that first day's route carefully, using Neil's precious *A-Z of London*, but because it was a bright September day, I cheered up as I walked. I was young and ever hopeful. In fact, I was quite excited, because Simpson's had such a reputation for its British food, its roast beef and roast lamb, carved in front of the customer – the carver traditionally gets a tip from each table – its steak and kidney pies, Yorkshire puddings and steamed puddings. Even my dad had heard of Simpson's! It was probably the most famous bastion of British cookery, and an interesting place for me to start, as I have since become such a staunch champion of British cooking and produce.

Opened in 1828 by a Mr Samuel Reiss, the Simpson's building was then known as the 'Grand Cigar Divan', because it was where men used to come and smoke, talk politics, drink coffee and play chess, all sitting on comfortable divans and sofas. For this they would pay one guinea a year, and it was an early version of the gentleman's club, many of which had developed in their turn from the coffee houses of the sixteenth century onwards. In 1848, Mr Reiss went into collaboration with a noted caterer, John Simpson, and the name of the 'club', now somewhere to eat as well, became 'Simpson's Grand Divan Tavern'. In 1961, a few years before I got there, the *Good Food Guide* described Simpson's thus:

> This restaurant is famous for one thing – its roast joints; they are not really successful with what they no doubt call "made-up dishes". White-coated carving-men patrol the restaurant with large heated trolleys on which are great joints under silver dish-covers, from which they will cut you an ample portion. Sirloin of beef and saddle of mutton (8/-), are as tender, flavoury [sic] and generously served as under Edward VII; so too is the roast duck, which is 10/6. Boiled silverside and steak, tripe and onions (very good indeed, 5/9), kidney-and-oyster pudding are also commended; plain cabbage

and boiled potatoes are included in the price. Stick to those, and the giblet soup (2/-), and drink good beer (Bass's) in tankards or the carafe claret. 1/- table money. Open till 3.30 for lunch, and 10.30 for dinner, approximately, weekdays only.

Even in the 1960s the masculine ethos was still in place, for the ground floor restaurant was for men only at lunchtime, from Monday to Friday.

Simpson's has a rather large, imposing front door, actually on the Strand, but I knew that staff weren't supposed to go in there. I found a side entrance off the Strand, up a little alleyway, and clattered over a metal staircase to the basement. Halfway down was a little shed belonging to the timekeeper, who facially resembled Charles Laughton's Quasimodo. 'What you want?' he demanded and, after ticking my name off in his register, he sent me further down into the bowels of the building. As I turned into a corridor to the kitchen, I bumped into a little fat kid from Weston-super-Mare, who almost knocked me over. This was Richard Shepherd – now chef extraordinary, running five major restaurants in London – who was to become a lifelong buddy. Thus are friendships made!

I went to see the chef, Arthur Moss, one of the few in the country who was allowed to wear a black cap, denoting seniority in British cuisine. He was quite old – at least to my eighteen-year-old eyes, he might have been fifty – and introduced me to the *sous-chefs*, Ray Gower, Joe Curly, Tony Gough and Graham England among them. They were influential in my life at that time, but none of them ever hit the big time; Tony went on to teach and I see him occasionally, and Shepherd and I went to Graham's retirement party in the mid 1990s.

It might be useful here to describe how a professional kitchen is organised. In French practice, it is headed by the *chef de cuisine*, who supervises all sections of the kitchen. Helping him is one or more *sous-chefs*, and then there are *chefs de partie*. In a full kitchen, there will be a *chef de partie* in each section – the larder chef or *garde-manger*, the roast section (*rôtisseur*), fish (*poissonier*), soups, vegetables, eggs and pasta (*entremetier*), desserts and pastry (*pâtissier*) and stocks and sauces (*saucier*). Depending on the size of the kitchen, each *chef de partie* is assisted by one or more *commis-chefs*, who can be ranked one, two or three, depending on the length of their service and on their skill. A first *commis* is sometimes known as a *demi-chef*. I was fairly junior, despite my two-year

The gentleman who asked the carver whether
the meat was English or Foreign.

DRAWN BY H.M. BATEMAN

*This classic Bateman cartoon decorates the menu at Simpson's,
reflecting its very British style. The carver is suitably shocked at
the deeply inappropriate question.*

training, and was designated *commis-tournant*, which meant that I would move around the various sections, where and when I was needed. I didn't mind that, as it meant I could gain experience in a number of sections: you have to master all specialities before you can reach the next rung of the culinary ladder.

I was put on the pastry section, and the first person I worked with was Sam Costa, the head pastry chef. He was English, but obviously of Greek or Spanish descent. About four feet six inches tall, he was the height of a jockey, but built like a heavyweight boxer, all muscle. (As a result, I tried never to cross him.) He'd worked in Simpson's since the year dot, and ran his section with an inflexibility that would have been frustrating had I been older and more experienced. To do things in an automated way is no bad thing, in that tried and proven methods make things easier, but I think it left little room for progression. If someone had come in and said, 'Why don't you change this?', it would have messed up the entire system.

So Sam persevered in his archaic, albeit effective, routine. He would make his pastry in bulk laboriously by hand on a marble work surface, when there was a perfectly good machine there, a Hobart, which would have done the mixing in a fraction of the time. This would be pressed into service when Sam was off duty, or on holiday, particularly by his deputy, Stuart Garrett. (I was secretly rather horrified by Stuart, as he never wore a hat, had his jacket neck wide open, and never fastened his boots. I, the new boy straight from college, was always properly dressed!) So, by hand and, occasionally, by machine, we made shortcrust pastry for individual apple pies, suet pastry for steak and kidney puddings, and the suet mix for steamed sweet puddings such as treacle roly-poly and jam roly-poly. Suet pastries and puddings were, and are, central to British cooking, as they were at Simpson's, and there was always plenty of suet there because of the amount of beef the restaurant cooked and sold.

My principal memory of working with Sam is helping him in September, that first month, to make the Christmas puddings and mincemeat. Both required suet, so we would have to painstakingly pull off all the skin on the outside. To meet a string of suet skin in your mouth isn't a good experience! As we were working with mixtures of at least 100 lb in weight (around 45 kg), which would require around 20 lb (9 kg) suet, this became a very tedious job. We juniors, many of us straight from college, also had to pick the heaped mounds of dried currants, raisins and sultanas clean of stems and stones, again about 50–100 lb at a time. I found it extraordinary, working with those sheer quantities, when I'd never before seen ingredients in other than small packets, even at college. Sam would put the pudding mixture into a dustbin and then into the walk-in fridge. The smell as the mixture matured was fantastic, the main reward for all the tedium in its preparation: heady, aromatic, alcoholic and spicy. You felt you could get drunk if you stuck your head too near! For me, used to nothing but fried kitchen smells, a new world was suddenly opening up. In fact, my worst habit probably developed about then. I tend to sniff at everything – plates, glasses, you name it – as there are lots of extraneous smells which might spoil food. Now, as then, I think there is so much beauty in the aroma of fresh, ripe or properly cooked food, and you don't want anything to interfere with it.

Other puddings I worked on were trifles, fruit salads and steamed and baked puddings. The fruit salad was made, in 17½pint (10 litre) bowls, from oranges, apples, pineapple (probably tinned), pears, lemon juice and a stock syrup. It was very basic, and served with ice cream or fresh cream. Nowadays we might put a bit of lemongrass, star anise or alcohol in the syrup to add flavour but, at the time, I thought it all very sophisticated and the cream seemed a great step up from the tinned evaporated milk we served at home. (I still dream of Carnation!) It was then that I learned properly the art of segmenting citrus fruit, and did oranges for the fruit salads, grapefruit for starters. I found it very satisfying to release those great meaty chunks from their skin, and to squeeze all the juices from the centre pulp. I ate a lot as I went along, so I suppose I was getting a lot of healthy vitamin C.

The trifles were made in big batches, the puddings in twenty-portion tins. Sam and his team, including me, used to prep everything during the day. Sam didn't work at night, so we would be left to do the actual cooking. The steamers we used were quite interesting, solid and made of cast iron like old Rayburns. There was a bank of about eight of them; I found them vicious in that I could never get the hang of their safety valves. If I wanted to get into a steamer, I'd have to turn it off first otherwise I'd get scalded. To me, it was a bit like Ronnie Barker's Mr Arkwright and his recalcitrant cash till in the TV series *Open All Hours*.

Hampshire roll was probably the first pudding I ever had a major hand in at Simpson's. It's a baked apple sponge pudding, with apricot jam adding sweetness and succulence. We used to make it in wonderful battered, half-moon tin moulds: brushed with butter, then jam, apple and sponge, and another layer of apple and jam, topped with more sponge. The sponge was very basic then – I've added a little cream and orange zest to my present-day recipe to make it a little tastier – but the flavours were still fantastic. There would be about half a dozen moulds per baking sheet. I'd carefully carry one full sheet to the oven, which was outside the pastry section, but Sam, despite his size, hefted two, one sheet per shoulder.

Sam would make a wonderful custard which, I'm ashamed to admit, he made with custard powder rather than with eggs. He would add some double cream for lightness and flavour, though, and we'd pass it through sieves to ensure smooth perfection. One of the major and time-honoured delights of eating puddings at Simpson's was reputed to be the huge bowls of steaming, golden custard.

Although we were fairly secluded in the pastry section, which was a little room separated from the pandemonium of the main kitchen, I did manage to meet a few other people. Opposite our door we could see the vegetable section which was run by Jimmy the Greek and 'the Archbishop', also known as Makarios (not surprisingly, a Greek Cypriot). I remember wondering why Makarios used to walk around with no socks on and his trousers rolled up. It was all due, I discovered, to the principal vegetable that Simpson's served at that time, the famous (or infamous) cabbage. This was blanched in huge vats of boiling water, the outside leaves left whole, the inner leaves chopped. As this was drained, so much water sloshed around the section that everyone in the vicinity got soaked. The cabbage was then 'plated': a blanched leaf would be put on a plate, with some chopped cabbage and another leaf on top. Another plate topped that, and then more cabbage. At least twenty plates and layers of cabbage were built up into a tower, and squeezed together to get as much water as possible out. To serve, the individual cabbage 'cakes' were put into a steamer to be reheated, then cut into eight wedges. An atrocious practice, and what a waste of what can be a delicious vegetable. I just accepted it at the time, as did the customers – and this in the foremost British restaurant, too – so it may have been about then that the British got their bad reputation for cooking vegetables. We have learned quite a lot since.

The Beatty twins, David and Willie, were over six feet tall, and ran the sauce section. They were from Scotland, had been in the Army, and were really quite tough and strict disciplinarians. The Catering Corps has never been known for its five-star cooking, and neither were these two boys. But they did an adequate job, I got on well with them, and in those early days learned from them how to work hard. David Beatty was the captain of the Savoy Hotel football team, so Shepherd and I volunteered to play. We used to train on the afternoons of split shifts in the St Martin-in-the-Fields crypt – yes, a curious sporting venue, but handy – and play five-a-side football. We also played in the Park, for the hotels and catering leagues. If you got hurt while playing, you had to limp back to the restaurant, go into one of the fridges, and pretend you'd fallen over and damaged yourself in there. We could go home then, without losing any pay, and without being banned from playing which was a fate worse than death.

Another new acquaintance was Leslie, a Billy Bunter lookalike with a wicked smile, who was on the fish grill, cooking soles all day. I also met a lot of transients, dossers, chaps who lived on the street or in hostels, who were used as kitchen porters or pot-wash men and runners. All alcoholics or unfortunates in

Roast Rib of Beef with a Horseradish and Coriander Crust
SERVES 6

The bigger the joint, the better the roast. Three bones will give you enough for six portions, but a bigger joint, like the six bones in the photograph, will leave some spare for second helpings and cold cuts – good with sauté potatoes and chutney. A herb Yorkshire pudding is good with this roast (see page 224). Simpson's would have simply roasted the beef without any adornment, but this recipe has a modern-day twist, which I think just adds a little something.

3-bone rib of beef

1 tablespoon English mustard

2 tablespoons horseradish cream

55g (2 oz) unsalted butter, melted

225g (8 oz) fresh white breadcrumbs

salt and freshly ground black pepper

1 bunch fresh coriander, chopped

Ask the butcher to take off the backbone from the beef, and trim the excess nerve and fat from inside the beef. Then clean the tips of the ribs and tie up again.

Preheat the oven to 240°C/475°F/Gas 9, and roast the beef at this temperature for the first 20 minutes. This helps to give the joint a good colour and gets the cooking off to a good start. Lower the oven temperature to 190°C/375°F/Gas 5, and roast using the following approximate times according to weight and your personal taste:

about 14 minutes per 500g (18 oz) for rare

about 21 minutes per 500g (18 oz) for medium

about 27 minutes per 500g (18 oz) for well done

Half an hour before the cooking ends, mix the mustard and horseradish together. Remove the beef from the oven and brush the back of the joint liberally with this mixture. Mix the melted butter with the breadcrumbs, salt, pepper and coriander. Push this on to the horseradish-mustard mix, and finish roasting.

Take the beef out of the oven and rest for 20 minutes before carving. Serve with Yorkshire puddings if making, a good gravy and lots of vegetables.

some way, they would start their work in the kitchen in relative smartness – stiff back, shaved, a suit on, with some degree of self-respect. But there was a cycle to their working lives. Eventually they'd have no money, would have drunk it all away, lost it at cards or in the bookies. When they got to that stage, they would walk along the Strand with a brick, throw it through the nearest window – usually Yates Wine Lodge, a local pub – and wait for the police to come and pick them up. They'd be put in the slammer for a few weeks, then social services would give them a new suit, a bath and shave, and they'd come out and get back to work. You'd notice every now and then that someone was missing, but they never got long terms, a few weeks maximum. They always seemed to look after us young guys, possibly because they didn't want us to end up like them. They recognised what had gone wrong in their lives, and didn't want it perpetuated.

Top: *A rare photograph of the six of us Turners together, taken in about 1967, the four children all in their Salvation Army uniform.*

Bottom: *The Grand Divan at Simpson's, also known as the Ground Floor, where I was to carve beef in front of the customers, a first taste of performing in public.*

I was in the Salvation Army at the time, and you can imagine how I felt seeing all this, but for them it was a way of life. Chalkie, Watson and Taff spring to mind. Chalkie's job in the morning was to do the brown bread and butter for the smoked salmon and oysters, which we sold at Simpson's by the bucketload. He'd start off with half a pound of butter and twenty loaves, cut as thinly as possible on a machine. He'd spread some butter on a piece of bread, and then he'd scrape as much as he could back into the butter bowl, so that the bread was just literally skimmed with butter. By the end of his session, the butter bowl would hold what looked like three pounds of butter, rather than the half pound he'd started off with, as it was so imbued with crumbs! He was proud of his buttering skills.

Taff, with whom I used to play an occasional game of cards (learning, not gambling!), was Welsh, and had been a leading and eminent lawyer in Wales, so the story went. He had a problem with a woman (we never did discover what) and lost his mind. One result of this seemed to be an inability to remember how to make use of hot water and soap. His accent was very strong, and he was always very eloquent, much to our embarrassment, at Christmas or on bank holidays, playing to the gallery of the roasting kitchen. Many of these 'regular' transients were extremely clever in their own way – calculating betting odds, how to get from one side of London to the other on the buses – and Taff played a mean game of poker. Watson, too, who wouldn't have been able to read *The Times*, was superb at his job, looking after the lift from the kitchen to the restaurants. This lift had to go to three different rooms, and when the chef ordered for one particular room, Watson had to make sure the lift went there. It was really quite a clever and responsible job, and I don't think he ever made a mistake. Like Chalkie, he was proud of his skills, limited as we might have thought they were.

I also made friends with the lads in the larder and roasting sections, very important people to know, especially when you wanted to get something to eat. Simpson's had a staff canteen, like many large restaurants at that time, but the cooks didn't often eat there. You got time off to eat, but you'd have to do it for yourself, and so a system of barter had developed. We'd go and ask the roasting lads if there was any chance of a few fillet steaks for dinner, and we'd do a swap. In the same way, the boys in the larder, who didn't cook, might provide the

Hampshire Roll
SERVES 12

I don't know whether Sam Costa would have approved of double cream in this recipe, because he certainly didn't use it. However, I think this adds a Turner touch and a bit of richness, which for me, along with clotted cream to serve, helps you to spoil yourself.

225g (8 oz) unsalted butter

175g (6 oz) caster sugar

3 medium eggs

2 tablespoons double cream

finely grated zest of 1 orange

175g (6 oz) plain flour, sifted

a pinch of salt

675g (1½ lb) apples (Cox or Granny Smith)

175g (6 oz) apricot jam

icing sugar

Preheat the oven to 180°C/350°F/Gas 4. Use 55g (2 oz) of the butter to generously grease a semi-circular tray mould (if you can find one), or a large pie dish.

To make the sponge, cream the sugar and remaining butter together until light, then beat in the eggs, double cream and orange zest. Fold in the flour and salt.

Peel, core and slice the apples. Spread 115g (4 oz) of the jam in the bottom of the mould or dish. Sprinkle over half the apples, then spoon in half the sponge mixture. Mix the remaining apple and jam together, place on top of the sponge in the mould, then cover with the remaining sponge. Smooth the top, and bake in the preheated oven for 40–50 minutes until golden. Serve sprinkled with icing sugar, and accompanied by something like vanilla clotted cream or hot custard.

ingredients, and we'd prepare and cook for them. It may sound primitive, but the system operated in most of the restaurants I worked in thereafter. It also meant that you could eat extremely well! What Shepherd and I used to love particularly was saddle of lamb; not so much the saddle itself, but the fillets that were still attached to the saddle when it was roasted. They had no use for these upstairs in the restaurant, so we used to tear them off when the lamb came out of the oven. Then we'd make a caper or white onion sauce and eat the lamb fillets, to me the best part of the animal. We'd have a plate of bread and butter, and dip the lamb in the sauce. Kings and queens didn't eat as well as us, we thought, but even at the tender age of eighteen, we did actually recognise how lucky we were.

While I was getting acquainted with the workings and personnel of Simpson's, things were changing in my life outside as well. Neil and I had moved to a flat in Princess Road in Primrose Hill, just opposite the school, and in the same road in which the model Jean Shrimpton – 'the face' of the day – lived. The nearest tube was Chalk Farm, right next door to the Salvation Army, and so I went in to offer my services. To me, the donkey-jacketed lad from the north, with no money, they all seemed rather posh, but they took me on. When I'd left Morley I'd been playing second cornet and drums, but they put me on the tuba. This was huge, and didn't have any straps, but I mastered it – just. However, marching with it from Camden Town to Chalk Farm on a Sunday night, playing three times on the way, was exhausting to say the least. But I stuck it out, and actually stayed with them for a very long time, taking on positions of responsibility, running the youth club, and even travelling abroad with the band. I had the reputation of being a 'rehearsal man': I'd always go to the rehearsals, but rarely managed the concerts themselves. Often in places like the Albert Hall and Festival Hall, these were usually on Saturday nights, when I'd be working. I became a good member of the Corps and enjoyed my life there. In fact after a month or so in London, my flatmate Neil moved on, and I went to share a flat in Chalcot Road, a bit further north from Princess Road, with Bob Humphreys, the Salvation Army band drummer.

But I also kept up with my new mates from Simpson's – Richard Shepherd, Brian Redmond, Paul Taylor, Michael Tucker-Bull, Tony Pickering and one or two others. Shepherd shared a flat in Prince's Square, Bayswater, with Tony,

The Chalk Farm Salvation Army Band taken outside Portsmouth City Hall in the late 1960s. I am in the second row, on the far left. We were just about to publicise our European tour.

Paul and Michael, and I spent a lot of time there, playing cards, laughing, eating, quite often sleeping overnight and going straight into work the next day. Michael was a waiter at Simpson's, with size fifteen feet, and he fancied himself as an impressionist and ventriloquist. He called himself by a variety of 'stage' names: Michael Chance, Dawson Chance, Dawson Bull, Tucker Chance etc. (It was hell if he asked you to pick up his dry-cleaning as you had to run through a telephone directory of possible name combinations.) He wasn't very good then, but years later, when I was working at the Capital, I was lucky enough to be invited to a Royal Variety Performance. Dawson Chance was on the bill, and I rushed out to telephone Shepherd at half-time – 'You'll never guess who's on stage at the Palladium!' Despite his dramatic ambitions, and ultimate success, Michael was actually rather shy and unsophisticated, and we used to tease him relentlessly. As we did everybody, in fact. Once, I remember, we'd been playing cards while Paul had gone to bed early. We went into the bedroom half undressed in the early hours of the morning – three of them slept in there – and said, 'Paul, are you coming or aren't you, it's time to go to work.'

He got up in all innocence, and went into the bathroom to get ready, while we went straight to bed. When he realised, the air was blue...

I spent a lot of time at Shepherd's flat. That was where we ate in our free time. The ingredients for our rather lavish meals were, I'm now fairly ashamed to admit, purloined from Simpson's. It wasn't so much that the head chef Arthur Moss was quite elderly, but that the taking of food from restaurants, despite internal security arrangements, was rife. Undeniably it was stealing in the strictest sense, yet it was accepted. And I suppose, as we all earned so little, we considered it fair game. You had to pass Arthur Moss's office on your way out from the changing rooms at Simpson's, and the window was probably four feet from the floor. As he was so small, he could see your face and shoulders, but not your body. We would put on our overcoats and this would bewilder Arthur: 'Why are you going out with coats on? It's warm out there.' 'Oh, but Chef, we found it really cold this morning.' The truth was that under our coats were sides of smoked salmon and fillet steaks and sundry other luxuries. We would work as a team, designing our potential meals: one would get the sausages, one the steaks, another the tomatoes and so on. My little Billy Bunter friend, Leslie, toted a carrier bag, and Arthur Moss would ask, 'What you got in your bag, Leslie?' Leslie would list, quite truthfully, the contents of the bag: 'Two sole, a side of smoked salmon...' and Arthur would say, never believing the worst, 'Oh, get on with you, get out of here.' As I say, we ate well, even if it was at Simpson's expense!

However, our first Christmas looked as though it might be a complete and utter disaster. By this time I'd moved to Prince's Square, next to Shepherd, and was sharing with Bob Humphreys and a guy called Ivor Gibbs. The two flatfuls of lads decided to have a club and save some money for Christmas presents, for I was definitely planning to go home to see the family. We all put some money aside every week, and the fund was growing when, two weeks before Christmas, Shepherd's flat was burgled and the money went. We all decided we couldn't go home, and so a bleak Christmas loomed – no money, no food, no presents... On Christmas Day we decided to walk down from Prince's Square to Queensway and, as we turned into Moscow Road, there was a guy coming towards us carrying a brown bag full of goodies (there were loads of continental shops open in the area). As we got close to him, he slipped on the snow and fell to the pavement. We all raced to help him, but he got up and ran off, leaving his bag behind. To this day I can't imagine why he fled – perhaps he thought we were going to attack him, perhaps he'd robbed a shop, who knows. Whatever it was, he lost out and we gained tins of salmon, steak and kidney pies, packets of biscuits, tea and sugar. As a result, we had a great Christmas! Whenever Shepherd and I tell this story today, we both end up in tears: our first Christmas in London, money stolen, no money to go home or buy food, then God sends us this man in a mac with tinned salmon.

Later in the New Year I was transferred to the smoked salmon and oysters section. We had to open the oysters – a specialist job – put them on ice and halve the lemons. Jimmy, who was in charge of the section, had been at Simpson's for years, a thin man with hunched shoulders and few words. All he did all day was carve smoked salmon. He would stand at the counter, legs wide apart, his feet never moving from one hour to the next. He could carve a hundred slices off a piece of smoked salmon and nothing would be wasted. He taught me how to carve a side from one end to the other, in one great long slice. It was so thin you could almost read through it. That, with lemon, pepper and some of Chalkie's brown bread and butter, was a great Simpson's starter. The skills Jimmy taught me have never gone, even now, and in fact I was the first chef ever to go upstairs to the restaurant at Claridge's, years later, to carve smoked salmon in front of the customers.

I worked two years altogether at Simpson's-in-the-Strand and progressed ultimately to the roasting section, which was the top section, responsible as it was for at least 90 per cent of the restaurant's food revenue. The size of the roasting ovens astonished me when I first arrived. They were like two huge wardrobes. There were huge trays underneath into which the fat dripped. The meat used to be put into the ovens in a special order, so that the beef fat didn't drip on to the chickens, although the chicken fat could drip on to the beef. Each day we used to roast about thirty to forty huge sirloins on the bone, wing rib and loin together, which each weighed about 30 lb (13–14 kg). The turnover was huge, thus the number of sirloins to be roasted each day. And the bones weren't wasted, for a special savoury on the menu was 'Devilled Beef Bones'. When the bones returned to the kitchen, we'd cut them into doubles, brush them with mustard then sprinkle them with breadcrumbs, and throw them under the grill. They were considered a real treat by many a city gent, serviette tucked under his chin, and fingerbowl by his side.

We also roasted thirty to forty saddles of lamb per day, and countless chickens and ducks. And of course there were Yorkshire puddings – we made 12 gallons of mix daily – which I didn't think much of, having tasted much better in my dad's transport café. They were considered to be the best in town in those days, though. Everything else on the menu was steamed, and it was so bland, as bland as the Beatty sauces and the plated cabbage. Tripe and onions, for instance, was a few pieces of tripe and a white sauce with half a boiled onion, reheated in the steamer, but people seemed to love it. I'm sure things are very much better today. Simpson's was a precursor of the massive restaurants in vogue now: we used to do some 1,200–1,400 covers a day through the three restaurants. A lot of work for us!

When I'd arrived at Simpson's, I had expected to work there for about a year before a vacancy turned up at the Savoy. However, it was done on rotation, depending on how long you'd been there, and after my first year, it was Shepherd who got the transfer, and went to work in the Savoy Grill. The next one due to be moved was Paul Taylor, but he didn't seem to be pursuing it, and they said I couldn't go until Paul did. After two years I got very frustrated, so decided to take matters into my own hands. One afternoon I took it upon myself to go and see Olive Barnett, the Personnel Director, who also happened to be a member of the D'Oyly Carte family who owned the Savoy. I remember I arrived at about three, and her secretary must have thought I was there by appointment, so I saw Miss Barnett straightaway. I told my story, she was very pleasant, and said she would see what she could do.

But when I got back to the kitchen, all hell had broken loose. By this time Arthur Moss had retired, Ray Gower was head chef, and Joe Curly was second in command, in effect running the kitchen. When I appeared, Curly, a tough man, came out of his office and shouted, 'Turner, get in here. Where have you been this afternoon? Who have you been to see?' Apparently when I left her office, Mrs Barnett had rung Mr Mumford, the general manager of Simpson's, and said, 'What on earth are you doing, letting young chefs come to my office to pester me about transfers?' Mumford got shouted at, he shouted at Joe Curly in turn, who shouted at everyone else, particularly me. It was the dressing-down of my life.

But I got my move, and Paul and I went together to the Savoy. By now I was considered to be a troublemaker, but I didn't care. I knew what I wanted, I knew what I could do, and I had decided to take my life into my own hands.

The Savoy

Although I'd been longing for this move for two years, I was still rather nervous at the prospect. I'd already been in the Savoy several times, because the hotel and Simpson's were interconnected by a maze of underground passages, through which heating and water-pipes ran and deliveries were made. When something was needed at Simpson's – very rarely vice versa – someone would be sent to the hotel to borrow it. I remember standing at the top of the stairs watching what seemed to be hundreds of chefs working in the Savoy Grill kitchen – there were actually around 120 to 140, a massive operation – determining to get there one day. (The opposite was true for my younger brother, Philip, whom I took into the underground maze of tunnels at the Savoy a year or so later. As we burst into the light of the kitchen, I was so proud because Escoffier's stove, his original stove, was there on the right-hand side. This meant nothing to Philip, of course, and he couldn't appreciate my pride about this place where I worked. The heat, the light, the noise, din, smells and energy were so intense that my brother burst into tears, thinking I worked in hell!)

However much I may have wanted to get into the Savoy, a distinct deterrent was the terrifying presence of the head chef, Silvano Trompetto. Although an astute businessman and a great influence on cooking in Britain, he was rumoured to be very fierce indeed. His appearance was no less intimidating. He was very tall anyway, but his elongated chef's hat – the higher your position in those days, the taller the hat – made him tower over everyone else, at least six and a half feet. I was told he'd had an unfortunate experience in his youth when he fell off a wall and ripped his nose; the nose had to be operated on and a false skin inserted, which sadly made the middle of his face look like the parson's nose on a chicken. He was self-conscious about this, and others were no less chary of facing him. Once when I went to borrow something from the Savoy, I had to confront him, and he demanded, 'Sonny, why are you not looking at me?' Terrified out

Mint-stuffed Shoulder of Lamb
SERVES 6–8

A cut which is much underrated today, but the flavour of an old-season or a large lamb shoulder, due to the fat distribution, is really wonderful.

1 x 1.6kg (3½ lb) shoulder of lamb, boned	salt and freshly ground black pepper
2 shallots, peeled and chopped	55g (2 oz) unsalted butter
3 tablespoons groundnut oil	Shallot *jus*
350g (12 oz) sausagemeat	2 shallots, peeled and chopped
1 bunch fresh mint, chopped	25g (1 oz) unsalted butter
1 bunch fresh parsley, chopped	175ml (6 fl oz) red wine
1 medium egg, beaten	85ml (3 fl oz) white wine
225g (8 oz) fresh white breadcrumbs	300ml (½ pint) thickened *Lamb Stock* (see pages 240–41)

Preheat the oven to 180°C/350°F/Gas 4. Bone the shoulder of lamb yourself – it's not hard – or get your butcher to do it for you.

To make the stuffing, sweat the shallot in 1 tablespoon of the oil until softened. Cool, then mix with the sausagemeat. Add the chopped herbs, egg and bread-crumbs, and season to taste. Stuff into the cavity in the lamb and tie up with string to a thick sausage. Seal on all sides in another tablespoon of the oil, then roast for 1–1½ hours. Allow to cool overnight.

Take off the string, and cut the stuffed lamb into steaks about 4cm (1½ in) thick. Preheat the oven to 200°C/400°F/Gas 6. Heat the remaining tablespoon of oil and the butter together. Sauté the lamb on one side in an ovenproof pan, then turn over. Roast for 15 minutes.

Meanwhile, for the shallot *jus*, sweat the shallot in half the butter until softened. Add the wines, and simmer to reduce by half. Add the stock, and bring to the boil. Add the remaining butter in small pieces, and season to taste.

Take the lamb slices out of the oven, and drain off excess fat. Serve with something like a *Rösti* (see page 143), and the hot shallot sauce.

Potted Lobster
SERVES 4

It was often a chore, but I grew to love it when my mum said, 'Just nip up to the corner shop and get some potted meat for tea.' One hot meal a day was all we had, and 'potted dog' (as we affectionately called it) was a typical teatime 'delicacy'. The style of potting remains almost the same today, although the ingredients change, and this luxury version, typical of a Savoy cold starter – and something I still prepare today at Turner's – is simple and delicious.

175g (6 oz) unsalted butter

1 tablespoon finely chopped spring onion

450g (1 lb) cooked lobster meat, in medium pieces

a pinch of ground mace

a pinch of freshly grated nutmeg

a splash of cognac

salt and freshly ground black pepper

Clarified Butter (see page 239)

Heat the butter gently, but do not colour it. Add the chopped spring onion, and stir for a minute. Add the lobster then the spices, and cook for 2–3 minutes to amalgamate well.

Remove two-thirds of the lobster meat from the pan, and put into a bowl. Put the rest of the lobster and the cognac into a food processor and blitz. Scrape into the bowl and mix with the remaining lobster pieces. Check the seasoning.

Pour into small ramekins and press down. Cover with a coating of melted clarified butter and leave to cool. Refrigerate for 2 hours before serving.

of my wits (and I wasn't one to be easily terrified), I stuttered in reply, 'Sir, I'm very shy, I never look at anyone.'

So I was a little reticent about the move, although enthusiastic, but it worked out well for both of us. Mr Trompetto was promoted to *maître chef des cuisines*, in charge of banqueting and the River Room, and I, as a new *commis* in the Grill Room, wouldn't have to run across him. The chef there was Louis Virot, a rugby-loving Frenchman who spoke with a very heavy French accent. (Happily, he's still around today at the time of writing, a member of the Academy of Culinary Arts, and I'm sure he's proud of what I've achieved.) I was put on the vegetable section, which depressed me a little, as we all considered it a bum job. We all wanted to gravitate to roasts, fish and sauces, the latter the height of glamour in any kitchen – and where Richard Shepherd was when I arrived, and already a star. Still, you've got to start somewhere, I suppose.

The veg section was a production rather than a creative area, but nevertheless, there was a certain amount of skill involved in what we did there. The prepping of the vegetables was paramount, of course. There would be about ten of us standing around a table trimming artichokes (a vegetable I'd never seen before), shredding cabbage, and turning potatoes and carrots. This latter operation involves taking a piece of root vegetable and cutting it, using a small sharp knife, into a neat barrel shape. It was the main skill I learned in the veg section, and I'm still a dab hand at it today. A mindless job, though, and we couldn't even chat to alleviate the boredom, as Paulo, the small fat Italian in charge, always liked to exercise his authority and ensure our complete concentration. Paulo wasn't around long, though. I thought he was extremely greedy – he never seemed to stop eating – and one day he was whisked into hospital with intense stomach pains. The rumour went round that a surfeit of spaghetti had formed a ball in his gut that could neither be passed nor digested. We never saw him again.

Another lesson learned very early in my years at the Savoy concerned the pots. I had already recognised how important pot-wash men were – and the pot-wash man I befriended in the Savoy, Ben, claimed to be an African prince – but here you had to make sure you had the requisite number of pots, dishes and pans you would need before service began. This involved quite a lot of organisation, if not mathematical genius, and led to a few disagreements between the sections. The thing about professional cooking is co-ordination –

if you've got four people sitting around a table, all wanting different main courses which require different vegetables, you need to get the timing spot on so that everything is cooked and hot at the same time. That's the primary side of the equation; secondary to that, but no less vital to us in the kitchen, was calculating the number of dishes we would need for each and every single such order. If the chefs had miscalculated, or not got in early enough, the pot-wash men at the Savoy, separated in one big room from the rest of the kitchen, had a very hard time as frantic chefs threw dirty pots and dishes at them to get them clean for an imminent order. Many an Ali – they were mostly Pakistani, and Ali became a collective name – would scuttle fearfully between pot-room and kitchen, wet to the neck from washing at high speed, ducking to avoid assorted missiles.

The senior *sous-chef* in the Savoy was Vladimir Piccoli, a Russian Italian, would you believe. He was almost as tall as Trompetto, and nearly as intimidating. I think he was disappointed with life, as he never made head chef, so he was inclined to bellow quite a lot, although at heart he was a good man. He instituted a ridiculous system for stores, for those were the days when they worked very much to percentages: the kitchen percentage always had to be right, and it was the *sous-chef*'s job to make sure nothing was wasted or thrown away. (It was so strictly controlled that the chef would occasionally walk around the kitchen kicking over dustbins in the sections to see what had been thrown away.) Piccoli made us write down our needs in a carbon copy book at the same time every day. Each section had different requirements – for butter, eggs, wine etc. – and we would have to go to him to get a signature on the relevant page. If you'd ordered twelve eggs, he would inevitably halve it to six; if you wanted four pounds of butter, he'd alter it to two. All it meant of course was that we would order double what we actually needed – twenty-four eggs to get our twelve – so it was all a waste of time, a game really. He was hoist with his own petard, though, one memorable day. One of the boys in the section started to make a stroganoff and, on seeing what he was doing, Vladimir, eager to demonstrate his national dish, leapt in insisting, 'Son, this is not a *real* stroganoff.' He then proceeded to make his own version, using so much butter and cream that we couldn't possibly compete and recreate it, as he didn't allow us to have the necessary ingredients!

That was one of the things that struck me most about the Savoy: the fact that there were so many continentals. Amongst the chefs were Germans, French, Austrians and Swiss who had come to London to learn about French cuisine in a different country, and to learn English (although the language of the kitchen was, and still is, French). Apart from the Alis, many of the lesser denizens of the kitchen were foreign as well. In a little room above the underground delivery entrance – the Savoy of course is built on a slope down from the Strand to the river – worked two elderly men. One, an old Pole, prepared all the poultry and game: he plucked them, cleaned them and tied them, an amazing sight, and I learned a great deal from him (I remember his woodcock lessons in particular). The other was a Jewish refugee from Europe, called Maurice, who was in charge of peeling the potatoes. A hunchback, and only about five feet tall, he would drag himself around the kitchen, like Rumpelstiltskin trying to pull his foot out of the floorboards, gathering all the gossip. He was a fount of information about others, not all of it flattering, so he was someone you wanted on your side. Both these old men were probably working in these fairly lowly positions through bad fortune, because of being in the wrong place at the wrong time, and through no fault of their own. But it was a lesson to me and my friends, and they and the pot-wash men certainly instilled in me a determination to rise well above that level, and to succeed.

After a while I was moved to the roast section, which pleased me. Sharma the Greek was the roast chef, a lovely man. So short that, even with his hat on, he only came to my shoulders, he reminded me a lot of Sam Costa in Simpson's; he was a great laugh, had muscles of steel, but you wouldn't want to cross him. Not only was he in charge of all the roasts, but he oversaw the chip cooking as well; this was because they didn't want the hot fat in the deep-fryers next to the inevitable water in the veg section. Those Savoy fryers were very old-fashioned, with cast-iron buckets, known as 'negresses', that slotted in and out. We used to have to take these buckets out, pour off the hot fat, scrub and dry them, then put the fat back in. We used to make perfectly square *pommes frites* and *pommes Pont-Neuf*, shaped to look like the ninth bridge in Paris, and crinkle-cut chips, all cut by hand. A Savoy speciality, something that was a very popular snack in the bars, was what we called *pommes soufflés*. We used to have to cut a potato into cylinders, and then in ⅛ in (3mm) thick slices. We cooked these in cool fat first so that the potatoes were sealed on the outside, but remained white.

I worked in the Savoy for about two years, but I think I only looked into the Savoy Grill itself about a couple of times. Our place was below in the kitchen, not above stairs.

When ready to serve, we would throw them into hot fat: they would balloon out into a pillow shape because of the expanding air trapped between the outside sealed coating and the inner potato. They looked great – a puffed-up crisp really – but they were difficult to do, and I think in retrospect rather a waste of effort and skilled time.

One of the *sous-chefs* there was Nino, a brown, fat Italian, who waddled around the section. He would think nothing of ripping the leg off a roast chicken and eating it, his reason being that he wanted to check the bird was cooked properly. But I think he actually just wanted to eat it. Once, when we got busy on a Saturday night, I saw him take a chicken out of the oven before it was ready, chuck it whole into the fish-fryer, and deep-fry it. This was ages before Colonel Saunders 'perfected' the art of frying chicken, and I dread to think what it tasted like.

I learned quite a lot in the roast section, but not really enough – none of us did. The experience of Clement Freud, who trained as a chef at the Dorchester, exemplified what was happening then in a professional sense and how ignorant we really were. The story goes that Clement's flatmates, wanting to impress some girls, got Clement to cook a couple of ducks, as he was always boasting about the ducks he cooked on the roast section. He duly roasted two birds in his oven at home, and they came out raw, all over the place and flavourless. What he was forced to acknowledge was that, although in one sense he could be called a chef, in another sense he couldn't. At the hotel, the purchase section bought the ducks, then the larder section trimmed them, readying them for the oven; someone in the roast section would turn the commercial oven to the correct temperature, and someone else would tell the *commis* how long to cook the birds. The *commis* only had to oversee one part of a detailed and highly skilled process, and until he or she had experienced each of the progressive stages of that process, and 'married' them together, they couldn't really call themselves a cook or chef. I don't think the story is apocryphal, because I, to be quite honest, was in much the same boat. And, sadly, I suspect some of my younger friends are still finding themselves, in larger restaurants, with the same problems. Because of the size of the business, they only get an opportunity to learn limited skills and don't have the advantage of working in small units where everything can be seen, done and learned.

After the roast section, I went into the larder for a while, where the cold preparation and the cold starters are done. The butcher's shop is part of the larder, so meat was cut there into its various joints, depending on the menu. No real cooking was involved, but it was useful knowledge to acquire. Not long thereafter, I reached my goal and was promoted to the sauce section. My boss there was Eric Scamman, an Englishman surprisingly, from whom I learned an amazing amount. I think I cook some fantastic sauces these days, and it's all due to Eric Scamman. I said as much on a radio programme not long ago, and had a very sweet letter from Eric, retired in Skipton, thanking me. Eric gave everyone nicknames. Shepherd was Baa-Baa – obviously because 'Shepherd' led to sheep and hence the noise a sheep makes – and I was known as Elsie, as Elsie Tanner was then the highlight of the northern television soap, *Coronation Street*. You can work it out, Turner, Tanner, Elsie… Eric was known to all and sundry in the kitchen as 'Dewdrop' (although not to his face), because of a tendency for sweat to gather, in the heat of the kitchen, on the tip of his nose.

Eric was very well organised. He insisted that we all start off the morning in the fridge, taking everything out, washing, checking, discarding. By doing this, at the beginning of every day, he had a very clear idea of what he had that was usable, and what he needed to bring in or prepare before service. It was tedious and pedantic, but a sensible and thrifty system: all the chefs that have worked in the past or that work now for myself, and indeed for Richard Shepherd, have been taught to do the same. To this day, all over the country in hotels, in large and small restaurants, brasseries and diners, there will be someone checking through a fridge making lists at the same time every morning because, ultimately, of Eric Scamman!

In those days, the classic French *espagnole* and *demi-glace* were the basic sauces, both of which involved hours of reduction. They were sauces based on a roux of dripping or clarified fat and flour, not on a reduction of stock as is the fashion today. In the Savoy, the roux would be cooked very gently for an hour in big copper pots in the oven until the mixture was *singé*, just starting to colour. (When these pots were full, it took two men to lift them out of the oven.) To make *espagnole*, we would add brown stock to this basic roux, bring it to the boil, then add a *mirepoix* of gently sautéed carrot, onion and bacon along with some wine and herbs. This would then in turn be cooked overnight, then skimmed, strained and reduced for a further couple of hours. To finish, tomato purée would be added, and the sauce would be cooked for a further hour then carefully skimmed to make an intensely flavoured sauce with a texture like satin. A little would then be used as a component in another sauce, usually *demi-glace*; some light stock and a smaller proportion of *espagnole* would be reduced by two-thirds, then a little Madeira would be added. The flavour of this *demi-glace* (known to Carême as *demi-espagnole*) was so intense that a couple of tablespoons would be enough to make another sauce sing with flavour – whether it was for beef, veal, poultry or offal. It's *so* important to get the basics right.

Before every service, Eric used to taste every sauce. With his head cocked to one side and his hat firmly wedged on (and often, that dewdrop at the end of his nose), he would make his way down the serving table, saying, 'Right, let's go, let's go', just like a hospital doctor doing his rounds. We would have made the individual sauces and put them in bain-maries. There would be a pile of plates, and a jug of water with spoons in it. He would spoon out a little from each sauce on to a plate, check the colour and consistency, then taste it. Every service he would check them all, he was so meticulous. Occasionally the chef would come over to us and taste a couple of sauces, potentially a time for criticism if things weren't exactly right. But that rarely happened because Eric was so efficient.

Eric was truly a great cook, but he could be difficult. In those days, you learned your culinary skills by example, by experience, by watching and reproducing, and to reach the heights of *chef de partie* could take years. Quite understandably, men in those positions (and they were invariably men) used to safeguard their knowledge, not wanting others to benefit too easily from what they had worked so hard and so long to achieve. As a result someone like Eric would actually explain and demonstrate the art of saucery to only one or two people, the ones immediately below him, while the rest of us floundered around, guessing at the basics, knowing nothing or very little of the subtle nuances involved in the finished sauces. Regularly when I'd asked Eric for something to do to help, he'd tell me to scrub the back table where we did all the vegetable preparation. As I'd probably just done that very table, I would be reluctant to repeat it. When I pointed this out to him, he said, 'Well, go and make me a Madeira sauce then.' 'But Chef,' says I, 'I don't know how to.' 'Well, why are you asking me for a job if you don't know how to do it?' 'Can you show me how?' 'I don't have time.' And that was very much the mentality in those days: you had to fight to be shown anything, but you eventually got there by dint of perseverance.

On Saturday nights, when Eric was off duty, an Australian called Garth Wilkinson took over the sauce section. He said he was a committed communist, demanding that all possessions should be shared – although he also did the Pools weekly and was adamant that if he won he'd share nothing with anyone! He was a boisterous type and got drunk quite often, in fact was often at his best when full of alcohol. He used to tie his apron up with metal toilet chains, quite functional as they never wore out. When he was drunk, he used to 'anchor' himself to the stove by means of two meat hooks through the chain belt and hooked over the safety bar protruding from the front of the stove. Many was the Saturday night when I would pass him meats, stocks, seasonings, pots and pans, and he would stand there unsteadily, but cooking like a man possessed, the hook and chain attachments preventing him from falling over!

During those years at the Savoy, I was sent back to Simpson's a couple of times. Once, not long after I'd been at the Savoy, it was for Pancake Day and they just needed an extra pair of hands. I enjoyed that day as I'd been keen on pancakes since my mum used to make them at home (see page 10). In the roast section at Simpson's, there was a defunct wood-fired stove, which for most of the year was topped by a wooden board on which we used to prep meats. But on Shrove Tuesday, the top would be removed and the stove would be fired up with wood for the making of pancakes, thus freeing the remainder of the stoves for normal cooking and service. A team of us would make and cook pancakes all day, thousands of them. We looked like grease monkeys at the end of it, covered in sweat and tiny particles of wood ash.

Another time was about six months into my time at the Savoy. Tony Gough, in charge of the roast section at Simpson's, was on holiday and it was thought his deputy, Polish John, couldn't run it by himself. I was loaned back for two weeks to run the section – the first time I'd actually done that, of course – and John, a little understandably, felt upset and threatened, and didn't actually do much to make me feel at home or at ease. Nevertheless, it was good experience, and it felt good being in charge of at least 70 per cent of the main courses, because a lot of roast meat was eaten then at Simpson's.

During those two weeks, I had to remake an entire batch of apple sauce. This had to be made by the boxload to go with the roast pork and ducks. You peeled and chopped up the apples, then cooked the apple down to a sauce, reduced it, passed it through a sieve into a huge stainless-steel bowl, covered it with greaseproof and put it on the floor of the walk-in fridge. If you were lucky, that might last you a couple of days. However, on one of those days at Simpson's, one of the kitchen porters slipped in the fridge, fell over, and sat in the bowl of apple sauce. As I've already mentioned, many of the kitchen porters were less than efficient in the matter of personal hygiene, and most would have only one pair of trousers to their name. Not wanting to risk anything, I of course had to throw that particular batch of sauce out and start again. I'm not sure what the porter did about his trousers.

I filled in my free time when I was at the Savoy by playing football and playing in the Salvation Army band. On many afternoons off, when there wasn't time to get home and back again for the evening service, a group of about four or five of us would go to the Empire in Leicester Square. There we'd share one afternoon tea between us (we still earned a pittance), and watch the tea dances from the balcony. Bands the likes of Ken McIntosh and Ted Heath would play, and I think my great love of big band music was born on those afternoons, watching elderly ladies strut their stuff with equally elderly men. Many kids of today might be scornful, but to us, needing somewhere warm and dry to sit, particularly in the middle of winter, it was a haven – and indeed very entertaining.

We still played football for the Savoy, and often afternoons off would be spent training in the St Martin-in-the-Fields crypt. The ceiling was arched, there was a flat stone floor and stone walls, and no windows. We played from end to end. Richard Shepherd once kicked the wall by mistake and broke two toes.

Smoked Salmon and Prawn Slice with a Chilli Lime Dressing

SERVES 4

Smoked salmon and prawns served separately were stalwarts of the Savoy first courses. This marriage of the two probably didn't work for the Savoy clients at that time, and would have been considered slightly adventurous. But it works wonderfully well now, particularly with the addition of the chilli and lime in the dressing, which are very much flavours of today.

4 large slices smoked salmon, about 300g (10½ oz) in weight

115g (4 oz) Philadelphia cream cheese

8 cooked giant Mediterranean prawns, shelled

2 teaspoons olive oil

1 teaspoon white wine vinegar

1 tablespoon chopped fresh chives

salt and freshly ground black pepper

12 whole chives

Chilli lime dressing

½ fresh red chilli, seeded and finely chopped

zest and juice of ½ lime

2 tablespoons soy sauce

4 tablespoons olive oil

1 tablespoon chopped fresh parsley

1 garlic clove, peeled and crushed

½ teaspoon caster sugar

Cut 8 x 5cm (2 in) circles from the 4 slices of smoked salmon. Chop the rest of the salmon, and mix with the cream cheese. Chop the prawns finely, and mix into the cheese. Whisk the oil and vinegar together, then mix into the cheese along with the chopped chives, salt and pepper. Leave to one side.

Have ready 4 x 5cm (2 in) metal rings. Lay one circle of salmon in the bottom of each ring. Spoon some of the cheese mixture on top, and pat it flat. Lay another circle of salmon on top, and pat that flat as well. Chill to set.

To make the dressing, mix the chilli with the lime zest, lime juice, soy sauce and olive oil. Add the parsley, garlic and sugar, and season with salt and pepper.

Carefully remove the salmon shapes from their rings, and arrange in the centre of each plate. Drizzle the dressing around, using the whole chives as a garnish.

We had to walk him back to the Savoy and go through the fridge trick, for the Savoy management frowned upon games which might affect work abilities as much as the Simpson's management had.

Although the Savoy management *could*, it appeared, be more enthusiastic when there was the lure of possible success. One year, when I was captain of the football team, we got to the final of the Catering Cup, which was quite something. There were two leagues, and all the big hotels had teams – Grosvenor House, the Dorchester, the Hilton, the Regent Palace, Strand Palace and the Cumberland. We got to that final by dint of sheer guts and determination, but we did have some great players. Peter Novack was a superb midfield player. Anderson, a Swede, should have been a professional centre-forward. And although Bill Cowpe, now general manager of the Goring Hotel, was one of the laziest players I ever met, he certainly knew how to stick the ball into the back of the net with his foot and head.

We usually played the league games in Hyde Park, but the final was to be at Highbury, home to Arsenal. When it was announced that we were to play there, against the Hilton – the hot favourites – I, a mere *commis-chef*, was summoned via the head chef, then the *sous-chef*, to see the Savoy directors. Mr Griffin told me how proud they were of us and that they would do everything they possibly could to help. They provided us with new kit and all promised to come. On the day itself, we changed in the Arsenal home-side changing room – great excitement for lads of our age – and then watched the beautiful actress Shirley Anne Field kick off. The crowd cheered us on – albeit only half-filling one stand – but despite all that support, we lost a goal in the first half, were one–nil down. When we returned to the changing room, the directors all came down and encouraged us: 'You're doing well, we're behind you, you can do it, go for it.' But by the time the whistle blew, we were two goals down and the directors had done a runner. None of us ever saw hide or hair of them again.

Playing for the Salvation Army was one of my other relaxations. I was by now sharing a flat in Bickerton Road in Archway, north London, with four fellow bandsmen. David Loukes became a trombonist with the Hallé Orchestra and taught trombone at the first brass band university in Salford. Malcolm Lucas had been in the Blues and Royals Guards band, playing tuba, as he still did for the Salvation Army. Mike Stubbins, who played the cornet, used to be

Tournedos Rossini
SERVES 4

The Savoy will always remind me of my classical upbringing, and this recipe is probably the classic of all classics of French cuisine – great ingredients married together. In my opinion, the success of this dish at the Savoy was entirely due to the care and attention Eric Scamman gave to his basic stocks and sauces.

4 slices white bread

2 tablespoons groundnut oil

85g (3 oz) unsalted butter

4 x 115g (4 oz) fillet steaks, about 3–4cm (1½ in) thick

salt and freshly ground black pepper

55g (2 oz) shallots, peeled and diced

75ml (2½ fl oz) Madeira

75ml (2½ fl oz) dry white wine

150ml (¼ pint) thickened *Beef Stock* (see page 240–41)

4 x 25g (1 oz) circular portions of good smooth pâté or *pâté de foie gras*

Cut the slices of white bread into *croûtes* the same diameter as the fillet steaks. Fry the *croûtes* in half the oil and 25g (1 oz) of the butter until golden brown. Drain and keep warm.

Heat a heavy-based pan over a fairly high heat. Turn down slightly then add the rest of the oil and half the remaining butter – it will melt very quickly. Add the steaks and sauté, allowing about 3 minutes each side for rare. Season after turning. Remove the steaks from the pan and keep warm.

Place the shallot in the fat in the pan, sauté until softened, then add the Madeira and white wine. Bubble this mixture until reduced and thickened slightly. Add the remaining butter in small cubes to the sauce, followed by the thickened stock. Season and bubble for another 2–3 minutes to allow the flavours to develop.

To serve, place a steak on each of the *croûtes* of fried bread, then put a circle of pâté on top. Spoon the sauce over and around the steaks. Serve with green beans and new potatoes.

a civil servant, and always seemed to be sleeping. He invariably got into work two hours late because of oversleeping, but had to work two hours longer to make up for it. Laurence Findlay, known as Fingers, was a keyboard man, a fantastic pianist. He had a dummy keyboard which he used to play, but without the sound. The only thing you could hear was the tap, tap, tap of his fingers, playing Mozart and Rachmaninov, like a little rat running up and down. Every now and then, while he was 'playing', he would exclaim, 'Oh no!', and we could never work out how he knew he had gone wrong! They were a good bunch of lads.

I'll come back to that particular flat later, but while staying there, I had the chance of a lifetime and was invited to travel abroad with the band on a tour of Europe. I'd played with them already in many distinguished places, including the Albert Hall, and all over the country at the weekends, playing and preaching. (I was still obliged to miss out on quite a few of the concerts themselves, although I'd been to all the rehearsals, because of working on Saturday nights.) The Chalk Farm Salvation Army Band was considered to be one of the best in the country, with a tradition stretching back to the beginning of the century, and a very famous bandleader, A.W. Punchard. It had retained its great reputation in my day because of the bandleader under whom I served, Michael Clack. I got very excited about the European trip as I'd never been abroad before, and we were booked to go to Belgium, France, Switzerland and Italy. In Brussels, a couple of us stayed in an apartment in the cathedral. It belonged to the caretaker, a friend of the Salvation Army. His wife, who had been in the Resistance during the war, entranced us with accounts of her horrifying experiences. It was really quite eerie, sitting in that huge and beautiful space, no television, dim lights, listening to stories about hiding from the Gestapo.

After Brussels, we crossed over the border into France and went up into the mountains where we had lunch in the Mennonite community in whose church we were to play. (The Mennonites are Protestant Christians opposed to infant baptism, taking oaths, holding public office or performing military service. The sect originated in Holland in the sixteenth century, and there are sizeable Mennonite communities in North America, where they settled in 1683.) That lunch to me, although it consisted simply of charcuterie, cured meats, air-dried ham and salad, was spectacular. Sitting in the sun, replete with new foods, tastes and sensations, I felt I'd come a long way from England and its Spam and corned beef! In Strasbourg, though, I had a gastronomic experience that I would rather forget. I can now appreciate the idea, and relate it to the culinary influences in that part of the country, but bowls of rice saturated with pork fat was not at all to our taste.

From France, we went to Switzerland, to Lausanne and Basle, where I fell in love with Dorly Tchopp, a Swiss Salvationist I met at a church concert. I wrote to her (in English, my French was virtually non-existent) for many years thereafter, and I think that visit (Dorly too?) inspired in me a desire to return to Switzerland. From there, we went to Italy, to Turin. After every concert, Dudley Dickens, the second euphonium player, and I would race off to the back of the concert hall and set up a stall to sell souvenirs and records. (The band had made a record especially to help us raise finances for the tour.) In Turin, over the books and discs, he and I met two South African mulatto girls, who were teaching English at the Berlitz School. We stayed out with those girls all night, only creeping back to our hotel in time for breakfast at about eight the next morning. They drove us to somewhere called, I think, St Margaret's Mount, where we parked to look out over the whole darkening skyline of Turin, then we went back to their flat. When we returned, we discovered that we were the talk of the band. That particular episode was fodder for the gossips for many a year afterwards, the band secretary Bram holding it up as a warning as to what could happen to impressionable young bandsmen in foreign parts. The trip became legendary in Chalk Farm, and was known as 'the dark nights of Turin'.

After those dark (but enjoyable) nights, the band went to the Eternal City, to Rome, where we played a few concerts. After a few days, word came that we had been requested by the Pope – at that time, Pope Paul VI – to play in front of him. We were all thrilled, it was such an honour, but Major Brindley Boon, the evangelical leader of the tour, got himself into a terrible lather, and was on the phone to England for hours seeking advice. We were a non-conformist English church. Should we play in front of the leader of the Roman Catholic church? Would it be looked on as paying obeisance to the Pope and his Church? We eventually got permission to play, on the condition that the Chalk Farm band would sing a song written by William Booth, the founder of the Salvation Army.

The night before, our preparations seemed worse than being in the real Army.

In 1967, the Chalk Farm Salvation Army Band played in front of Pope Paul VI in Rome, probably one of the most exciting experiences of my life. I am circled, left of the flag.

We had to iron crisp creases into our trousers and polish our shoes until they gleamed. But it was worth it when we formed up in St Peter's Square. We played some rousing tunes, before marching into the audience chamber where, in front of about three thousand people, including the Pope, we sang our song. There were loud cheers and applause, although I suspect nobody had much idea of who and what this *Esercito della Salvezza* was. The Pope was carried through close to us, and I found it all quite emotional. An Irish Colour Sergeant, Arthur Forbes, was very upset about it all, because he was a staunch Protestant, but we were all Christians together, recognising and acknowledging our differences. To me it was a unique experience, and I shall never forget it as long as I live.

After spending a relaxing day on the silver sands of Ostia, we went back to France, to Paris, where we were to finish off our fortnight's tour. We were supposed to be sleeping on a barge-hostel on the Seine, but most of the young bloods stayed up all night, drinking in the smells and atmosphere of that wonderful city (but not of course *literally* drinking, as the Salvation Army was a temperance organisation!). I reacted to the unfamiliar beauty of the architecture particularly, and I still have notes taken as I wandered around looking at menus

Spring Onion, Garlic and Prawn Risotto
SERVES 4

This is a more appealing combination of rice and fat than the one we had in Strasbourg. Some fish dishes taste just too fishy for many people's tastes, thus I have included the chicken stock as well. I also add Parmesan, not usual in fish risottos, because it too adds a different and good flavour. (To be honest, I often add a tablespoon of cream as well, but I wrote – and ate – this recipe when I was in strict dietary training for the 2000 London Marathon.)

1 tablespoon olive oil

2 bunches spring onions, chopped

4 garlic cloves, peeled and sliced

325g (11½ oz) arborio rice

600ml (1 pint) *White Chicken Stock* (see page 243)

600ml (1 pint) *Fish Stock* (see page 242)

20 large raw prawns

juice of ½ lemon

2 tablespoons freshly grated Parmesan

salt and freshly ground black pepper

1 tablespoon chopped fresh chives

Heat the oil in a large saucepan, add the spring onions and garlic, and sweat, but do not colour. Stir in the rice, and allow the rice to become coated with fat, sweating it until it changes colour.

Meanwhile, bring the stocks to the boil together.

Add a fifth of the boiling stock to the rice pan, and bring back to the boil. Stir in, then leave to simmer until the liquid disappears. Stir regularly. Repeat, each time adding approximately one-fifth of the stock. Stir to allow the rice to absorb the stock, but it should still be quite liquid when ready.

Meanwhile, season and grill the prawns lightly, then shell and chop them. Add the prawn pieces to the rice with a squeeze of lemon juice and the Parmesan. Check for seasoning, then stir all well together. Pour the finished risotto into a hot dish, sprinkle with chives and serve.

pinned to the side of restaurant doors. The food I experienced in Europe was not great, as we couldn't afford to eat out in really good places, but I was still interested and willing to learn.

It was a fantastic trip, with many highlights, and I still remember the silliness of our return journey. Whenever we travelled by bus or coach on the way to a concert, one of our pastimes was to hold a moustache inspection and competition. We were all young men, and growing a moustache was, I suppose, a way of expressing our individuality, a form of defiance even. We used to compare upper lips, giving points for content, thickness, shape, colour and aesthetic value. We also had a secret sign which consisted of rubbing our upper lip, whether hairy or not. We participated in all that sort of nonsense on that trip back from Europe, but when I reached north London I made a beeline for the local barber. There I had a shave, a haircut and a hot towel before, feeling utterly shattered, going home to Bickerton Road with relief, where I slept the sleep of the dead.

Bickerton Road wasn't to remain a haven for long, though. I was the only one of the five of us to do my own washing and ironing (the others got their mothers to do it), and one day I was ironing at home, and alone, when the paraffin heater in the kitchen blew up. We later discovered that someone had been accidentally mixing petrol with paraffin, a terrifyingly flammable combination, and had distributed it around the Kentish Town/Archway area. When the heater burst into flames, I picked it up, opened the door, walked down a flight of stairs, opened a window and pitched it out. The flat was on fire, though, and I ran out into the street seeking help. With burned hands and face, I flagged down a car, asking the occupants to phone the fire brigade and police. Remember there were no mobile phones in those days. I asked several people to help me try and fight the fire, but in vain. The Salvation Army preachers told this story as a modern parable thereafter, but after several rejections, a West Indian guy unreservedly came in, looked after me, and organised things. (I'd still like to thank him properly.) The fire brigade eventually arrived, and the ambulance, and I was taken to the Whittington Hospital with very badly burned hands. I had less severe burns on the face and one of my feet. They sprayed me, put gauze on my hands, told me to keep my hands upwards, and kept me in for a day or two.

The police came to interview me, partly because of the paraffin scam, but also, bizarrely, to ask me about loads of silver jugs, teapots and cutlery they'd found in the back garden of the building. I think they thought I was a burglar trying to get rid of evidence when the flat went on fire. But the explanation was even more bizarre. A mad woman lived in the studio flat upstairs from us; we used to hear her pacing from one side of the studio to the other, talking to herself. She frightened us a little, but never harmed us in any way. It was she who had thrown her silver out of the window when the fire started – quite sensible really (although we later discovered she did this regularly when the madness came upon her) – and it was the last straw so far as the landlords and the local council were concerned. She was taken away to a sanatorium, and sadly later threw *herself* out of a window.

Anyway, there was no flat to come home to after that episode, so we all had to find somewhere else to live. I was taken in by a couple of Salvation Army officer friends who lived round the corner. Because of my hands, they had to do everything for me, even take me to the bathroom. The wife was a very good-looking young lady, and when her husband was out, she had to take over, which caused great hilarity amongst the bandsmen. After a few days there, though, the boys took me home to Yorkshire. I hadn't told my parents the full extent of the accident and my mother was horrified. She rushed me straight to Leeds Infirmary which had, and still does have, a renowned burns unit. The doctors there were equally horrified by the state of my hands. Apparently, the worst thing to do was put gauze bandages on as burns should be allowed access to air. They cut the bandages off, cut a ring off my finger, and sprayed my hands then and regularly thereafter with a plastic film rather like a new plastic skin.

The net result of that stupid accident was that I had to take a few months off work at the Savoy (ironically, the only real holiday I've ever had!). My hands are still affected, being very heat-sensitive – a disaster in a kitchen! – although there was no nerve damage. My right foot was very painful, so I had to wear slippers for a couple of months; there is a scar to this day. My face wasn't very badly burned, but I still have a slightly bald spot on my beard.

Meanwhile, interspersed with my sick leave, my fortnight in Europe and various other excitements, I had actually continued working. I was enjoying the Savoy, and was learning an enormous amount, but I had already begun to hanker for something different. I'd had a good time in Switzerland with the Salvation Army, and I'd since heard that the country had some magnificent hotels as well as a world-famous hotel school. If any one nation knew about food, hotels, and hotel and kitchen management, it was the Swiss. I thought it might be a good idea to get some experience there, so I allowed the idea to begin bubbling in my mind. I also decided that I needed to do a management course, always remembering that they'd thought at college in Leeds that I might make a better manager than cook. The next stage was membership of the Hotel and Catering Institutional Management Association, the HCIMA, and you could acquire that by examination. So I applied to and was accepted by Borough Polytechnical College to study part-time, for a three-year course.

As I was still working, I asked the Savoy head chef if I could have time off. No joy. I then had to ask Eric Scamman if I could reorganise my hours slightly. He was rather more amenable, but it cost me in terms of hours, so I was committed to working like a dog. Often I would be working from early in the morning to half-past midnight to make up for the three hours or so I'd spent at the college. To boost my rocky finances (now about £15 a week, but still not enough) I had taken a job as an office cleaner with the Century Office Cleaning Company. This happened in the very early morning, so you can imagine how tired I was to become.

However, as I was determined to pass that course (I've never failed an exam since the two during my GCEs), I worked constantly, which was very hard when all my mates were out having a good time. I got through the six parts of Part One of the course at Borough after that first year, and was ready and willing to go for the second year. I had to make a big decision though, whether I could do it while still at the Savoy. Conscious of my thoughts of Switzerland, and my determination to become a member of the HCIMA, I decided that I was going to have to leave. I just couldn't keep all those hours going. I got myself a job at St Ermin's Hotel in Victoria, next to Caxton Hall, and said farewell to everyone at the Savoy.

Working there had been a huge move forward in my career, for a few years at the Savoy Grill looked good on anyone's CV. At the Savoy, the dishes were more complicated, part of the classic French tradition, which after all was what I had been trained in. To have had promotion there would have been good, but I never made it beyond *demi-chef*, and could see no immediate chance of profitable advancement. But stepping stone it had indeed been, another few teaching blocks in my culinary education. It still had not given me the whole picture, though – the catering industry was just not designed in that way – and although I now had experience in quite a few sections, I still had many pieces of the commercial kitchen jigsaw to slot into their correct places.

St Ermin's Hotel

St Ermin's, now the Stakis St Ermin's Hotel, was in culinary terms much more down-market than the Savoy. The management and chef were fully aware of my intentions – to do Part Two of the course at Borough, and then to go to Switzerland – but they were happy to have a chef from the Savoy Grill, where I'd learned lots of good dishes. I was appointed *chef-tournant*, relief chef. This meant that whenever a *chef de partie* was sick or had a night off, I would step in, so I worked in all sorts of areas. The chef, Dieter Sondermann, was very good to me and we got on well. I also became friends with Herbert Streiznig, the general manager (later general manager at the Mayfair and Savoy Hotels), David Date, the larder chef, and the second chef, Moser, a German who went on to teach at Westminster College. It wasn't a big team, but they were nice guys and we all mucked in together.

Impatient as I was – and certainly workaholic (as I still am) – I decided to sign on for Part Three of the HCIMA as well, at Ealing College, and do both simultaneously. This wasn't really permitted, but I wanted to save a year, so that I could get to Switzerland sooner. Borough was quite happy as I'd passed Part One, but Ealing was less amenable, although I was taken on: I merely said I'd done all I needed to take Part Three. About forty-eight students had signed on for the course at Ealing – the class was massively oversubscribed – most of them public-school johnnies who were trainee managers at hotels like the Savoy, Strand Palace and Grosvenor House. They would be doing daily management tasks, which I wasn't of course, and they rather mocked me and two others – a publican from Oundle, Peterborough, and Jeremy Taylor, a *chef-tournant* at Claridge's – because we were cooks, not managers. However, he who laughs last... Fifteen of us actually finished the course and not all of those passed it. We three did, though, and once again, dedication and perseverance

Caramelised Lychees on French Toast
SERVES 4

Much as I love fresh lychees, it really is a fag to peel and stone them and try to keep them whole. For this dish, just use tinned. And this French toast is an upgrading of what we used to eat at home for breakfast, using an enriched bread like brioche instead of white sliced.

4 medium eggs

150ml (¼ pint) single cream

85g (3 oz) unsalted butter

8 small slices brioche

55g (2 oz) unrefined caster sugar

32 pieces tinned lychee

4 tablespoons maple syrup

Mix the eggs and single cream well together. Heat 55g (2 oz) of the butter in a frying pan. Dip the brioche slices into the egg–cream mixture, then fry in the butter, colouring lightly on each side. Drain and keep warm.

Meanwhile, in another pan melt the remaining butter and add the sugar. Allow to start to caramelise whilst drying the lychees on a clean cloth. Put the lychees into the caramelised sugar and warm through well.

Serve the lychees on top of the French toast, and pour the maple syrup over and around.

had paid off. Because we were so highly motivated, and the prize was so much greater so far as we were concerned, we had succeeded.

The first management lecture was given by a guy called Chalky White, who was the course tutor at Ealing. He asked us all for our definition of management, and I can't remember what any of us said. But I do remember what *he* said: 'Management is the ability to get others to do what you want them to do.' That has stuck with me, and dominates my management thinking. I believe I have developed an ability to get people to do things for me and to do them my way – although of course I still like most of all to do things myself!

The two courses ran simultaneously, the Ealing one from six until nine at night, on two days a week, the other from three in the afternoon until nine at night one day a week. From Ealing, I would race back to St Ermin's and do the closure, which involved tidying up, prepping things for the next morning, overseeing the washing and cleaning. They were extraordinarily good to me there and I enjoyed that year. Because it was small in size, it had a happy, family atmosphere. If nothing else, I learned about team spirit there, that it was far better to operate as one unit with a shared goal in mind, than to work in many disparate units, as at the Savoy, with each unit 'fighting' another, as they looked after number one.

But I also learned about a new way of 'cooking' (which I was to encounter again years later). A lot of the foods used in the St Ermin's kitchen came out of tins, packets and jars, as it was a hotel which specialised in banqueting, being next to that prime wedding venue of the time, Caxton Hall. The restaurant was not considered too important in the scheme of things. One of the restaurant and banqueting specialities was something called Cocktail Oriental, which consisted of tinned orange and grapefruit segments, with tinned lychees. Although I'd never used tinned ingredients before, I grew to love tinned lychees. In fact, I used to spar with Dieter Sondermann in the larder over who would finish the tin once it was opened. I still use lychees today, albeit fresh, caramelised on top of French toast (see page 85). I also learned from Dieter ways of improving on rather dull basic ingredients when cooking in bulk. He used to take a powdered soup such as asparagus, make it up with water, and cook it. He would then strain it to remove the little lumps of dried asparagus. To the basic soup he'd add some fresh chicken stock, some fresh chopped asparagus and double cream. After a judicious re-seasoning, the soup would emerge, from the least likely of beginnings, as a product which was really not at all unpalatable.

At the end of that year – which was marking time as far as my cooking education was concerned – I learned that I had passed both Parts Two and Three. I got the whole lot, despite the accounting exam being the toughest I've ever had to sit, and I was very chuffed. I wrote immediately to the HCIMA to say that I now wanted the letters MHCIMA, Member of the Hotel and Catering Institutional Management Association, after my name. Despite all my catering experience, at Simpson's, the Savoy and St Ermin's, they refused, saying I had no management experience. I needed to have run at least two sections simultaneously, with responsibility for things like accounts, reception, housekeeping and maintenance, to prove I had practical managerial skills. Upset, I got my father to write to them, saying that in the transport café, and from the age of twelve, I'd run the plate wash, larder preparation, sales and accounts. Mr Streiznig was very kind and wrote to them as well, but all to no avail. It wasn't until I came back from Switzerland that I actually managed to acquire and utilise those useful and tantalising letters. In fact, I've now been elected a fellow of the association, and as there aren't many chefs who are fellows, I feel the long wait was well worthwhile.

Switzerland

Once I'd passed my exams, and gained enormous amounts of confidence, the next part of my life was about to begin. I started applying for jobs in 1968 and, as luck would have it – or divine intervention – I was offered a place at the Beau Rivage Palace Hotel in Lausanne. I'd been to Lausanne when on the Salvation Army band's tour of Europe, so that struck me as the ideal place to go. I have to say that the trepidation with which I left Leeds to come to London was nothing like the trepidation I felt leaving London to go to the Continent. For one thing, I didn't speak any French. I hadn't taken it to any examination stage at school as Mr Brookes, the French master at Morley Grammar School, had taken me aside at one point and said, 'Turner, I don't know why you're wasting your time, you won't be allowed to sit the O-level.' It didn't matter a jot to me then, because when on earth was I ever going to need to speak French? Anyway here I was, regretting that I hadn't concentrated more on French vocabulary and grammar, and really rather apprehensive about it all.

I travelled by train, Channel ferry and train. On the boat I met a rather pretty nurse, so there was an unscheduled night's stop in Paris... Once in Lausanne, I took a taxi to the Beau Rivage Palace, a wonderful building on the edge of Lake Geneva, looking across to Evian-les-Bains, with the Alps and Mont Blanc in the distance. That view never ceased to amaze me. The staff at the hotel, mainly Swiss German, who saw it every day, thought I was mad to be so emotional about it. But to see that panorama against a clear blue sky, every day as I went to work, quite took my breath away.

I worked in the larder section the whole time I was in Switzerland, but didn't in all honesty advance my culinary skills that much. What I did learn were the great and useful skills of organisation, as the Swiss are efficient organisers. The head chef in the kitchen was a Frenchman, Roger Barbate, but the man who really ran the larder was a huge Swiss German called Richard Frei, a gentle giant and a lovely man. Jean Connu was the larder butcher, who cut all the meats. He used to make a spectacular hamburger, more a steak haché really, using the tails of beef fillets: he'd put them through the mincer, and beat the meat up with cream, chopped gherkins and shallots, salt, pepper and some mustard.

We were catering for the hotel's dining room, which had that fantastic view over the lake. It offered a *menu du jour* with choices. In the larder we prepared the first courses, the meats and fish, and much of our work involved pre-preparation in order that the hot kitchen chefs could cook the ingredients straightaway. This was an aspect of organisation that I'd encountered previously, of course, but I had never really been 'hands on' before my time in Switzerland, and in typical Swiss fashion they had it down to a T. Another, to me, uniquely Swiss touch, were the banks of efficient hotplates for putting serving plates on. The waiters would serve dishes from a small separate table: they would leave a little of the meat or vegetable in the serving dish, so that they could come back and offer you more. I thought this very civilised: the customers didn't have to eat too much, and felt they were getting more for their money!

Once a month we used to have a *buffet froid*. As you know, this literally means 'cold buffet' or 'cold table', but the pronunciation in French needs to be spot on.

The verb *buffer* in French means to gobble, to eat hungrily, and I just couldn't get it right. The parents of one of my friends out there, on asking what exactly I did, were somewhat bemused to learn that I worked with 'cold gobbles'! For those buffets, we used to work for up to three days, sometimes half the night, preparing great aspic flats – wonderful silver serving trays coated with an aspic jelly with embedded floral and vegetable decorations. There would be saddles of lamb, ribs of beef, air-dried beef from Grisons, smoked ham from Engadine (both areas in the Swiss Alps), roast turkeys and, unusually but very Swiss, ribs of veal.

Most days, people finished their first courses quite early, so we in the larder were usually finished by about nine-thirty to ten, so for once I could enjoy some social life. There were about twenty to thirty other English people working in the hotel, so groups of us, after changing, used to go to the Café d'Angleterre and drink café Viennoise at the tables outside. It was good fun, but after a month I had to excuse myself from such nightly forays. I had come to Switzerland to learn French, not to speak English, so I cut those evenings down to about two a week. The rest of the time I devoted to the local Salvation Army band, which I'd joined as soon as I had settled in. Georges Donzé was the bandmaster, a kind man, but the chief motivator of the band was the young euphonium player, Jean-Pierre Chevalier. He was a very talented musician, and used to get quite frustrated that the rest of us weren't quite up to the same standards. His parents were retired officers, who ran social services locally, and had a second-hand shop in Lausanne which bought and sold for the Salvation Army. Brigadier Emil Chevalier would dissect damaged second-hand books, and salvage the prints and lithographs. He'd paint them – using a magnifying glass – then frame and sell them to make money for the cause. I have one in my home, of the chateau at Lausanne. He is still alive today – he must be over a hundred – and I had a wonderful relationship with him and his wife, Jean-Pierre's brother André and sister Rosemary. They were like a second family to me. I ate with them regularly on Saturdays, the meal preceded by prayers and a refrain of 'God Save the Queen' for my benefit. Jean-Pierre became and has remained one of my closest friends, and is godfather to my two sons. That family typified the Swiss character to me – generous, warm-hearted, gently humorous. They would say, shaking their heads in mock despair, 'The trouble with us Swiss is that we haven't really got it right. You English people work hard all your lives, and buy your own homes, so that when you die you can leave it all to your children. We don't do that. We rent our homes, spend all our money and go and have a good time. Why can't we be more like you?' It was all very tongue-in-cheek, and indeed they did live life fantastically well.

There was a gang of us in the Salvation Army band who hung around together, among them Rudolf Richenbach and Bernard Polletti. Jean-Pierre would pick me up after service in his Alfa Romeo sports car and we'd go into town, to Rudolf's flat or Bernard's room. There I was forced to speak French which caused much amusement, but at least I was trying. As we chatted about life, music and girls – the important subjects – they teased me about my accent and attempted to correct my pronunciation. In fact, what I was learning was Swiss French from the canton of Vaud. The Vaudois always say that they don't speak but sing, and they do have a wonderful lilt to their voices. When I speak French today – and I'm much more competent now – a lot of French people think that I am Swiss. In fact, an article about me in *Le Chef* in October 1987, entitled '*Le Chef dans le Monde*', says: '*Brian Turner aime la qualité de produits frais et bien choisis. Et cela lui suffit. Car comme il le dit si bien, avec une pointe d'accent suisse: "Plus ça change, plus c'est la même chose!"*' (Brian Turner likes quality, fresh and well-selected produce. And that is sufficient for him. For as he says, with a hint of a Swiss accent: '*Plus ça change, plus c'est la même chose!*')

The gang of us went to band practice as often as we could, and all became good mates. I was often invited to people's homes for meals. On Sunday afternoons, the young daughters of Georges taught me how to ski, slipping and sliding about on wooden skis, a sight to behold. They must all have been under ten then and I remember how they burst into tears when some French visitors started denigrating the English. 'But Brian, *notre ami*, is English...' I've been out to visit several times since then, and the girls, now grown-up of course, have been across to see me and my family. I befriended another youngster, the ten- or eleven-year-old son of a Scots pastry cook at the Beau Rivage Palace. The latter had married a Swiss woman three times his size and twice his age who ran the local *tabac*, or corner newsagent. I worked when I could in the *tabac*, not for money, but for the chance to practise and improve my French, and I took myself off to the local Berlitz School, I was so determined.

I also made other friends, outside of the Salvation Army. Helmut Reichart was my room-mate at the hotel, a German who spoke immaculate English. Keith Timewell is still in my life, and I occasionally see Linda Berry, daughter of the then manager of the Adelphi in Liverpool, who is now a television presenter. I also met an American girl called Betsy Paige-Bent who worked at the *tabac* kiosk in the hotel for three months. I fell desperately in love with her (as did a few others of my cohorts). During that time with Betsy, I persuaded my parents to come out for a few days' holiday. My mother had never before

Mum and Dad came to visit me in Switzerland in 1969, the first time my mum had ever been abroad or on a plane.

left the shores of England, and had never been on a plane, but they arrived with one of my brothers, Philip, and we had a wonderful time. Betsy and I took them to one of my favourite places, the village of Gruyère. We all visited the modern dairy where they now make the cheese, and we sat in the sun afterwards, eating fresh Gruyère cheese with blackberries and Gruyère cream, with our backs against the walls of Gruyère castle.

I went on holiday with Betsy before she left. She had two weeks, but I only had four days. We bought a train ticket around Switzerland, and stayed in youth hostels in places like Gstaad, St Moritz and Zurich. It was a great way to see the country. I had to leave her at a place called Chur, which was very emotional, and make my way back to the Beau Rivage Palace. She returned to Lausanne for one night only before flying back to the States, and I tried very hard to stay with her then, but she couldn't be persuaded. I went back to my own place somewhat disgruntled, and set my alarm so that I could see her off in the morning. But I overslept, and thus missed her, not getting the chance to say goodbye. I've seen her since, though, as she comes occasionally to London.

There were two other highlights of my Swiss sojourn (apart from Betsy).

The Best Burger in the World
SERVES 4

I still think that the hamburger is much maligned, and I suppose when we eat some of the mass-produced ones, we can see why. For me, the comfort of a burger is something we should never lose sight of. I often find myself with fellow chefs (you wouldn't believe the names if I told you) after an official dinner at 2 a.m. on Chelsea Bridge, all of us eating burgers in our dinner jackets. That for me is a sign I've had a great night. But this recipe I found in Switzerland still makes the best burger in the world.

> 2 shallots, peeled and chopped
>
> a splash of olive oil
>
> 675g (1½ lb) tail of beef fillet
>
> 4 tablespoons chopped gherkins
>
> 2 tablespoons double cream
>
> ½ teaspoon Dijon mustard
>
> a splash of Worcestershire sauce
>
> salt and freshly ground black pepper

Sauté the chopped shallot quickly in the oil to take off the rawness, then allow to cool.

Mince the fillet of beef through the fine plate of the mincer into a bowl. Add the shallot, chopped gherkins, cream, mustard and Worcestershire sauce. Beat well together, and season to taste with salt and pepper.

Using a little oil on your hands, shape the mixture into 4 even-sized burger shapes. Leave to rest for 10 minutes.

Preheat the grill, then cook the burgers medium-rare, about 4 minutes on each side. Season well. Serve with *Rösti* (see page 143) and a green salad. Bottled tomato ketchup would not be very Swiss, so use some of our home-made one on page 22.

The first was the invitation to Richard Shepherd's wedding. He had been working in the La Réserve restaurant in Beaulieu-sur-Mer, some ten kilometres from Nice, had met a girl and fallen in love. He phoned me up out of the blue, and I was determined to get there. I was in charge of the days off in the larder section, so I organised myself a couple of extra days and went down by train from Lausanne a little in advance of the actual wedding day. One of those days we went into Italy to buy Richard's wedding suit from his tailor in Ventimiglia. Richard warned me to wear loose clothes, but it wasn't heat he was considering, it was smuggling. Richard bought another couple of suits at the same time, and we came back each wearing a new suit under the old!

The night before the wedding, I ate one of the best meals of my life. Richard and I went to a little wooden restaurant up in the hills looking down over the bay. We had charcuterie to start with – a whole smoked ham carved in front of us, local air-dried meats – which was served from a wooden table with castors. With it we had salad and *anchoïade*, an anchovy vinaigrette. Then we ate *côte de boeuf grillée aux herbes de Provence*, ribs of beef with a crust of rosemary and thyme, both herbs native to the area. It was carved at the table again, and served with potatoes, and then we had cheeses, real French cheeses. It was a wonderful evening, not least because of the occasion, and the food, but possibly, in retrospect, because it was the first time I had eaten superb food in a real restaurant and relaxed into it, talking, eating and laughing (I still wasn't drinking). It brought home to me the difference between the British and the French. In England, we would have eaten and drunk, then gone on to play cards or the piano, or have a sing-song. In France, they take the serious things of life very seriously, and spend the whole evening talking, drinking, eating and more talking. This concentration on sitting at table and eating as sheer pleasure was a revelation to me, another piece of the jigsaw slotting into place.

After we got back to Beaulieu, we joined Richard's mates and had a stag party. My memory is usually good, but could it really be true that we all painted each other with make-up? The wedding itself passed in a blur. I was the only Englishman there, apart from the bridegroom, and nobody could quite believe I was from England – this time they thought my accent was Parisian! But I was in trouble when I returned to the Beau Rivage Palace. I'd been back at work for a day when there was a call on the tannoy from the kitchen. Roger Barbate

Chocolate and Hazelnut Terrine
SERVES 15

Whenever Switzerland is mentioned, we all think of cheese, clocks, mountains and cows, but how can we forget Swiss chocolate, everyone's favourite.

Brownie

75g (2¾ oz) unsalted butter, softened

125g (4½ oz) caster sugar

1 medium egg, beaten

30g (a good 1 oz) plain flour

30g (a good 1 oz) cocoa powder

35g (1¼ oz) shelled toasted hazelnuts, chopped

¼ teaspoon vanilla essence

Truffle mix

375g (13 oz) dark chocolate

225ml (8 fl oz) double cream

25ml (1 fl oz) dark rum to taste

100g (3½ oz) hazelnut paste

4 medium egg yolks

225ml (8 fl oz) double cream, whipped

Ganache

100g (3½ oz) dark chocolate

50g (1¾ oz) unsalted butter

25ml (1 fl oz) double cream

Preheat the oven to 180°C/350°F/Gas 4. To make the brownie, cream the butter and sugar together. Add the egg, and sift in the flour and cocoa. Fold in with the hazelnuts and vanilla. Spoon into a 30 x 20cm (12 x 8 in) tray lined with greaseproof paper, smooth over, and bake for 15–20 minutes.

To make the truffle, put the chocolate, cream, rum and hazelnut paste in a bowl in a bain-marie, and heat to melt. Whisk the egg yolks in a bowl over simmering water until they have thickened and turned pale and frothy then fold into the melted chocolate mixture. Fold in the whipped cream and mix gently.

Line a 1 litre (1¾ pint) terrine mould with clingfilm, and pour the mixture into this. Cut an oblong the same size as the terrine out of the brownie mix, and place this on top of the truffle mixture. Put in the fridge overnight to set. (Cut the remaining brownie mix into squares and serve as a teatime cake or a dessert.)

Make the ganache by melting the chocolate, butter and cream together in a bain-marie – not over direct heat – then whisk until smooth. Carefully unmould the terrine on to a serving plate. Pour the hot chocolate mixture over the chilled terrine and allow to set. Slice with a hot wet knife.

demanded that I go and see him and, in French, I got the biggest dressing-down of my life for taking off two unauthorised days. I would have made up for them, and he knew it, but I'd always had a fairly hard time with him.

The other highlight of my stay in Switzerland involved some leave that was actually authorised. The Lausanne Salvation Army Band went on trips, playing and evangelising, in much the same way as the Chalk Farm band. This year they were going to Vienna to take part in the annual Music Week, involving four days away. To my Swiss colleagues, going from Switzerland to Austria was like a trip from London to Cardiff. For me it was a great adventure, but from the very first moment, it became a real saga.

About thirty of us boarded the train at Lausanne. Those of us with easily portable instruments carried them as hand luggage, but the larger basses and euphoniums had to travel in the goods van. This was all done at Lausanne, then again at Zurich, where we changed on to the Vienna train. When we were approaching Buchs, on the frontier between the two countries, a customs man got on the train to check passports. He was a small Austrian, very correct, and Jean-Pierre was suddenly seized with a desire to deflate that pomposity. Jean-Pierre took the plastic lining from his Salvation Army cap, and put it on rather like shower cap, put in a set of false teeth (with fangs) and a pair of glasses. He sneaked behind Herr Customs Man and sat down in the next compartment, waiting for his passport to be checked again. He was giggling so much (as were we) that when he tried it a third time he was rumbled. Our own little Nazi called the police as soon as the train reached Buchs, and Jean-Pierre, our star bandsman, was arrested and marched off. 'You cannot enter Austria, you are a hooligan.' We had to negotiate for about an hour, explaining that we were evangelists, that we were booked to play music in churches in Vienna, that we really were quite responsible people. Only when Jean-Pierre apologised was he released and the train allowed to go on its way. Hundreds of people had been held up because of that stiff-necked little man – although I must admit, laddish tomfoolery had played a part as well.

But worse was to come. When we reached Vienna, we discovered, much to our chagrin, that the goods coach had been disconnected from the train, and thus the bass end of the band had no instruments. This was mid afternoon, we had a concert in the evening, and we panicked. A series of frantic telephone calls elicited

Flan au Gruyère
SERVES 10

I'm a great cheese fan, and would be hard pushed to name my favourite cheese. Gruyère must figure there somewhere though, and I think it eats really well when warm. I remember staying with my family in Jean-Pierre's flat, having returned there on holiday. He lived five floors above a boulangerie, and guess what my favourite dish was?

1 x recipe *Shortcrust Pastry* (see page 17)

Cheese filling

6 medium eggs

2 medium egg yolks

125ml (4 fl oz) double cream

280g (10 oz) Gruyère cheese, grated

1 teaspoon salt

freshly ground black pepper

500ml (18 fl oz) milk

Preheat the oven to 190°C/375°F/Gas 5.

To make the pastry, follow the instructions on page 17. After chilling, roll out to line a large flan ring of 25cm (10 in) in diameter on a baking sheet. Blind-bake this, using foil and dried baking beans, about 15 minutes. Remove the foil and baking beans, and leave the baked case in its ring to one side on a baking sheet. Reduce the temperature of the oven to 160–180°C/325–350°F/Gas 3–4.

To make the cheese filling, put the eggs, egg yolks, cream, 55g (2 oz) of the cheese, salt and some pepper into a bowl, and whisk together. Warm the milk to blood temperature and stir in.

Scatter the rest of the cheese over the bottom of the pastry case on the baking sheet, and gradually add the milky mixture until full. Carefully lift the baking sheet into the preheated oven, and bake until the filling is set, about 35–40 minutes. Serve warm, with a nice salad and a glass of chilled white wine.

apologies and the promise of instruments being returned to us – but sadly not until the next day. Reluctant to cancel the concert – most of the tickets had been pre-sold – Georges Donzé decided that we would sing, rather like a male voice choir, with only the tenor horns and cornets as accompaniment. There was no time for rehearsal, although we always had songs and hymns in our repertoire, but the evening was a disaster waiting to happen. I'm afraid that I was the innocent who precipitated that disaster. We stood in rows, the cornets raised on steps behind, with Georges Donzé in front conducting, his back to the audience. As we were about to begin, with Georges' baton raised, I remembered that I had not fixed my denture with glue. The pressure of a cornet on your embouchure, on your lips, is quite great, so the glue was vitally necessary. As I prepared to play, my denture shot forward, half out of my mouth, and Georges collapsed with laughter. As his baton twitched uncontrollably, the band, unable to see what was happening, thought this was the signal to start playing and singing. That first piece was an absolute and utter shambles, but we got through the rest of the concert, God only knows how.

Apart from those mishaps, the weekend was a total success. The instruments duly arrived the next day, and the concerts thereafter went without a hitch. We all enjoyed Vienna, in spare moments going to the fairground with its huge ferris wheel and into the wonderful parks. I saw the famous Sacher Hotel (although I missed out on the *torte*), and travelled about by tram. The Viennese Salvationists were wonderful, very hospitable, and Rudolf Richenbach, as was his wont, fell in love with an Austrian Salvationist, Elizabeth, and bought her an engagement ring a day or so after meeting her (sadly, he never got her to the altar, but there again, that was Rudolf!). We ate mostly in the hostels where we were staying, but I managed to taste some Austrian specialities such as *Wiener schnitzel*, *Sauerbraten* and *Bratwurst*. It wasn't inspiring, but again I was learning.

However, back at the Beau Rivage Palace, I was beginning to feel homesick. I had been away from England for twelve to fifteen months and I was missing my family. I had learned to speak French quite well, considering I only knew how to say '*oui*' and '*non*' when I arrived, but I longed for the ease of speaking in my native language. I was surrounded by good friends, but I just had the urge to go home. In retrospect, that was a huge career mistake. I should have stayed and moved on to one of the other hotels, perhaps done a winter season somewhere in the Alps, or another summer down at the lakes. My French would have improved, as indeed might my German, for I had started to be taught by my room-mate, Helmut. One thing I've learned since about life is that once you do something, you should consolidate it, but foolishly I didn't. Switzerland was a valuable experience, but I should have taken the skills I'd acquired on to somewhere else, to expand and build on them, instead of returning to my own country.

Back Home and Claridge's

And so I returned to Yorkshire in the September of 1969, to the home comforts of Morley. Everyone was pleased to see me, and it was great to be back. I had grown up a bit, laughed and learned a lot, played lots of music, acquired a fondue set (inevitably), and started a new collection of Swiss stamps. I had no money, though, and no immediate prospects, but I wanted to throw myself back into work and try to save up for the next stage of my culinary journey. From the want ads of the *Caterer and Hotelkeeper*, the trade magazine, I applied and was accepted for the post of head chef at Kildwick Hall, a hotel near Skipton (where the television version of *Wuthering Heights* was filmed). It was owned and managed by Mr Donald Hart, an eccentric antiques dealer.

As I arrived at Kildwick Hall, the previous chef was just leaving. This was Michael Quinn, a fellow Yorkshireman, who was later to cook at Gravetye Manor and then at the Ritz (the latter job he got indirectly through me). Michael hadn't stayed long at Kildwick and history was to prove that I wouldn't either. I loved the cooking and leadership opportunities, but I felt that Donald Hart, clad always in slippers and cardigans festooned with holes, did not give me enough autonomy. After six weeks I'd had enough and went back home. My mother suggested I get back in touch with Michael Smith for some advice as to what to do next. She had been going with Michael's sister to night classes at the EAW, the Electrical Association for Women, where they learned how to change plugs and do domestic things that weren't considered too difficult or dangerous. With some trepidation I went to see Michael, now in the vanguard of British food journalism, at the Kitchen, his café-restaurant in Leeds. His counsel was to return to London. 'Look lad, if you've got it, you'll make it, and if you haven't, you might as well find out, then you can come back home.' So once more I wrote to hotel restaurants

Caviar and Sole Rolls
SERVES 4

I suppose the inclusion of caviar might put you off this recipe because of the cost factor, and many would argue that cooking with caviar is a waste anyway. However, the idea is good, as is the taste, so a simpler and cheaper method is to use keta, a salmon roe – but please, *never* lumpfish roe!

8 Dover sole fillets

8 large spinach leaves

salt and freshly ground black pepper

175g (6 oz) unsalted butter

55g (2 oz) caviar, the best you can afford

1 shallot, peeled and chopped

150ml (¼ pint) *Fish Stock* (see page 242)

175ml (6 fl oz) dry white wine

3 tablespoons double cream

juice of ½ lemon

2 tablespoons chopped fresh chives (optional)

To serve

25g (1 oz) caviar, as above

some whole chives

Preheat the oven to 180°C/350°F/Gas 4. Tap out the sole fillets carefully to flatten them a little, and cut in half crossways.

Blanch the spinach leaves and refresh quickly in cold water. Drain and lay on a work surface. Season with salt and pepper and place a piece of sole on top. Melt 55g (2 oz) of the butter, and brush some over the sole. Place some caviar sparingly on top and then another piece of sole. Brush with melted butter again. Wrap this tightly in a spinach leaf and put to one side. Repeat so that you have 8 rolls.

Brush a suitable ovenproof dish with melted butter. Sprinkle with the shallot and place the rolls on top. Gently pour in the fish stock and wine, and season with salt and pepper. Poach in the preheated oven for 10 minutes covered with foil, then take out and keep warm. Pour the juices from the dish into a preheated small pan and boil to reduce by half. Add the cream and reduce again by about half. Slowly add the remaining butter, cut into cubes, and then the lemon juice. Season, and stir in the chopped chives if using.

Put 2 reheated sole rolls on each hot serving plate, and cut one of the rolls in half. Top the cut edges with a little caviar, and garnish with some whole chives. Pour the hot sauce around and serve immediately.

and chefs in London to offer my services. I could have been chef saucier at the Ritz, under Jacques Viney, but I accepted a job as *chef-tournant*, relief *chef de partie*, at Claridge's, under Felix Soubrand.

I was to start just after Christmas, but meanwhile my Salvation Army pals from Lausanne – Jean-Pierre, his brother, André, and Bernard – had decided to pay me a visit in Yorkshire. I got Ken Evans, the flugelhorn player at Chalk Farm, to meet them at the airport and get them to King's Cross. They came up on a Royal Mail milk train, which stopped at every station in those days. These tough boys, for all of them had been in

Richard Shepherd and I met in 1964 in Simpson's, and we have been close mates ever since. I think this photograph, taken more recently at an Academy do, typifies our relationship – convivial, bucolic and full of laughter.

the Swiss Army (it's still compulsory), shivered for five hours all the way to Yorkshire in an unheated train, the freezing damp affecting them much more than the dry cold of Switzerland. They must have thought they were going to hell, or Siberia. I met them at the station in Leeds and took them home to get warm. My mum, in full Yorkshire welcoming mode, asked, 'Would you like a treat, boys?' And she presented them with platefuls of beans on toast! This was indeed a family favourite, but goodness knows what they must have thought. They could have expected something a little more glamorous from the mother of their chef friend, not what was virtually Swiss Army rations!

We travelled back to London together and stayed in a bed and breakfast place in Earlsfield for a few days. When the boys returned to Switzerland I went to live with Ken Evans and his family in Edgware. I started work at Claridge's in mid January of 1970, and stayed for about fifteen months. Richard Shepherd was back in England, too, happily ensconced as larder chef at the Dorchester. Claridge's in those days was known as the hotel where royalty and heads of state would stay when in London. Its kitchen wasn't particularly rated, and in all honesty, I can't remember much about the food that we produced, even though I worked in so many different sections over those fifteen months. What I do remember is the kitchens flooding regularly, with silver dishes floating in three feet of water. And I'll certainly never forget achieving a 'first', both for myself and certainly for Claridge's. Just as I'd carved beef on the trolley at Simpson's, that summer I had to go up to the restaurant to carve smoked salmon (those hours spent watching Jimmy, the carver at Simpson's, and all my practising, had not been wasted). This was usually performed by one of the waiters, but they were short-staffed. I felt immensely proud to be doing something I was good at in front of an audience. I also *enjoyed* it, seeing the customers and feeling the buzz of a busy dining room. This was my first taste of playing to the public, valuable experience in terms of what was to happen the next year, and in the years thereafter.

I made friends, though, among the lads: Brian Wallace was a sauce chef; Michael Smith (another one) was on roasts; Kipper and Michael Joyce were on fish. I met Ian Calver and Chip Fry (John Fry, known as Chip), a couple of jack the lads. (When I was at the Capital, I persuaded Calver to come and work with me, which he did, and he's now back with Richard Shepherd.) I also got on very well with Michael Bentley, the assistant manager. He was a stickler for correctness in dress and behaviour, a necessity in his job, dealing as he did on a daily basis with crowned heads, diplomats and important international figures. He is a lovely man, and I still see him occasionally. I learned a few things from him about dealing with colleagues and customers, and I believe that it was he who taught me how to dress well, speak well and carry myself well. At some time, though, I must have overstepped some mark, because I can never forget his gentle but admonishing words, 'Brian, never mistake friendship for a weakness.' People can and do take liberties with friends they wouldn't with others, but now, some twenty-five years later, I still don't know what it was I'd done.

Michael and I had many dealings over the Claridge's football team which I captained. He was a great supporter and very keen that the boys should get some good healthy exercise. We had a good team, played in Hyde Park in the Catering League, but we never reached the heights I'd achieved at the Savoy. I was still so keen that many a night after a banquet – as relief night chef,

I would have to work until two or three in the morning – I would be playing three-a-side soccer with the banqueting staff. The venue, Claridge's ballroom, the ball made out of rolled-up serviettes. And this after a supper of leftover caviar from the banquet, usually accompanied by chips! That was actually one of the primary perks of being a night chef. There would always be food and drink left over, which we could have, all above board. At about eleven-thirty or twelve, depending on who was on duty around the place, you could cook dinner for three or four senior members of staff. You had the keys, the doors were open, you could have what you wanted. Someone would bring some wine down, and things like caviar would be left over from the banquets. Notables like the Sultan of Brunei would bring in their own supplies of caviar in those days, for which Claridge's used to charge 'caviarage', like corkage.

But some things were not above board. The primary thing I remember about Claridge's was its problem with corruption. We had taken foodstuffs at Simpson's, but that was for subsistence, so could in a sense be 'justified'. Here there was outright thieving. Behind the backs of more senior employees goods were sold for profit by certain staff in the larder. They took specific orders for meat and pocketed the cash. It was all rather frustrating for me, as I was and am basically very honest at heart. I remember one afternoon when I was on duty as soup cook. The duty manager came and told me that the breakfast cook had been caught going out with a side of smoked salmon, fillet steaks and a cake under his raincoat – the whole shooting match for his child's birthday party. The hotel had him arrested, but the police wanted to know a rough value of the goods. Off the top of my head, I estimated around £70, a lot of money in those days. We never saw that particular breakfast chef again.

Richard Shepherd was experiencing the same sort of thing at the Dorchester. Perhaps because we were a little older, and more responsible, we had become more aware of such behaviour and could not disregard it. Memories must have come flooding back to him, as they did to me, of the days when we were so young and inexperienced, and thought dining at the company's expense was acceptable behaviour. How things change. Anyway, we often discussed our problems over the telephone and the occasional drink when our shifts allowed us to get together. But it was one particular telephone call from Shepherd that was to propel me into my next culinary phase. That call was to change my life completely.

part three
THERE'S A SMALL HOTEL

The Capital Hotel

I had been sent on a course at Ealing College by Claridge's in May 1971, and some time during that month Richard Shepherd phoned to say that he had been offered and had accepted the job of head chef at a new small hotel in Basil Street in Knightsbridge. Did I want to come as second chef? Shepherd intimated that there were great excitements in store, and that this might be the start of our future. So I went for an interview at the Capital Hotel with the owner, David Levin, and the newly appointed general manager, Michael Demarco, heard about their plans, and accepted with enthusiasm. It was Richard's first head chef post, my first as *sous-chef* (for my sortie into head chefdom at Kildwick had been terrifyingly brief, and didn't really count).

It was a completely new hotel, built to David Levin's specifications, and had been transformed into what the *Good Food Guide* would describe as 'an aeroplane-age hotel' by the interior designer, Nigel Clark. He had done this in close collaboration with David and Margaret Levin, who had very clear ideas about what they wanted. Small

The Capital Hotel in Basil Street, Knightsbridge, which opened in May 1971. It was brand new, a small hotel masquerading as a large one, and it was where I became Richard Shepherd's second in command.

It was nice to meet my former employers, David and Margaret Levin, at Anton Mosimann's
splendid fiftieth birthday bash – at the Natural History Museum – in 1998.

hotels did not exist in London at the time, only huge hotels like the Ritz, Dorchester etc., and it was these that people were most familiar with. David Levin had long wished to open a small hotel in London, but one which would be more in the style of the small country hotels beginning to spring up throughout Britain. The concept was to make this particular small hotel *look* like a large hotel, and in that they succeeded admirably. It was described in the 1972 *Egon Ronay's Dunlop Guide* as a 'brand-new, conveniently sited hotel whose pleasing modern lines blend well with its period neighbours'. Inside it was streamlined and smooth, with lots of space, and to quote the *Egon Ronay Guide* of 1974, had an 'excellent blend of luxury and functionalism in the décor'. The reception area was stainless-steel, space-age silver and grey, inspired by the surface of the moon – quite avant-garde for that time – with wonderful marble floors. On the right you could either go into the bar or into the restaurant. The latter was spectacular to my eyes: it had a very high ceiling, long windows and well-spaced tables. The colours were browns and beiges, the walls were lined with hessian and there were mounted oak carvings. The 1974 *Egon Ronay*, perhaps unwittingly, recognised the aim of the Levins in saying, 'Here you have the illusion that you are eating in a private room at a high-powered grand hotel, instead of at a quiet little spot in an attractive corner of Knightsbridge.' The bedrooms, about fifty of them, had all mod cons, and the marble bathrooms offered all sorts of thoughtful touches such as sachets of bubble bath and disposable razors (a new idea at the time). The upper floors were reached by a silver-panelled lift, and the short corridors were hung with modern abstract paintings. All in all, no expense seemed to have been spared.

David Levin was not well known then in the food world, although he has become so since, through an acute business sense and an unerring eye for what would become desirable and fashionable in both the hotel and restaurant scene. His initial concept, so far as the Capital restaurant was concerned, was to produce food on the call-order system – easy eating such as steaks or omelettes, with one or two more sophisticated dishes. But, perhaps foreseeing one of the trends that he has so cleverly exploited over the years, and very fortunately for us, he decided to make the Capital Hotel restaurant a centre of gastronomy. That's when Richard Shepherd was approached, through the recommendations of Michael Demarco. The latter had left the Royal Garden Hotel to join David Levin in the new venture, and appeared to know everything there was to know on the hotel, food and social scene. The restaurant might not make all that much money, they reckoned – the rooms would be the main earner – but it could be a great draw.

To understand just how revolutionary – and exciting – the concept of the new Capital restaurant was, it's necessary to describe a little of what was happening on the British culinary scene at that time. 'Posh' dining was dominated by the great London hotel restaurants, where most of the chefs were foreign and the principal style was classical French. This is what I had experienced at the Savoy, and Richard at the Dorchester. Apart from some French bistros, and a few other reasonable international restaurants, the standards of cooking in Britain then were not high. But out of London, different things were happening. Inspired by a few food writers – and food writing then was not the prevalent and popular art it is today – a number of gifted amateur cooks had opened hotels and restaurants, some of the latter with rooms, which were beginning to be famed for serving some of the best food in the country.

In 1949 Francis Coulson opened the huge oak doors of Sharrow Bay in the Lake District, following his own love of good food and the teachings of first, Constance Spry, and later, Elizabeth David. Brian Sack soon joined him, and by the early 1970s, the hotel had received many professional accolades. George Perry-Smith began cooking at The Hole in the Wall in Bath in 1951, just after Elizabeth David published her seminal first book, *A Book of Mediterranean Food*, and in the same year as Raymond Postgate published the first *Good Food Guide*. These luminaries were soon joined in the 1960s by others such as Kenneth Bell at the Elizabeth near Oxford, then Thornbury Castle, by Patrick and Sonia Stevenson at the Horn of Plenty in Tavistock, and by John Tovey's 'Tonight at 8.30' experience in Windermere (to be followed by his classic small country hotel, Miller Howe, which opened the same year as we did at the Capital, in 1971). John Tovey was inspired by another British food writer, Margaret Costa, but Elizabeth David was pre-eminent in re-introducing the post-war and rationed British to the joys of good food, and the wonders of French provincial cooking. She was soon joined, though, by writers such as Claudia Roden, Robert Carrier and other food journalists writing in such outlets as the *Sunday Times* colour magazine, who opened our northern eyes and hearts to the flavours of the warmer rest of the world.

A renaissance of good food and good eating in Britain was well on its way, and David Levin was quick to see the possibilities. He was still wedded to the classical French tradition, though, as were Shepherd and I, and indeed the style predominated in London – the Roux Brothers had opened Le Gavroche, their first British restaurant, in Mayfair, only a few years before, in 1967. But the concept of a top-flight classical restaurant inside a small hotel was new and exciting. He determined that the Capital would be less daunting as a dining experience, for many temples of gastronomy then were great echoing rooms where people were restricted by formal clothes (those worn by themselves and by the serving staff!), talked in whispers, and felt guilty if they clattered fork against plate. Another of his innovations was also slightly influenced by what was happening in the new British establishments. In George Perry-Smith's Hole in the Wall, and a few other restaurants, the kitchens were in full view of the diners, which made service easier and the atmosphere more convivial. The kitchen at the Capital was to be largely open plan, so that we could see out, and diners could see in. After being locked away in a dungeon–basement for years, this seemed fantastically attractive to me.

All these plans were outlined to me by David Levin and Michael Demarco during my interview and, although they painted a picture that was bright and full of life, it was Richard who really fired me up. It was he who said that in effect we would be in charge of our own destiny: we would of course work with the hotel owner and manager, but the kitchen, although small, was to be our total responsibility. This meant menu planning and designing, ordering from suppliers, preparing food and cooking it, managing the kitchen and its staff, as well as being seen by and dealing with the public, all new steps for us. For the first time in our lives, we could see a truly new and exciting future full of possibilities. For years we had both worked on sections in commercial hotel kitchens, perfecting one stage of a dish or meal, never seeing nor often caring about the final result; the chance to oversee both the finished dish and see the reactions of the recipients was tantalising. The thought of being appreciated by face and name was attractive, too. We had no illusions about stardom – television cookery and its mass audience were light years away – but a potential recognition both within the industry and the public was a whole new ball game for us. The backroom boys might now become more visible, and to a large extent I think this was due to the influence of those gifted amateurs mentioned above. Because of their enthusiasm, skills and sheer sociability, they had become household names, at least within their own individual fields. We, the ones with the professional experience, and with their example before us, could transform that enthusiasm into passion. I truly believe that it was in those first few weeks and months at the Capital that cooking, once a vital part of our lives, actually took over our lives completely. It was probably true for many young chefs in that all-important time of the early 1970s, but it was undoubtedly true for me!

That first month, though, was very hard work. The hotel opened on 11 May 1971, and I cooked virtually on my own, for Richard had jumped ship and gone to France. On David Levin's instructions, he was spending time with Pierre Gleize who had a two-star Michelin restaurant, La Bonne Etape. This was in Château-Arnoux in Provence, not all that far, but inland, from where Richard had worked at La Réserve in Beaulieu. Pierre Gleize had undertaken to work on the Capital's menu with Richard – designing it and showing Richard the dishes – for which I'm sure he was paid a fee. (He and his son, Jany, who worked at the Connaught, are still doing this, flying off for 'free' holidays in places like Mauritius, while advising on menu planning. As indeed are a number of us, and it's a great incentive for cooks. I've been on the QE2 and to Mauritius and Bermuda doing much the same thing.) For that month, then, we offered a very limited menu of simple plain fare, which we made up as we went along, but it gave me a chance to acclimatise myself and to meet the other staff.

Helping me in the kitchen was David Townsend. He had worked with David Levin at the Royal Oak, Yattendon, before he moved up. He was a good cook, a workhorse. He went on to cook for the Vesteys for many years, then married a Portuguese girl and now lives in the sun. I see him about every three or four years. Because the Capital was a hotel, we had to serve breakfast as well as lunch and dinner, and for that we employed Doreen, a cheeky Scouse. Often, though, she wouldn't turn up for one reason or another – a series of domestic excuses – and we would have to do breakfast as well, which was a bit of a pain, particularly if we'd been late the night before. We had two great Spanish kitchen porters, Rodriguez and José. The latter came with me to Turner's fifteen years later, and took early retirement in January 2000 because of his wife's ill health. I shall miss him; he was an integral part of our lives at the restaurant.

But when Richard came back, the action really began. He had spent four weeks with Pierre Gleize in the Alpes-Maritimes, looking, planning and learning. David Levin had decided that the Capital was going to boast a gastronomic French restaurant, which would be quite different from other hotel restaurants. He wanted people to come into the hotel to dine, and to come and *stay* in the hotel in order to dine. Most hotel restaurants at that time were mainly functional, serving as a dining room for the hotel guests, not in the business of attracting people in from the outside. Hotel food certainly wasn't much talked about, and Levin wanted to change all that. In fact, the Capital started a trend thereafter. As we became better known, it became the vogue for people to ring and ask if there was a table at a certain time a few weeks hence. If there were, they would then book a room; if there weren't, they'd book to stay elsewhere. The rooms were lovely, but the principal reason for staying in the hotel was the restaurant.

One of the first decisions made was that the menu, *La Grande Carte*, would be written entirely in French (the only things in English were the details of service charge and, later, VAT!). It was divided up into *Les Potages*, *Les Hors d'Oeuvres*, and three categories of main course: *Les Entrées Cuisinées*, *Les Entrées au Feu de Bois* (cooked on the wonderful charcoal grill in the centre of the kitchen) and *Les Entrées Gastronomiques* (mainly fish, and indeed later these were listed, intermittently, as *Les Poissons*). These terms were probably taken directly from Pierre Gleize's menu, his romantic way of differentiating between cooked and sauced meat courses, cooked and sauced fish courses, and grills. *Le Panier des nos Maîtres Fromagers* was on offer, as were various ices, sorbets, fruit dishes and gâteaux. The menu also included a small recommended list of selected wines which were separate from the main wine list. But most important to us in the kitchen was the note at the foot of the menu: '*Si par hasard un plat manquait à cette carte, c'est uniquement parce que nous ne disposerions pas d'éléments assez rigoureusement frais pour le préparer aujourd'hui.*' ('If by chance a dish is unavailable on this menu, it's only because we could not find the quality and freshness in ingredients necessary to prepare the dish today', or words to that effect.) This wasn't a way of excusing ourselves if by chance we hadn't managed to get an item that day, or had run out: it was an insistence on the quality we were offering.

The menu was to change roughly quarterly, primarily the soups and hors d'oeuvres, but core elements there were virtually permanent, and indeed some of them are still on the menus at Turner's and Langan's, where Richard was to go. The *Carré d'Agneau Persillé aux Herbes de Provence (deux personnes)* is a wonderful rack of lamb with an aromatic crust composed of Provençal herbs, which was one of Pierre Gleize's dishes. At La Bonne Etape he used the lambs of Sisteron, grazed during the summer on pastures rich in Provençal herbs, which gives them a very distinctive flavour. We were using the wonderful lamb from the Welsh Borders. Our rack was carved at the table, as was the *Côte de Boeuf aux Aromates* (also for *deux personnes*), an echo of the magnificent dish Richard and I had enjoyed in the Provençal hills the night before his wedding. Another French-inspired dish was sea bass, which we called '*Loup Capital*'. '*Loup de mer*' or 'sea wolf' is the southern French name for sea bass, and there it would be grilled with fennel. I think Richard had encountered this at La Réserve. *Gratin de Jabron*, a variant on *Gratin Dauphinois*, was a usual accompaniment.

Another dish which was new to us, and probably to London, was an hors d'oeuvre, *Coeur d'Artichaut Farci à la Nissarda* ('Niss' was apparently an old word meaning 'of Nice'). I'd seen and prepared artichokes before at the Savoy (most artichokes available before this time came from a tin), but now we stuffed them with a mushroom duxelles and served them with a paloise sauce (hollandaise plus mint). I only recently found out that Richard Shepherd invented this dish in his back garden along with his wife, Christine; it was inspired by the great dish, *artichauts barigoule*.

Another stalwart of the *carte* was *Mousseline de Coquilles St Jacques à la Crème d'Oursins*, once again a Pierre Gleize dish. It was a light mousse of scallops and hake which we used to make in large blocks and freeze. The outer mousse was lightly flavoured with curry powder, new to us then, but something that the French use quite often, subtly adding the spice mixture much as they would any other seasoning. In the middle was a bright orange blob, made from sea urchin and scallop roes. Sea urchins were virtually unknown then in England, but were used a lot in Provençal cuisine. A speciality of the region is sea bream with a sea urchin sauce. The dish, which we served with a horseradish cream and a Cumberland sauce, was immensely popular, primarily because of the sea urchin content, I think. People seemed to be attracted by the unknown – that spiky black ball which is a pest on Mediterranean shorelines? – and we had to constantly remind the waiters that, no, the sea urchin wasn't in either of the sauces, but in the orange centre of each slice. (The *Good Food Guide* inspectors often got it wrong, too.) The dish was great for parties on the mezzanine floor as well, as we could get twenty portions, two slices each, out of every tray. We served it on a silver flat, and it looked lovely, with the white and orange, some greenery in the middle and a garnish of tomato roses (yes, they may be passé and laughable now, but we thought they looked very chic then).

The Gleize-influenced dish that I remember most, though, was quite revolutionary for its time. On the *carte* a line in quite large type stated, '*Pour faire palais net: le Sorbet à la Fine Champagne*'. A palate-cleansing sorbet was unknown in London, I think, and although it was exorbitantly expensive – at 65p (main courses were around £2!) – it became almost a signature dish of the restaurant. Its name caused a bit of confusion with the waiters and the restaurant manager, Dieter Schuldt. None of them ever seemed to grasp that the main ingredient was not champagne, but a cognac brandy. Made with a three-star cognac, dry white wine, sugar syrup and lemon juice, the sorbet would not freeze properly because of that alcoholic content, or at least would start to dissolve as soon as it came out of the freezer. (It most resembles an alcoholic Slush Puppy!) Shepherd and I had to make it each evening just before service and because there were so many variables in the wines used or the intensity of the sugar syrup the only way of testing whether the mixture was correct was by taste. Richard was used to alcohol, I wasn't, but this tasting on an empty stomach (often we wouldn't have had time to eat during the day) would render us very merry indeed. I must say, though, that often between the two of us, giggling away in the kitchen downstairs, we would have some of the best evenings ever in terms of flavours, presentation and efficiency! However, one of the kitchen porters, a Nigerian studying to be a doctor during the day, called Mardy Gibson, would quite often finish off the remnants of the sorbet from the returned glasses, and get quite high. On one memorable occasion, he turned to Shepherd and said: 'Don't you talk to me like that, or I'll cut your "bollingers" off'!

We had to cope with desserts as well, but that was no problem as both of us had worked with Sam Costa so many years before at Simpson's. The basis of the dessert *carte* was a selection of gâteaux served from cake stands on a trolley by the waiters. I'd never tasted anything like the banana and strawberry one before: so much Kirsch had soaked into the sponge that a spoon placed on top would sink in as if through whipped cream. We also had a *gâteau aux marrons* (chestnuts), and a *pommes Bourdaloue* (syrup-poached apples in a frangipane cream with, on top, crushed meringue and what was known as *temps-pour-temps*, a lightly grilled and coloured mixture of caster sugar and ground almonds). We made these gâteaux fresh every morning.

Even though I hadn't been part of the menu-planning part of the process, helping Richard make the recipes work in the kitchens of the Capital was an education in itself. Wherever I had worked before, I had cooked what was already on the menu, with no creative input at all, but here was a new, exciting and inspiring *carte*, which was to be produced entirely between the two of us – albeit with the help of a few others. It was a steep learning curve in every way. Not only were we cooking, but we were also choosing and buying produce. In those days in a large hotel, most chefs never got to meet suppliers, but here we were, having to deal with them on a daily basis. It was good to talk to them about the quality of their wares, and they often came in and ate in the restaurant as well. Before, if I needed a chicken or a potato, I just had to go to the larder and it was there; now I was having to get on the phone and specify variety, size, quantity etc. Before, we had been managing one part of a large operation. Now we were in total charge of all parts of an admittedly smaller operation, responsible for a staff in the kitchen of about six chefs and others. Although he wasn't ultimately in control in a financial sense, Richard was allowed to run the kitchen very much as a chef-patron, with me as his deputy, often working all day and night, never too rigid about who should do what and when. Many was the time that service would go on long after the kitchen porters had gone home, so one or two in the morning would see Richard and me stacking plates and dishes in the washing machine and cleaning up for the next day. It was all great training.

So in late 1971, we felt that we really were in control of our own destiny. We're buying, we're choosing who we buy from, we're selecting produce, looking at ingredients we haven't seen before, we're bringing it in and controlling it, preparing and cooking it. We're doing our own time rotas, our own work schedules, making sure that everything is ready for lunch and then for dinner. Working in the open-plan kitchen was an eye-opener too. We had to look smart all the time, and couldn't shout or swear, because of the nearness of the customers. People would engage you in conversation, ask what you were doing, what was good tonight. We were nervous about this at first, but we both took to it like ducks to water, Richard rather more successfully than me. Nothing like this had happened before, social skills hadn't been part of a chef's mandate. Even head chefs wouldn't often have much contact with clients. When a Virot or Käufeler did talk to clients, usually in his separate office in the kitchen, it would be in company with the restaurant or hotel manager, a group conversation rather than a one-to-one. We found it all rather exciting.

The fame of the Capital spread gradually, helped along by some powerful publicity in the autumn. On 1 September, the late and much missed Quentin Crewe, a friend of David Levin, wrote a wonderful review in the *Evening Standard*, entitled 'Lobsters and Miracles'. Later, Sheila Hutchins published a piece in the *Express* about 'Dishy Dicky', the English chef of a French-style restaurant who was good-looking, and could cook and talk as well as play the amiable host. Richard became a bit of a star, and was known by name in the press: another first. The 'names' prior to that in the catering industry were all restaurant managers, the men (usually Italian) who greeted you as you came in, who represented the public face of the establishment. And as Richard acquired a certain notoriety, he would go into the bar after service to have a drink and talk to customers. He was also going out to eat occasionally with David Levin – they had become good friends – to see, experience and taste what was happening elsewhere in London. He'd always been part of that eating-out culture, primarily because of his French cooking stint, and indeed his French wife. I never had been, though, but I used to listen with fascination to the description of the dishes, and revel in the discussion of what we might use or adapt. I'd never really 'talked' food before, and it laid another foundation stone in my ambitions. But I, too, was getting my own small share of this new and exciting world. Someone would say, 'Thank you, that was the finest meal I've ever had', and you would be in cloud-cuckoo land. We both felt that we had become people, instead of just automatons who clocked on and off. It was very exhilarating, and I was suddenly aware that this was what I wanted to do, I knew where I was going, and I determined to have a restaurant like this myself, one of my own, at some time in the not too distant future.

One of the most attractive aspects was that we had only forty covers in the restaurant and at both lunch and dinner we would usually only have one sitting. Even if we had ten tables going at one time, what we were doing for the first time was cooking for individual people on individual tables. When we worked in larger hotels, we had been cooking for faceless people, but here we could actually see them eating and, to be hoped, appreciating! I'm still working like that today, cooking a sauce for an individual dish, for a particular individual at a certain table in the restaurant. The nicest way of doing it, I think. However, quite early on at the Capital we had a bit of a problem. Michael Demarco had agreed to take on a wedding buffet, much to our horror, as we felt it wasn't our style, we'd left that sort of thing behind. But even though Shepherd went to see David Levin, we were obliged to do it. Demarco flattered us, saying we could do it standing on our heads, so we knuckled down. We worked all Friday afternoon and night on the *mise-en-place*, as well as cooking for the restaurant, snatching a couple of hours' sleep under the tables on the mezzanine floor. As we got the

Roast Rack of English Lamb with Provençal Herbs

SERVES 4

It must be obvious to everyone that I'm a beef fan, but in actual fact red meat is where it's at. I think English lamb in springtime, when the lambs have had enough sun on their backs to develop some fat and flavour, will beat any lamb in the world. This is a dish that has stood the test of time. Nothing new, nothing unusual, just a great dish – although the sauce is more Turner's than Capital.

2 best ends of lamb, chined and trimmed for roasting

salt and freshly ground black pepper

2 tablespoons dried mixed herbs (*herbes de Provence*)

1 tablespoon groundnut oil

Dijon mustard

Coating

55g (2 oz) shallots, peeled and chopped

2 tablespoons dry white wine

115g (4 oz) unsalted butter

55g (2 oz) mixed fresh herbs (rosemary, thyme, parsley), chopped

225g (8 oz) fresh white breadcrumbs

Cream sauce

600ml (1 pint) *Lamb Stock* (see page 240)

4 garlic cloves, peeled

1 bunch fresh rosemary

1 bay leaf

300ml (½ pint) double cream

25g (1 oz) unsalted butter, chilled and diced

salt and freshly ground black pepper

2 tablespoons chopped mixed fresh herbs (chives, parsley, thyme)

Preheat the oven to 200–220°C/400–425°F/Gas 6–7.

Prepare the coating. Cook the shallots in the white wine for about 4 minutes, to soften and flavour them. Drain. Melt the butter and mix in all the other ingredients, including the drained shallots, well. It should be soft but not sloppy.

Heat a roasting tray in the oven. Season the racks of lamb with salt, pepper and mixed herbs. Add a little oil to the hot roasting tray, place the lamb in the tray, fat side down, and cook in the oven for 4–5 minutes. Turn the lamb on to the bones and cook for a further 4–5 minutes, or until pink. Remove the lamb from the tray and leave to rest for 5 minutes in a warm place.

Meanwhile, preheat the grill, and make the sauce. Bring the lamb stock to the boil with the garlic, rosemary and bay leaf. Reduce by half, then add the double cream and reduce again by half. Pass through a fine sieve, and return to a clean pan. Beat in the butter, then check the seasoning. Add the herbs and reheat just before serving.

Brush the back of the lamb with Dijon mustard. Spread the coating as thinly as possible over the lamb, pressing firmly to make it stick to the mustard. Glaze under the hot grill until the coating is evenly browned, then carve into cutlets and serve, along with the cream sauce. Gratin de Jabron (see page 211), mangetout and strips of tomato make good accompaniments.

Sea Bass with a Wild Mushroom Topping
SERVES 4

When I first met sea bass in the early 1970s, it was still regarded as a scavenging, bottom-feeding fish, and consequently we Brits hadn't really rated the flavour of its flesh. Simply grilled or roasted on the bone, though, sea bass (if you can't afford it, try fresh grey mullet) is a wonderful fish to eat.

4 x 225g (8 oz) sea bass fillets, skin on

salt and freshly ground black pepper

175ml (6 fl oz) dry white wine

300ml (½ pint) *Fish Stock*
(see page 242)

300ml (½ pint) *White Chicken Stock*
(see page 243)

2 bay leaves, cut into thin strips
with scissors

1 sprig fresh thyme, leaves picked
from stalks

2 garlic cloves, peeled and thinly sliced

Topping

115g (4 oz) unsalted butter, softened

2 tablespoons chopped mixed fresh
herbs (parsley, chives, dill, tarragon)

225g (8 oz) fresh white breadcrumbs

115g (4 oz) dry *Wild Mushroom Duxelles*
(see page 238)

Sauce

150ml (¼ pint) double cream

115g (4 oz) unsalted butter

2 tablespoons chopped mixed fresh
herbs (as above)

Clean the sea bass fillets of all scales and pin bones. Mix the butter for the topping until soft and smooth, but not melted. Add the herbs and breadcrumbs, season with salt and pepper, and then slowly stir in the *duxelles*. Smear the mixture evenly on the flesh side of the fillets and leave for 20 minutes. Preheat the oven to 200°C/400°F/Gas 6.

Lightly grease a baking tray with sides, and arrange the fillets in this, topping side upwards. Gently pour the wine, fish stock and chicken stock in around the fillets. Add the bay leaf strips, thyme leaves and garlic slices to the liquid. Bake in the preheated oven until the fish is just cooked, about 10 minutes. Take the fillets out of the liquor, and carefully put on to a baking sheet. Preheat the grill.

To make the sauce, strain the cooking liquor then simmer to reduce it by about half. Add the cream and continue to reduce until the consistency of double cream. Add the butter cubes and whisk in. Check the seasoning, then add the fresh herbs. Meanwhile, colour the fillets, topping side up, under the grill. Serve immediately, surrounded by the hot sauce.

Timbale de St Jacques, Beurre Nantaise
SERVES 4

Scallops are one of those ingredients that one could argue should not be 'messed about with'. However, the *mousseline de St Jacques* at the Capital Hotel convinced me that perhaps some dishes do work where just the flavour of the scallop is evident. This dish takes that *mousseline* one step further, and is served hot.

115g (4 oz) boned and trimmed hake

4 scallops

salt and freshly ground black pepper

2 medium egg whites

300ml (½ pint) double cream

a pinch each of cayenne pepper, paprika and curry powder

a dash of cognac

butter for greasing

Sauce

150ml (¼ pint) *Fish Stock* (see page 242)

2 tablespoons white wine vinegar

2 tablespoons dry white wine

2 shallots, peeled and chopped

150ml (¼ pint) double cream

175g (6 oz) unsalted butter, cold and diced

2 artichokes, cooked and hearts diced (see page 194)

Clean the hake and scallops, then leave in the fridge to drain and chill for about 30 minutes. Meanwhile, preheat the oven to 180°C/350°F/Gas 4.

When the hake and scallops are cold, push through a fine sieve into a chilled mixing bowl over ice. The fish must remain extremely cold. Add a pinch of salt, mix, then very slowly add the egg whites. To stop the mousse splitting, the whites must be added in small amounts, and well amalgamated each time. Slowly beat in the cream. Season with the spices and cognac.

Butter 4 dariole moulds, fill them with the mixture, and cover the tops with buttered greaseproof paper. Place them in hot water in a bain-marie, and bake in the preheated oven for 10 minutes until cooked.

Meanwhile, make the sauce. Reduce the fish stock, vinegar and white wine together with the shallot until the shallot is soft, about 3 minutes. Add the double cream and boil until the sauce starts to thicken. Gradually add the butter cubes until they are all absorbed. Check for seasoning and consistency; if the sauce is too thick, add a splash of white wine. Stir in the diced artichokes.

To serve, turn out the timbales on to individual plates. Surround with the sauce.

buffet going the next day, we saw Michael Demarco climbing into his car with his golf clubs. The general manager was not staying to oversee the wedding he had booked, he was leaving it to us, knowing we could do it. As we could, of course, and it was a lesson to us in management strategy. You must always create a good team, you must encourage, not criticise unconstructively, and you must trust people to manage on their own. That afternoon, though, we both devoutly wished that Demarco would get caught permanently in the rough, or even lose his balls...

When I look back on those early days at the Capital, what amazes me is how basically simple the food was. Many famous chefs of today such as Ramsay, Marco, Nico and Novelli, cook food that is quite complex in execution, and I think the average person wouldn't contemplate attempting two-thirds of their recipes. But although what we were doing at the Capital seemed quite complicated in comparison with what we'd done at the various hotels of our apprenticeship, it was in essence based on good principal ingredients, a few simple flavourings, and a wonderful accompanying sauce or two. At that time, the secret dawned on me that this industry I had chosen to work in was not one in which you could count the hours. It was and is a way of life, and I often say now that I never start work because I never stop work. My life is my business and vice versa, and this all gelled during those initial Capital months. All I did at that time was work, cook, eat, meet people, serve and talk about food and drink. There was the occasional sortie to a rugby, football or cricket match, but basically I was living a life that was inextricably interconnected with my job.

An Interlude

However, *plus ça change*. In 1973, I got married to Denise, whom I'd met again after college, and decided that my priorities had to change. I was living at that time in Barnet with, as my lodger, Keith Timewell whom I'd met in Switzerland. Denise and I then bought a house in Luton, as she was flying out of the airport there as a stewardess for Court Line, the charter company with the then famous pastel-coloured planes. Although I loved my work at the Capital, I thought it was very unfair to ask my wife to put up with such unsocial hours. I'd always

I married Denise in March 1973, and this photograph was taken in the garden of Denshaw Grove before the wedding. From left, Philip, Robert, Mum, Dad and the rather nervous bridegroom. Gillian must have been behind the camera.

thought that I might like to teach at some time – it was often a natural progression for young chefs – and I heard about a job going at the South-East London Technical College. Via John Bertram of Claridge's, later head chef at Scott's, I met John Peart, who had also been at Claridge's but was now teaching. It attracted me, not least because the hours would be more civilised, but also because I thought I could do a good job: I had my Salvation Army upbringing, I'd been a Sunday School teacher, I'd run the youth club, I knew how to relate to young people, and I was enthusiastic about sharing my considerable knowledge of cooking. Denise was delighted, as her father was a headmaster, and she was very familiar with school life and school holidays.

I went to be interviewed at the College by Dr Dean, the principal, and Wendy Dudleston, head of the catering school. When it was over, I didn't feel I'd done very well, but they asked if I had anything to say. Although very nervous, I admitted, perhaps too truthfully, that 'I only really came to the interview because I wanted the experience for a future date. I personally don't feel that I am ready to teach just yet, that I haven't learned enough in my industry.' The answer came, 'Mr Turner, if we decide that you're ready to do the job, please don't presume that you know better than we do.' The net result was that I was virtually bludgeoned into taking the job, although I wasn't all that confident after I'd heard what was involved. Retrospectively, education was in the position (and probably still is), that you can't ever get the right people at the right time – so you take the right people whenever you get the chance!

Gâteau Florentine
SERVES 8–10

Bananas and strawberries might seem unlikely, but I think they make a great flavour and texture combination.

Genoise	*Filling*	*Topping*
175g (6 oz) caster sugar	150ml (¼ pint) *Sugar Syrup* (see page 124)	2 tablespoons strawberry jam
6 medium eggs	100ml (3½ fl oz) Kirsch liqueur	green colouring
175g (6 oz) plain flour	300ml (½ pint) double cream	175g (6 oz) good marzipan
55g (2 oz) unsalted butter, melted	350g (12 oz) strawberries	a sprig of fresh mint
	2 bananas	icing sugar
	2 tablespoons icing sugar	

To make the genoise, grease and line a 23cm (9 in) cake tin. Preheat the oven to 180°C/350°F/Gas 4. Whisk the sugar and eggs in a bowl over a pan of warm water until the ribbon stage, i.e. when a trail of the whisk is left in the mixture after the whisk is removed. Gently fold in the flour using a large metal spoon. Add the melted butter, stir in, and then pour into the prepared tin. Bake in the preheated oven for 35–40 minutes. Remove from the oven, turn out of the tin, and allow to cool on a wire rack.

To assemble the gateau, cut the genoise in half horizontally and place the top of the cake in a 23cm (9 in) ring, curved top down. Mix the sugar syrup and Kirsch together and dampen the cake base thoroughly with about half this mixture. Whip the cream and put to one side. Cut the strawberries in half vertically and carefully place the cut side outwards against the ring on the cake base. Chop the remaining strawberries (except for 2) and the bananas. Mix with the icing sugar and then fold into the whipped cream. Taking care not to move the strawberries round the outside, put the filling in the middle of the cake base and smooth it evenly.

Put the bottom of the cake, smooth side up, on top. Brush this with the remaining sugar syrup and Kirsch, and then spread with the jam. Mix green colouring to taste into the marzipan, and then, using some icing sugar on the work surface, roll out flat. Cut this with a 23cm (9 in) round ring, and place smoothly on top of the cake. Place the remaining strawberries on top of the cake with the mint sprig. Shake icing sugar over, then remove the cake ring. Chill before serving.

So, sadly, I left the Capital, and travelled with great trepidation to London from Luton, and then to New Cross. I started at the beginning of the summer term, and didn't do any actual teaching for about three weeks. The very first day was an eye-opener. I was shown round by Jack Alcock, who was running the refectory, with some of his students cooking the lunch. We queued up, and I chose a cream of cauliflower soup. 'It tastes very nice,' says I, 'but it's very different.' Mr Alcock then quickly tasted it, and had to admit, rather ruefully, that they didn't always make cauliflower soup with fish stock!

The first class I was scheduled to teach was of management students, who were bright, but not particularly interested in cooking. I was told to teach them puff pastry, at which I demurred: 'I'm a cook, not a pastry chef.' Came the reply, 'That doesn't matter, Brian, you're a teacher now, you teach what has to be taught.' So I swotted up on all the theory of puff pastry, the many layers, the air trapped between, the chilling, the meticulous rolling: I even calculated the number of layers you might have after the requisite amount of rolling and folding. I was red-hot on puff pastry by the time I stood in front of the class, but when we came to the practical side – making some *millefeuilles* – mine were the only ones to remain flat as a pancake! I was very embarrassed and felt like giving up straightaway, but it taught me a lesson: when you're teaching, you're concentrating on what you're teaching, not on what you're doing. I resolved never to let that happen again.

I'm afraid I realised by the end of that first term that teaching catering was not what I wanted to do. It was very hard work for a start, although I was used to that, but planning classes, adapting my ideas to the set curriculum, and dealing with the amazing amount of paperwork, was not the sort of work I was used to. Neither was it as rewarding as I thought it might be. The people I had to teach were mainly on day release, mature students, and a lot of them were fairly uninterested. As they all worked in different types of establishment, as their ages ranged from nineteen to forty-five, and were from different social and ethnic backgrounds, it was very difficult to have to teach them all the same things at the same pace. Teaching classes of up to thirty-five or forty is a horrendous task anyway, but there were some good moments, and I did basically get on with most of the students. I also became a student myself. Because I had no real teacher training, I started going to classes at night with

Sorbet à la Fine Champagne
SERVES ABOUT 10

This was considered to be revolutionary and possibly decadent when we first offered it at the Capital. Why would anybody attempt to freeze a really great fine champagne cognac? To this day, I think it was a brilliant addition to our gastronomic learning curve, and what's more, it wouldn't surprise me if it were to be seen on Turner's menu soon.

500ml (18 fl oz) dry white wine (Sauvignon Blanc)

325ml (13 fl oz) fine champagne brandy

juice of 1 lemon

Sugar syrup

250ml (9 fl oz) water

250g (9 oz) caster sugar

To make the sugar syrup, put the water and sugar in a heavy-based pan, and heat gently to dissolve the sugar, stirring occasionally with a wooden spoon. When there are no traces of grittiness remaining, bring to the boil, then remove from the heat. Leave to cool.

Mix all the sorbet ingredients together, along with the sugar syrup, then strain to remove any lemon flesh etc. Put into the pre-cooled sorbet machine, and churn until frozen. At Turner's our machine takes about 45 minutes, a domestic one may take a little longer. (I'm afraid that this is one of those sorbets that can only be made in a machine.)

Mrs Harmshaw, a Yorkshirewoman whom I much admired. The secret of teaching, she claimed, was to get the students to want to learn what you wanted to teach. If you wanted to teach it, you'd teach it so much better. If it was something you didn't want to teach − puff pastry, for instance − you'd have a very difficult time (as I'd already proved!).

The first three months of that summer term were stressful, but I felt I was getting somewhere, even if it wasn't what I ultimately wanted to do on a permanent basis. During the six to eight weeks of the summer holidays, I got a part-time job in the kitchens at the Perivale Maternity Hospital, part of Ealing Hospital. Most of my students were cooking in industrial situations, not in restaurants, so I thought this job might enlighten me and make me better able to relate to them and the experiences with which they had to deal. The chef didn't take to me much; I think he thought I was a bit condescending, a real chef, a teacher, coming down-market. The job mostly involved opening tins, but I enjoyed it, primarily because I garnered so many horror stories. One of them involved a crème caramel, which was written on that day's lunch menu. I'd made crème caramel at college, and knew it should be cooked long and slow, then left to set and cool. As the morning wore on, I kept asking the chef whether I should start the crème caramel now. He kept putting me off, until about half an hour before the dishes were to be loaded on to the ward trolleys. He got a very large roasting tray out, and squirted into it from a large tube of what looked like toothpaste. It was instant caramel. Then he put some milk in a big bowl − no sign of cream − and whisked some sort of powder into it. This he poured on top of the caramel and, I kid you not, it suddenly set just like a junket, but with an audible 'crack'. To this day, I can't work out what that setting agent could have been. My jaw dropped to my chest, and I couldn't take anything very seriously after that. It made me realise, though, why it might be that we as a nation had a bad reputation for cooking. My experience in hospital catering did nothing whatsoever to disprove it.

When the academic year started again, I was back, having done quite a lot of work on my courses during the summer holidays. I was teaching basics − basic knife skills, sauces, stocks, soups and roasting − and I'm certain that, although my heart wasn't really in it, I did a good job. One of the most important things, I felt, was teaching the students how to taste. At the end of every class, I had to taste everything, and I encouraged them to do it, too. One lad's soup was so salty I knew he hadn't tasted it, and he agreed. I made him taste it to prove how over-seasoned it was, but his reply was, 'Chef, that's how I like it.' That taught me that taste, as with everything, is very subjective. I also had to deal with troublemakers. One boy in particular − ironically, potentially the most talented in the class − I had to become physical with behind the large walk-in fridge. 'Listen, son, we've got to work together for the rest of this term. We can do it on my terms, or we can do it on my terms...' Although bullying and physical force are alien to me, it worked, for I never heard a contrary word from him thereafter (although he must have complained, as I was slightly reprimanded by my superiors).

But, in general, I had a good rapport with the students, and I made a few friends. Johnny Vigurs and Peter Carstairs had been there for years, and were great teachers and characters − but, to be honest, I wouldn't ever have wanted either of them to cook for me! Vigurs was in charge of the production kitchen and the restaurant for people who came in from outside. He was a master at portion control, very important in any restaurant. A typical shout would be, halfway through service, 'How many more portions do I have to get from this piece of roast meat? If you close the windows and give me a razor blade, I'll get out as many as you need'!

I stayed for the whole academic year after the summer holiday, learning more about the theory and practicalities of teaching. I'm glad I did it, and have no real regrets, because I was still learning and I was honing my social skills. However, despite Denise's happiness with me being home at night and weekends, I knew I had to do something − but what? Luckily, I met Richard Shepherd again − we'd stayed in touch − and he said, 'Why don't you come back to the Capital?' They hadn't replaced me with anyone at the same level, or with anyone he empathised with so well. There was no doubt in my mind that that was the most exciting thing anyone had said to me in a long time. So I accepted, recognising that I missed cooking at the Capital, missed the smell of the greasepaint and the roar of the crowd.

The Capital and the Greenhouse

Coming back to the Capital in the summer of 1974 was like a homecoming. It was good to be working with Richard again: the old camaraderie hadn't changed. The dishes were familiar, as were the suppliers, and the Capital staff still formed the same efficient team. I felt comfortable.

In retrospect, that was one of the most impressive things about David Levin: his ability to pick the right people to work for him or at least to pick one person and then pick his or her brains in a sensible and creative way. It was he who had pulled in Michael Demarco, but it was Demarco who had suggested Richard Shepherd, who then suggested me. Later David Levin discovered Shaun Hill at the Montcalm, but it was me who brought in Gary Rhodes. Levin found Philip Britten after I and my successor, John Elliott, left, and in 1999 he brought in the talented Eric Chavot. He was no less successful at choosing staff elsewhere in the hotel. Bob Gould, John Parr and Bobby Evans were on the front desk. Bob had been a great concierge at the Royal Garden, so was probably persuaded to come by Demarco, but he stayed the entire time I was there, and left after me. John and Bobby stayed for years, too; John retired, and Bobby sadly died while still employed by the hotel. The bar staff were good too: Michael White (a charming rogue), Noel O'Connor, Joe Elliott and David Thompson spring to mind.

And the restaurant manager, Dieter Schuldt, was a star in his own right, a real 'schmoozer'. He had this knack of charming the customers as he showed them to their tables: 'Let me take you to the royal box' and 'My lord, how are you?' He would regularly congratulate a customer on his or her order: 'What a wonderful choice, I would have selected that for myself, too.' Richard and I used to cringe when we heard him answering the telephone to someone wanting a reservation: there would be no one booked, but he'd still say, 'Let me check for you, sir. Yes, I have one table left.' We thought he was taking a huge risk, but somehow his instincts were spot on, and the tables always managed to fill up. He did his job superbly, adding style and a heart to the restaurant. Richard and I learned a lot about conversing with customers from Dieter, and he's still around today, working for Richard at Odin's.

We had an efficient team of suppliers, too. Many people today might think that the 1990s were the peak time of the small top-quality supplier, but the produce we used was of paramount importance to us even as early as the 1970s. Because we were such a small operation and our cuisine was so simple the basic ingredients simply had to be the best, and we used to spend hours talking to suppliers. This was rarely on a cost basis at first. Much more important to us were quality and service: how many times a day and when each day we could expect deliveries, and where the produce came from. I think we probably led the way in this respect. Insisting on top-notch food suppliers and supplies is not a new thing; what is different now is that people talk about it more. George Simcock and CST used to supply our lamb. Arthur Allsop used to ship beef down direct from Aberdeen for several London restaurants, the Capital among them. Five or six loins of Aberdeen Angus – sirloins for the *steak au poivre* and ribs for the roast ribs – would almost fill the small walk-in fridge. Once a barman at the Carlton Tower, Danny O'Sullivan of Downland Growers, decided to change his way of life and his direction. He leased fields in Storrington in Hampshire on which he would grow soft summer fruits. He'd pick a field of strawberries one night, pack them and drive them up to London to fulfil several orders. We'd always go down and have a look in his van to see what else was there – and to see what others were ordering – and then we would place an order for the next day or week. He would turn up a few times a week, not every day, and later on he was one of the first suppliers of less usual ingredients such as courgette flowers and mangetout, again well in the vanguard of fashion.

David Levin encouraged us to be as serious about our wine suppliers. There were regular wine tastings in the hotel, in which Richard and I participated, and we learned an incredible amount. We would spit the tasted wines out, as was only right and proper, but the varying flavours lingered, and it was probably at about this time that my passion for fine wines was born. I still didn't drink much, but I was beginning to get the taste! Once again, this was a totally new concept for us as cooks, being involved with and learning to understand wines. By talking to the wine merchants, the food suppliers and, increasingly, the food writers who were now flocking to the restaurant, we were made much more aware of our being an integral part of a much larger business. All the parts of the jigsaw were beginning to slot together.

Life was expanding for Richard and me in so many ways, and our happiness was crowned in 1975 when the Capital Hotel restaurant was given a Michelin star. This was the second year that the *Guide Michelin* had been published in the UK, and until then only large hotels like the Connaught, which had French chefs, had achieved that coveted award. We were small, we were British, but we had joined a very select and distinguished band. Things suddenly went into the stratosphere; Levin and Shepherd were interviewed all over the place, and were the new confirmed culinary superstars, possibly the first the country had ever seen. Although David Levin might have been aware, Richard and I had known nothing about being considered by Michelin which is not like today when chefs import new this or that, or spend thousands on décor or napery to gain Michelin notice. What we had done was produce food to a certain standard – doing the right thing for the kitchen, for the restaurant and having pride in it – and we had kept to that standard. Consistency was our watchword, and the Capital was to hold that star for another decade or so, until the year after I left. I think we got it because the restaurant was French, and the chef and *sous-chef* were classically French trained and had worked in France (well, the French-speaking part of Switzerland as far as I was concerned). The fact that we were British running a French restaurant must have been influential; I suspect Michelin wouldn't have given us a second thought in those days had we been British running a British restaurant.

We were thrilled to bits, and that accolade took us to a new level. The restaurant was full all the time, Richard and David Levin continued to give interviews, we worked enthusiastically, consolidating what we had done, and we enjoyed ourselves. Shepherd got very much involved at this time with Club Nine, a group of top chefs, which was the precursor of the Académie Culinaire de France in this country. Nine of them (obviously) would meet regularly, go on trips and eat out together. They were, apart from Richard, Michel Bourdin of the Connaught, Guy Mouilleron of Ma Cuisine in Walton Street (who sadly retired two years after I moved to Turner's to become his neighbour), Bernard Gaume of the Hyatt Carlton Tower, Peter Kromberg of the London Inter-Continental, John Huber, pastry lecturer at Slough College, Uwe Zander, Felix Muntweiler (both working in and around Heathrow Airport) and Anton Mosimann, who had just taken over as *maître chef des cuisines* at the Dorchester at the tender age of twenty-eight. (Incidentally, it's said that this is the job Shepherd turned down two years after moving to the Capital.)

It was around this time that the influence of *nouvelle cuisine* began to be felt in Britain. The term had been coined in 1973 by Gault and Millau in their magazine, in an article entitled *'Vive La Nouvelle Cuisine Française'*. It described a new, lighter and flourless cooking being practised by a group of French chefs, among them Paul Bocuse, the two Troisgros brothers, Roger Vergé and Michel Guérard, who had been influenced by Fernand Point at La Pyramide in Vienne. Interestingly, the chefs concerned did not much like the label *'nouvelle'*, apparently, and would have preferred *'moderne'*, but whatever the name, the new

Matthew Gloag of the Famous Grouse whisky asked me to go on a publicity shoot – literally – on the Glorious Twelfth in the mid 1970s at Gleneagles in Scotland. I was in Switzerland on holiday at the time, so you can imagine the journey I had to undertake. We were successful though, as you can see – though why our whites didn't frighten the birds away, I don't know! From the left, me, the chef from the Atheneum Hotel in London, Jean Cotté, head chef at Gleneagles, and Stuart Cameron, his sous-chef.

ideas were enthusiastically embraced on both sides of the Channel. When Michel Guérard's book *Cuisine Minceur* was published in 1976, the health aspects of the new way of cooking were emphasised (and re-emphasised some ten years later by the publication of Anton Mosimann's *Cuisine Naturelle*). *Minceur*, which was associated with dietary regimes at Guérard's spa in Eugenie-les-Bains, began to be confused with *nouvelle*. This helped to lead the way to an extreme interpretation, particularly in this country, of the tenets of *nouvelle cuisine*: not only did portions lack cream, butter and flour, and anything remotely 'unhealthy', but they became so small in some restaurants that you almost had two peas, a green bean and potato as a garnish. And the plates got bigger as the portions got smaller!

Things got so ridiculous at one point that a newspaper defined a *nouvelle cuisine* restaurant as one in which the chef came out of his kitchen, not to ask how good your meal was, but to *tell* you how good it was. And then he would say, 'As you have enjoyed it all so much, I'm going to give you my latest creation, a Perrier sorbet.' A highly satirical definition, but it did point out that, however inventive and pretty things were on the plate, many cooks had forgotten that food should *taste* good as well.

I tend to liken the rise and fall of *nouvelle cuisine* to the drunken man syndrome, where the drunk goes six steps forward, then staggers back four steps. He is still two steps further on than before, though. The *nouvelle cuisine* road was a necessary one to go down, but it was also necessary to come back a few steps from it. So the actual legacy of *nouvelle cuisine* is quite a strong one. It's made us think about what we're eating and serving, about the balance, about the size of portions, and about the amount of fat we put into our dishes. Cream- and butter-rich sauces were so much part of the *haute cuisine* tradition that at one point the attitude was almost that you weren't getting your money's worth unless the dish was virtually too rich to finish. People often said that at the Capital we were cooking in a *nouvelle cuisine* way, but this wasn't a following of current fashion. We had been getting inklings of what was happening in France for years, via Richard's French connections, and a few of the new concepts had already been absorbed and digested into our cooking, which was to remain fairly constant throughout those early Capital years. We still had good-sized portions, though, used cheese in potato dishes, and had cream in sauces. We were probably among the first to use *jus*, reduced stock thickened with potato flour, a pre-cooked, gluten-free flour. We'd always tried to make our food look good, too, which is another positive aspect of the *nouvelle cuisine* legacy. Now people seem, in general culinary terms, to be turning completely away from *nouvelle cuisine*. Think about the currently fashionable plates of lamb shanks with mashed potatoes, a hearty combination which harks back to pre-*nouvelle* times. But that lamb shank is now shaped and trimmed, and arranged carefully and artistically against a mound of olive-oil-smooth, glistening mash.

Nouvelle cuisine was also very instrumental in the development of plate service. In many of the large hotels in the old days, the emphasis was more on waiter service than on the food. Dishes containing food would be taken from a trolley or *guéridon*, and served on to the plate at the table. Roasts would be carved alongside the customer's table, as would smoked salmon. Waiters could be less than efficient at this service, and often the food would be carelessly put on the plate and, most importantly, would often be cold by the time the customer started to eat. I'll never forget a Capital diner, Herb Stone, saying he'd just enjoyed my 'sole-burger'; the waiter had so mangled the boning of a Dover sole that it looked like mincemeat on Herb's plate. *Nouvelle cuisine*'s emphasis on a plate of food looking good empowered chefs to start insisting that they should be in control of the plates and send them direct from kitchen to table. At the Capital, our rack of lamb and rib of beef were an echo of the era that was disappearing, but we had chosen to be a food-based rather than a service-based restaurant, and we soon went over to plate service with our other dishes. In fact the old ways make no sense in many of today's smaller restaurants: in Turner's, for instance, there just wouldn't be *room* for *guéridons* or trolleys.

At some point after the Capital gained its Michelin star, David Levin started to expand his empire. The proposal to open another restaurant had been on the cards for some months, at least since I returned to the Capital fold, and ideas started to gell after we gained that Michelin star. What was to become the Greenhouse was situated in Hay's Mews in Mayfair, and had been the Vanity Fair restaurant. Levin and Shepherd spent a lot of time planning the concept. Once more in the vanguard of culinary vogue, Levin wanted a restaurant that was very much more British in style, a simpler eating experience than the Capital. He wanted more covers as well, at least one hundred as opposed to the Capital's forty, and to run an altogether more commercial set-up. He also recognised that his Capital guests might not want to eat in the Capital every night, so the Greenhouse could serve as a cheaper, more accessible dining room. Richard was to be in sole charge of the Greenhouse, but would become executive chef of the two, while I would be promoted to head chef of the Capital. This was a huge challenge for both of us.

There were one or two hiccoughs, though. The Greenhouse was at the foot of a large building which was divided into apartments, and many of the elderly residents had eaten their meals in the Vanity Fair, primarily breakfasts. So Richard would have to cook breakfasts for a while, and Mr Levin had to offer some kind of discounted incentives, until all the leases were sorted out. After that the restaurant would have to close for refurbishment. The Greenhouse menu was causing a few problems as well. Although I wasn't directly, even indirectly, involved, I heard whispers occasionally whenever Richard and I managed to snatch some time together in the many months during which the Greenhouse concept evolved. Although it was meant to be basically British in approach – Barnsley chops, sausages, steaks and other grills, fish and chips, wonderful mashed potato – one or two 'foreign' ideas had crept in, due to David Levin. A Jewish style chopped liver on matzoh was one of the starters, included, I later learned, because Margaret Levin made it better than David Levin's mother! Another starter was cod's roe pâté on thick toast, which was to become the bane of my life. I never found out where David Levin had found the idea – probably in one of the restaurants he regularly ate in – but apparently he was adamant that it should be offered on what was supposed to be a British menu. The pâté was in essence a Balkan taramasalata, but made with cod's roe instead of the more authentic grey mullet roe. The popularity of the dish today confirms that David Levin was quite right to include it on the Greenhouse menu at that time.

In the meantime, while Richard was preoccupied with the new venture and all its ramifications – designing the menu and revamping the interior, particularly the kitchen – I was to all intents and purposes in charge of the Capital, and revelling in every minute of it. This continued for about twelve months, and the Greenhouse was due to open in the second half of 1977. Because I had not been privy to the discussions about the new restaurant, I was unaware of any tensions developing between Levin and Shepherd. I'm still no wiser to this day. There must have been some major falling-out, but all I know is that I got a call from Richard one Sunday afternoon. I was due to go into the Capital late on the Monday, but Richard said I should come in early. This I did, whereupon he sat me down, and told me he was leaving. 'It's not going to work out at the Greenhouse, I've given in my notice, and I've recommended to Mr Levin that you take over as executive chef of the two. Mr Levin would like to see you.' With great trepidation I went to talk to Mr Levin, and discovered that Richard felt he should go sooner rather than later, and that he was actually leaving at the end of the week.

I was horrified. Richard was my pal, my boss, my mentor, my guiding light, and it was a complete and utter shock. I didn't know what to say or do, but had to agree that if Richard wanted to go he shouldn't be made to work his month's

When Richard Shepherd left, I became executive head chef of the Capital restaurant and the Greenhouse (the Metro was yet to come). This photograph was taken in the kitchens of the Capital in around 1978.

Chopped Liver
SERVES 4

Chopped liver, a stalwart of the Jewish tradition, has been described by those who may not understand it as being mundane in flavour. But this recipe, thanks to the Tabasco, cognac and – dare I say it – smoked back bacon, really comes alive.

25g (1 oz) unsalted butter

1 medium onion, peeled and finely chopped

4 smoked back bacon rashers, finely chopped

225g (8 oz) whole fresh chicken livers

1 tablespoon cognac

salt and freshly ground black pepper

3 hard-boiled medium eggs, shelled and finely chopped

a dash of Tabasco sauce

1 tablespoon chopped fresh parsley

¼ teaspoon made English mustard

Melt the butter and add the chopped onion and bacon. Allow to sweat and colour lightly. Carefully put in the livers – they must not touch each other – and seal on both sides. Cook for 2–3 minutes, keeping them pink inside. Pour in the cognac and flame or flambé to burn off the alcohol, then reduce quickly.

Pour the contents of the pan on to a board and chop coarsely. Season with salt and pepper and put into a bowl. When cool, mix with the chopped hard-boiled eggs, Tabasco, parsley and mustard. Serve with well buttered toast.

notice. That would serve no meaningful purpose, I knew, and we would just have to knuckle down and get on with it. I didn't mind that in one sense, but running a Michelin-starred restaurant completely alone, without the back-up, energy and foresight of the man who had actually *gained* that star (albeit with my help), was a little daunting. And not only that, I had to take on a new restaurant about which I had very little inside knowledge. I was being asked to be executive chef without feeling that I had really proved myself as a head chef. The whole thing was a bit of a mess.

Staffing was a major problem at first, and continued to exercise me over the next few years. I needed head chefs in both establishments, plus reliable deputies, to run the kitchens on a daily basis in order to allow me, as executive chef, a proper overview of the whole dual operation. A priority was the opening of the Greenhouse, and PJ, an Irish boy who had worked in the City and was to have been Shepherd's second, was not quite up to it. Although honest and hard-working, I didn't think he could maintain our high standards by himself. However, PJ and I did manage to open the Greenhouse together at the appointed time (Margaret Levin being in charge of the room was a great asset), but David Levin soon brought in Don Smith, previously famous for his chopped steak at Annabel's.

At the Capital, my own deputy was the able Ian Calver, whom I had met at Claridge's. However, he was not experienced enough either to assume complete responsibility while I was here and there trying to oversee everything, so David Levin brought in Shaun Hill from the Montcalm Hotel. Shaun, one of the most intelligent of chefs – he had turned down a chance to read classics at university to take up cooking – had worked at Carrier's, the Gay Hussar in Soho and with Kromberg at the Inter-Continental. He took over as working head chef at the Capital, with Calver as his deputy.

I must admit that I found it all rather difficult. I wasn't really used to controlling my own staff, apart from our six or so at the Capital, and here I was now trying to cope with Shaun and his individualistic ideas, and the very much older Don Smith. The latter's approach to cooking – to stand watching others doing it while he bellowed, his arms folded on top of his gargantuan beer belly – was as far removed from our established style as it was possible to be. It was all a totally different ball game for me, a steep learning curve, and I had to work excruciatingly long hours. I was somewhat nervous about it all, wasn't sleeping well, and lost quite a lot of weight. It was at this time of pressure that Richard and I fell out. We didn't speak properly for about eighteen months, a huge crack in our long friendship. It wasn't so much that he was bad-mouthing me, or I him – as rumour had it – but that our lives were so inextricably bound to our jobs that we literally had no time or inclination to see each other. (If I was stressed, so too was Richard. He had just arrived at Langan's to be told that the business was in severe financial difficulties. That the restaurant managed to pull through in the next couple of years was largely due to Richard's talents.)

There were some financial strictures too, which added to my general angst. Brian Hartley, David Levin's accountant, was adamant that the finances of the two restaurants should be kept separate, presumably to prevent any repercussions from a potentially unsuccessful Greenhouse affecting the Capital. However, if on paper this seemed possible, it was less so in actuality. At the beginning, quite a lot of the basic preparations were done at the Capital, under my supervision, and shipped over to the Greenhouse, usually in the boot of my car. Meat, for instance, was ordered by the Capital, because of the reliability of our suppliers, stored in our fridges, and then taken across (again, to the detriment of the lining fabric, in the boot of my car!). We didn't really care about the finances, and how closely linked they were; we were all under pressure, and were just trying to get enough food produced to satisfy two hungry restaurants.

Don didn't stay very long, which pleased me as the Greenhouse after a while actually began to frighten me. Then I had a brainwave. I had shared a room in Lausanne with Helmut Reichart, and had kept in touch with him since. His career had advanced, he had married an English girl, and was now working at the Saunton Sands Hotel in Devon. He would be perfect at the Greenhouse so, when I went on holiday to Saunton with my family, I persuaded him to up sticks and move to London. This was a huge success, and during the years he was in charge, I was able to relax much more. He even introduced a few Swiss and Germanic touches. We served *spätzli* for a while, and *Pommes Rösti* became a basic. It was based on a recipe given to me by the grandmother of my good friend Jean-Pierre Chevalier, so was truly authentic! (I'm not quite sure to this day whether we were the first to introduce *rösti*, or if it was the Swiss Centre or Mosimann at the Dorchester.)

Cod's Roe Pâté on a Cucumber Yoghurt Salad

SERVES 4

The very thought of cod's roes fills me with dismay. I hated to look at them, I hated to touch them, and I always pulled rank and gave the job of skinning them to someone else in the kitchen. I never understood how such a great dish could evolve from such an unpromising ingredient.

175g (6 oz) smoked cod's roe

½ small onion, peeled and very finely minced

1 medium slice white bread

150ml (¼ pint) olive oil

juice of ½ lemon, or to taste

cayenne pepper

Salad

1 cucumber

salt

140g (5 oz) natural yoghurt

2 tablespoons finely chopped fresh dill

To start the salad, peel and seed the cucumber. Slice thinly, sprinkle well with salt and leave to marinate, in a sieve or colander over a bowl, for about 20 minutes.

Peel the skin from the roe, then mix the flesh with the minced onion. Put the bread to soak in a little water. When soft, squeeze dry and mix with the cod's roe and onion. Beat the three well together, then slowly beat in the oil as if making mayonnaise. Season with the lemon juice and cayenne. Cover, and leave in the fridge to cool.

To finish the salad, squeeze the liquid out of the cucumber. Mix the drained slices with the yoghurt and dill, and divide between 4 plates. Spoon the pâté mixture on top, and serve with toast or pitta bread.

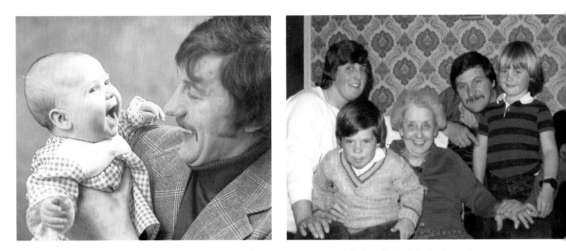

Left: *My eldest son Simeon was born in 1974, and I was a very proud father. I think he looks rather like I did in the photograph on page 2, don't you?*
Right: *Benjamin was born in 1976, and here he is with Denise, Simeon and me at Grandma Riley's ninetieth birthday in 1981.*

Neither did Shaun Hill stay long. He went to Blake's, and we then employed Remy Cruaud at the Capital, a little Frenchman with a moustache and a classical tall chef's hat. He was focused, and a little arrogant as he had come from a Michelin-starred restaurant in France, but he was effective and imaginative. He was less easy to deal with than Helmut, but nevertheless his skills allowed me to spend more time with customers, to work out problems, plan staffing and menus. We always seemed to be changing something, and it all became a bit of a balancing act. I was trying to teach Remy our ways so that regular customers would not notice too much of a change, while at the same time trying to acquire new ideas from Remy, some new dishes, so that those same regular customers would know that we were thinking, that we were not standing still.

During this time, too, we were still training chefs from Buckingham Palace at the Capital. A few years earlier David Levin had met a Richard Winship, the assistant master of the Household, and they did a deal. David Levin met Prince Philip once and, so the story goes, HRH, on hearing of the Capital connection, made a plea that, 'If you could just teach them to serve *hot* food, we'd be very grateful.' (Of course, the kitchens and dining room were so far apart that even the most skilful of chefs could not guarantee that the food would be hot.) Lionel Mann, one of the guys I trained, became head chef at the Palace later, and I like to think that I had a little input into feeding Her Majesty, as I am a very proud Royalist.

It took some time, but eventually the two restaurants were back completely on track. The Capital was still acquiring good reviews, was full every day, and retained its Michelin star every year. The Greenhouse, too, began to have a good reputation. Many people think that it was only when Gary Rhodes took over that it became a success. Not so. We were full day in, day out, and it started to be a pleasure to me, popping over to the Greenhouse from the Capital in my whites to see what was going on. I could have gone in my car, but often David Levin and I made a point of taking taxis – Hay's Mews was so off the beaten track that we wanted as many cabbies as possible to be aware of where we were.

During those busy years, once things had sorted themselves out a little, I was able – at last! – to go out and about to see what else was happening on the London restaurant scene. In fact, for a while I was the only member of the company to have my own American Express card for precisely that purpose.

The last recorded family picture of my mum with us four children, our spouses, and seven of her eight grandchildren.

At first I used to go mainly to large hotels and dining rooms, particularly when chefs from France would come in to cook their menus for a week or so. I remember taking the staff from the Capital to dinner at the Grosvenor House when Louis Outhier came across (he had the three-star L'Oasis restaurant at La Napoule, near Cannes, and was one of the Point disciples who had stuck most closely to the precepts of *haute cuisine*). It was also a delight to visit famous and highly revered places in London like the Connaught where Michel Bourdin cooked, the Roux brothers' Le Gavroche, Guy Mouilleron's Ma Cuisine in Walton Street, and Pierre Koffmann's La Tante Claire in Royal Hospital Road. But the latter street was also home to Foxtrot Oscar, a place of lesser culinary status perhaps, but of infinitely greater social attractions to me: I used to meet and gossip with many of my culinary peers there, as well as many businessmen who have remained friends over the years. Another haunt was Pomegranates in Grosvenor Road. This was the brainchild of Patrick Gwynn Jones, an extremely eclectic chef-patron, who was responsible for introducing many new ideas, including the best *gravadlax* in town, buying in Scottish salmon and Scandinavian dill.

I was also travelling abroad on buying trips, on eating trips and just-looking trips. I did several of these with David and Margaret Levin, and on one memorable occasion we drove down to Lameloise, an eponymous, three-starred restaurant in Chagny, in the heart of Burgundy (I chauffeured for part of the trip, the first time I had driven abroad). This was a top-class restaurant with good rooms, exactly the description the Levins had decided should characterise the Capital, and we thought we should have a look to see if we could glean any new ideas. We had a wonderful meal there, and David Levin was very anxious for me to meet the chef, the son of the owner. He seemed reluctant to come out of the kitchen, though, so I went in to see him, mentally brushing up my French as I did so. There, much to the Levins' surprise, I gave the young chef a huge Gallic embrace, which he reciprocated with much laughter. I'd never known his surname, but Jacques Lameloise had been one of the fish chefs at the Savoy, and had played a very competent right wing for my football team!

My first trip abroad by myself was to Bordeaux in June of 1981. This was to honour the cuisine of Aquitaine – *La Grande Carte d'Aquitaine à Bordeaux* – and was organised by a gentleman from the local Chamber of Commerce who has

Goat's Cheese, Bacon and Tomato Rösti
SERVES 4

Lots of different kinds of goat's cheese will work for this dish; I like the chalkiness and slight acidity of Crottin de Chavignol. We have used here the basic *rösti* mix and put the other ingredients – the tomato and bacon – on top, but if you feel really adventurous, mix pre-cooked crumbled bacon and finely chopped tomato into the potato before you form and cook the *rösti*.

> 4 back bacon rashers
>
> 4 tablespoons olive oil
>
> 4 plum tomatoes
>
> salt and freshly ground black pepper
>
> 2 Crottin de Chavignol (round goat cheeses)
>
> *Rösti*
>
> 900g (2 lb) baking potatoes, scrubbed
>
> salt and freshly ground black pepper
>
> duck or goose fat, or lard

For the *rösti*, bring a pan of water up to the boil. Carefully drop the potatoes in, and bring back to the boil. Add salt. Cook for about 20–25 minutes until just cooked, then drain off and leave to cool. Peel and put in the fridge for 1–2 hours.

Preheat the oven to 200°C/400°F/Gas 6.

Coarsely grate the potatoes, and season. Using a 10cm (4 in) frying pan, heat enough fat in it to cover the bottom. When hot, drop a quarter of the grated potato into the pan. Push down with a fish slice, but not too much. Colour for about 6 minutes, then carefully turn over and colour on the other side. Do the same with the remaining grated potato, making 4 *rösti*.

When the *rösti* are cooked, place them on a baking sheet lightly oiled with a little of the olive oil. Cut the bacon into fine strips, and sauté quickly in a frying pan in a little of the oil. Slice the tomatoes and place on top of the *rösti*. Season with salt and pepper. Cut the cheeses in half horizontally, then place a half on the tomatoes. Sprinkle this in turn with the crumbled bacon, then drizzle with the remaining olive oil. Bake in the preheated oven for 10 minutes. Serve hot.

since become a great friend, Lionel Delbancut. John Bertram, who had been on the hotplate at Claridge's and had then gone to Scott's, was also on the trip. The idea was that a group of chefs should visit six young chefs from Bordeaux (only one was nearing fifty years old), watch them cook, and taste the food. We were also to go and see where *foie gras* and Armagnac were produced (I've been a great lover of Armagnac ever since), where truffles were found, and visit the newly instituted Vin Expo. We were also – the height of ambition of any French chef worth his onions – to spend the night in the company of the master himself, Michel Guérard, at Eugénie-les-Bains. For a council-house lad from Yorkshire, this was absolutely mind-blowing, awe-inspiring, wonderful.

The whole trip could be similarly described. I ate some of the best food I have ever tasted, but more than that, I was being introduced to proper French food in a France that I had never truly appreciated before. Everything I had done up until then I had done with a British attitude (despite that sojourn in Switzerland), but now I was seeing the real McCoy. Because Richard had moved on, and I had depended on him and his knowledge in so many ways, I knew now that *I* had to move on and do my own thing. I had to set my own standards, and that trip helped coalesce many thoughts and ideas, and indeed gained me some enduring friendships. I kept in touch for years with three of the participating local chefs I met, all with one Michelin star – Francis Garcia (Le Clavel),

We chefs have to turn our hands to a variety of tasks. Here I am demonstrating how to fold a napkin.

Christian Clement (another eponymous restaurant), and Jean Ramet (Le Chapon Fin). Those three also helped confirm an enduring affinity with Bordeaux, a city and area I love, which I have visited at least once every year since, and where I hope to buy a property for my retirement (if that day ever comes).

Sadly, the wonderful Restaurant Christian Clement is closed now, but when we visited it on one of our teaching courses it was magic. We had dinner with the irrepressible Christian the night before and then reassembled the next morning to watch him demonstrate five of his dishes. At 9.30 a.m., this apparently mad Frenchman asked if anyone wanted a drink. All said no except me. An hour later, and several drinks and dishes later, Lulu, Madame Clement, was instructed to close the restaurant for the rest of the day as he wanted to enjoy himself. Lulu remonstrated, reminding him that the Mayor of Bordeaux was coming to lunch, and he had to capitulate, only specifying that no more bookings were taken. The six or eight of us dined in some hilarity at one end of the restaurant, Christian and I not surprisingly to the fore in the laughter stakes, while the Mayor's rather more dignified party ate at the other. Quite apart from the fun he engendered, Christian was someone who suddenly embodied everything I felt and aspired to. He wanted to cook for the sake of cooking, and was happy to do so with people watching. He showed me that a chef can be a performer, and indeed watching him produce about thirteen dishes (many more than he was contracted to), in a very short space of time and using whatever he had to hand in his kitchen, was a faint foretaste of the skills needed for *Ready Steady Cook*. I couldn't keep up with him.

The story has a slightly sad ending, though. I went back to see him several times, and one of my lads from the kitchen did a *stage* there (working and learning for a period in the kitchen, normally unpaid), but when I last saw him in 1998, his circumstances had drastically changed. I was in Saint-Emilion on a wine-tasting trip with Michael Proudlock of Foxtrot Oscar, his manageress and my chairman, Michael Mills. A racehorse trainer pal, Andy Smith, got us a lunch invitation to a box at the Bordeaux Derby as guests of M. Rougier, the champion trainer in the region. We were having *foie gras* and steak, and as she moved around the table, I thought I recognised the waitress. It was Lulu, and Christian was in the kitchen of this rather decrepit stadium, cooking private lunches. I don't know what went wrong, he wouldn't talk about it, but it was a great lesson for me (one I wish I had paid more attention to): that however brilliant a chef you may be, you must have financial acuity as well.

Other chefs I met on that 1981 trip were André Daguin (an ex French amateur rugby player and chef at the two-star Hôtel de France in Auch), Jean-Marie Amat (two Michelin stars at Restaurant Saint James), Jean-Jacques Bureau (the one-starred Restaurant Dubern) and Jean-Paul Male (two stars, at the Auberge Saint Jean in Saint Jean de Blaignac). At the end of the course we all got diplomas, and I have mine to this day. Those seven days were a great learning experience for me. The visit to Vin Expo confirmed my burgeoning interest in wine, and I have been back several times since. Another door had been opened in my culinary thinking, another facet of my world exposed that I hadn't seen or experienced before. I loved the fact that cookery could be spontaneous (although I recognise the value of recipes), and that it could be deemed a 'spectator sport'. It appealed to me immensely because I love to talk to people, and if it's about my favourite subject – food – I'm happy. The realisation that I could be cook, teacher, raconteur and showman, all rolled into one, was like the icing on my own personal cake.

Still relishing that first trip, I went on another in March 1982, to Paris, for a course run by L'Institut de Cuisine Vatel (Vatel was a famous French chef centuries ago). Kevin Kennedy from Boulestin was going as well, which dismayed me a little as he had rather a reputation as a bon viveur and chef-about-town, and I didn't want to be out partying all the time. I hadn't met him, but I'm afraid I telephoned him and virtually threatened that if he were going to keep me up to all hours of the day and night in Paris, then I wasn't going. God knows what he must have thought, but it just shows how serious-minded I still was (although I was getting there), and how pompous as well. Despite that introduction, Kevin and I got on very well together – his then girlfriend and my wife came out for a couple of days and we all went out to eat – and we're still good drinking and socialising mates now, eighteen years later.

That trip was a huge success, too. We ate at some of the best places in Paris, among them the three-star Lasserre, where Marc Daniel cooked. I had already been there a couple of times before in the company of Ted Koryn and Abe Landau. These Jewish New Yorkers, friends of David Levin, were very influential in all my excursions to Paris, introducing me to everyone that mattered, to new

I first met Kevin Kennedy in 1982 in Paris. Despite my initial stupid doubts, we got on like a house on fire – and still obviously do!

restaurants, to my first cigar… It was also Abe who defined the most successful businessman as one who doesn't have a key to his own business. As he explained it, if something disastrous happened to his biscuit-making business, the general manager, who holds all the keys, would phone and say, 'Mr Landau, I've got some bad news and some good news. The bad news is that the cookie factory burned down last night, but the good news is that I've got everything under control and the insurance cheque is in the post.' The point is, of course, that when you reach the top, you can leave everything to your carefully chosen subordinates. I took all that on board at the time, but I still – workaholic that I am – carry my own keys!

Other chefs and restaurants included Pierre Androuët at his eponymous, one-starred restaurant which served only cheese: *Gault et Millau* at the time said that he was 'the greatest living expert in cheese in France'. I also met Dominique Bouchet, who cooked at the three-starred La Tour d'Argent. The restaurant was famous for its duck dishes, and Dominique said that a certain consistent percentage of the orders was for duck every day. Wanting to show that I could speak French, that I was knowledgeable and sympathetic, I mentioned that this must make his life easier, that he could organise things in advance. He flew off the handle, thinking I was denigrating his talent, suggesting he had an easy job! Kevin Kennedy teased me about that for hours afterwards, but I still maintain that if I knew I was going to sell fifty per cent lamb in the restaurant, it would make ordering, prepping and cooking very much easier.

We also went to eat at a two-star restaurant called Pangaud, run by Gerard Pangaud, who cooked, according to *Gault et Millau*, 'the best food to be found anywhere in Paris'. The restaurant itself was slightly odd, obviously two buildings knocked together. But between the two parts – one the kitchen and one the restaurant – there was only a hatch to pass food through. If M. Pangaud wanted to visit his own restaurant, he had to come out of the kitchen back door and walk round to the front door of the restaurant, a matter of a few yards. While we were there, talking to M. Pangaud, we saw the blue flashing lights of an ambulance and fire engine outside. M. Pangaud had to rush out of the front door and round to the back of the building to find out what was happening in his own kitchen. (A *commis* had unfortunately burned himself on the fat-fryer, and was taken to hospital.) A ludicrous situation, but the food was wonderful, and Gérard Pangaud has become a bit of a hero of mine. Unlike many young French chefs, he had made his own way to the heights of a three-star restaurant named after himself. He had not inherited a restaurant from his father or grandfather, as Jacques Lameloise had done, so I think Gérard Pangaud was probably the first proper chef-patron I met. It made me feel that I, too, could do what he had done, open my own restaurant without a family tradition behind me, and he was a great inspiration.

A visit to the kitchens of the two-star Hôtel Crillon (it so reminded me of the Savoy) wrapped up our trip, and we all came back to London bursting with new recipes, our blood transfused with Parisian ideas and French influences.

I felt I was still learning, that there was more I could take in, and these trips were very educational. I was thirty-six at the time, and it occurs to me that we matured then in a gastronomic sense at a much older age than the boys do today. But, even though I do say so myself, I feel that the boys of today have the benefit of what we did then, as the paths to enlightenment had been already explored and revealed.

L'Hôtel and Le Metro

At some point in the early 1980s, the Levins bought the hotel next door to the Capital. They did it up and christened it L'Hôtel, after the one in Paris. It was to be a cheaper and simpler version of the Capital, and many people transferred their allegiance to L'Hôtel fairly swiftly. L'Hôtel would not have a restaurant, but guests could eat breakfast at the Capital – and lunch and dinner too, if they chose. It was probably one of the first exclusive bed and breakfast hotels in the city, another first for David Levin. Some time after it opened, they were wondering what to do with its basement. Should they make it into a society hairdresser, and get Princess Margaret and several other famous people to come along? Or should they turn it into a wine bar? I fought for the wine bar option, as half my social life (when I had the time for any such) was spent in wine bars like Motcomb's, Draycott's and Bill Bentley's, all the rage in the late 1970s, early 1980s. Both Draycott's and Motcomb's were rather plush, in décor and clientele, and the former was actually rather reminiscent of a Paris café with bushes in tubs and a few tables outside on the pavement. This was the approach David Levin favoured once he had decided on the wine bar, and we separately made several trips scouting around Paris, Lyons and Bordeaux for ideas. The wine bar was actually a uniquely British phenomenon, but the French had been perfecting the art of serving wines and spirits in harmonious surroundings for years in their bar-restaurants and brasseries. A major idea came from L'Ecluse in Paris, where the owner had shipped in marble from the south as an integral part of the décor; this we echoed in the new wine bar, with a marble bar and marble tables.

One of my planning and eating trips to Lyons was particularly poignant for me. As I sat down to eat at Paul Bocuse's restaurant, the first time I had been there, I was called to the telephone. It was Carol from the Capital, telling me to get home as soon as possible as my mother had taken a turn for the worse. Mum had been ill for some time, but I had spoken to her daily on the phone until that trip. The staff at the restaurant, particularly Jean Fleurie, who was in the kitchen with Bocuse, were extraordinarily helpful and sympathetic, but I could not get a plane home that night. By the time I flew from Paris the next morning, my mother had left us.

David Levin, once again, had foreseen a new trend, the alliance of wine bar camaraderie with good wines, good company and good food. As we were so close to Harrods, it became obvious to him that the store's customers – particularly the ladies – might like somewhere to eat a light lunch of a single dish possibly, plus a glass of good wine. In fact the wine bar became almost a canteen for the staff at Harrods, it was so handy.

It was christened Le Metro, its sign was a direct copy of the Metro sign in Paris, and from the very beginning it was a huge success. It was small, and its kitchen was even smaller, but I knew that, because the two were almost physically connected, we could supply some of the basics from the Capital kitchen, particularly the stocks and sauces. We planned a menu that would be easy to eat at lunchtime, for someone coming in for a quick snack, but we would serve food in the evening as well. We had *ballotines*, stuffed chicken legs, and a *confit* of duck, sold as crispy duck, which we pan-roasted once it was out of its preserving duck fat, which made the skin crisp. I still maintain that my *confit* is better than most I have eaten in France for that very reason. We might have *rillettes de canard* to start, with something like *saucisson à la lyonnaise* to follow. Each day we would offer four specials – two starters, one main course and one dessert (the latter often what was left over from the Capital). Warm salads, *salades tièdes*, I had encountered in France, so I created one with chicken livers plus a mustard and Madeira sauce. I thought I was being very economical, as I could use instead of waste the chicken livers from the chickens we cooked at the Capital. However, within two months of opening the Metro, we had to buy our chicken livers separately, as the Capital supply just couldn't keep up!

So here I was involved in three food operations, each of them representing a distinct market sector: there was the up-market Capital, the middle-market Greenhouse, and now the wine bar. Because I had been involved in its planning from day one, I revelled in the Metro from the beginning: the look, the ambience and the food. I had enjoyed the occasional chat with customers at the Capital and, once I had gained my confidence concerning the Greenhouse, walking among the tables there, asking whether people had enjoyed their meal, greeting acquaintances and friends gave me great pleasure. But the informality and friendliness of the Metro was absolutely up my street and, because I was happy with the brigades in both the other restaurants, I began to spend a great deal of my free time there. This was very valuable in a culinary sense, as it meant I could more closely understand what people were looking for in food. I could actually look them in the eye and ask them, much more directly than I could at either the Capital or Greenhouse. I could have real conversations with them. I felt very much at home in the Metro wine bar, and although we didn't have an actual 'happy hour', we were always happy!

I also met many people in the Metro who were to become very important in my life. Michael Mills, now chairman of my company, very quickly became a Metro regular, along with his friends Stephen Greene and Stuart Courtney. All were businessmen, and loved to entertain and make merry four or five times a week. They were party animals, good imbibers and eaters, and the Three Musketeers fairly swiftly became the Four Musketeers, as I was included in their adventures. They kept me abreast of new restaurant openings, and when I could afford it I would go along with them. They were earning far more than I, but as often as not, they would insist that I be their guest. They were of course a great asset to the Metro, being so sociable – networking, introducing people to the wine bar and each other – and what we called the Mills Trick became a masterpiece of salesmanship, adding considerably to the Metro's profitability. Michael would always come in at about five in the afternoon, just before we opened, he and I would stand at the bar, and I would buy us glasses of champagne. As soon as the doors opened at five-thirty, people would stream in, and as if by osmosis, seeing what we were drinking, they would order champagne as well. The Mills Trick was so successful that David Levin would always ask if Michael (or Champagne Charlie as he became known) was on holiday when the weekly sales of champagne diminished!

That time of my life was happy. It was all about social skills, meeting people, talking to people, watching how people reacted to what we did. Because I was

Confit of Duck
SERVES 8

Ever since I fell in love with Bordeaux and the south-west of France, Armagnac, *foie gras* and *confit* have been great favourites of mine. The principle of preservation involved – cooking and storing in fat seasoned with garlic, herbs and spices – gives marvellous textures and flavours, and is so simple to do.

This duck *confit* that Turner's head chef Jon Jon and I have perfected is delicious. Although *confits* may not make the healthiest of eating, I think in autumn and winter there is nothing to beat them.

8 large duck legs

2 tablespoons Maldon sea salt

2 bay leaves, chopped

2 sprigs fresh thyme, leaves picked from stalks

freshly ground black pepper

2 whole garlic heads

1 medium onion, peeled and roughly chopped

1 carrot, peeled and roughly chopped

enough rendered duck fat to cover the legs

Madeira sauce

2 shallots, peeled and chopped

85g (3 oz) unsalted butter

175ml (6 fl oz) Madeira (rich Bual)

175ml (6 fl oz) dry white wine

300ml (½ pint) thickened *Veal Stock* (see pages 240–41)

Make sure the duck legs are free of quills. Lay the legs on a tray, and sprinkle with sea salt, chopped bay leaves and thyme leaves. Season with some black pepper. Cut the garlic heads in half and pile around the duck legs. Cover with clingfilm and leave to marinate for 24 hours.

Preheat the oven to 140°C/275°F/Gas 1.

Wipe the herbs off the duck legs, and pat the legs dry. Put them in a deep, heavy-based ovenproof pot. Add the onion, carrot and the halved heads of garlic. Cover with melted duck fat, then with the lid, and cook in the low oven for 1½–2 hours. Make sure the fat does not boil. Do not overcook. When cooked, take the pot out of the oven and leave to cool.

Decant the duck legs into a clean bowl. Strain the liquid through a fine sieve over the duck legs and refrigerate for 2 days. The legs will actually keep like this for ages if well covered with the fat.

To serve, remove the legs from the fat and put into a hot pan, skin side down. You don't need to add any extra fat, as there will be enough still on the legs. Roast to a good colour on all sides, turning over frequently to reheat the legs all the way through.

To make the sauce, sweat the shallot in 25g (1 oz) of the butter until softened but not coloured. Add the Madeira and white wine and simmer to reduce by half. Add the thickened stock, bring back to the boil, and check the seasoning. Stir in the remaining butter, cut into cubes.

Serve the duck legs with the hot sauce and, as in the photograph, with some mashed potato and some spring onions sweated in butter.

Ivor Robbins, fruit and vegetable man extraordinaire, with whom I became friends when I was at the Capital. I was checking fruit at his stand in the old Spitalfields market.

eating out more often, I was developing an overall restaurant sense, rather than just a kitchen sense. I also became even more of a wine enthusiast because of the Metro. I drank a lot of champagne, but I occasionally had some of the excellent wines which we served from a Cruover machine. This we had seen in Bordeaux and imported, and it grabbed a lot of attention in the wine media when we opened. The basic principle involved an inert gas: once wine had been siphoned off into a glass, the gas would replace the vacuum left by the wine, and thus prevent the wine oxidising. The good wines, good food and the ambience obviously made for a successful combination because in the first year we opened we won the National Wine Bar of the Year award, and the *Evening Standard* London Wine Bar of the Year in our second year.

So all in all, David Levin's three food outlets were doing extremely well. The Capital was still going from strength to strength and the Greenhouse was doing phenomenal business. The Capital restaurant had been transformed into an elegant peach and pink oasis by Nina Campbell, the leading interior designer of the day. She also utilised some antique wallpaper that David Levin had found at an auction in Monte Carlo, and had had copied to make four pieces. We had these framed and mounted on the walls, and the flowers in the 'murals' were echoed by the fresh flowers on the tables. She also refurbished elsewhere in the hotel as well. As the small hotel concept had proved successful, now the small hotel could stop pretending to be a big hotel.

At the Metro, I was entertaining people, and being entertained by clients, friends and suppliers. One of the suppliers, Ivor Robbins, has become a good friend, having been introduced by the Levins. He ran a company called Hotel Purveyors, and I said I would try him out. His face lit up at that, but fell again when I gave him possibly the smallest order I could, 'I'll have a sack of potatoes and some cabbages.' I repeated that order for a few weeks, just to see how it would work out, then took him on permanently. My philosophy concerning suppliers was, and still is, that so long as they are doing a good job there's no real point in changing. You should be loyal to suppliers, just as you expect them to be loyal to you. At that time I was slightly upset with our then current vegetable and fruit supplier, thus the Robbins experiment. About two weeks after this, the first supplier rang up wondering why he hadn't had an order. 'What's the problem?' 'That's the problem,' I said. 'It took you two weeks to notice that there was no order, which means no one was looking after us properly.'

Ivor was instrumental in another aspect of my business. He, his wife Sue and I went out quite a lot, and one day he told me about a young chef who thought I was the 'bee's knees' (to use his expression), and wanted to meet me. So the three of us went to Winston's Eating House, an English pie and pudding type restaurant. The food was good, but the chef wasn't happy there and wanted to move. Although a little suspicious of his Duran Duran haircut and earrings (I insisted on him getting rid of the latter, much to the horror of my wife and Margaret Levin), I took him on as third chef at the Capital. Gary Rhodes – for it was he – stayed with us for about eighteen months, during which time I sent him to do a *stage* at Lameloise in Burgundy. I employed Gary's future wife Jenny too, as *sous-chef* at the Greenhouse under Nigel Davis: Gary, Jenny and Mark Clayton, my trusty second, had all trained together at Thanet Technical College in Broadstairs. Gary and Jenny left to open up a new restaurant in Essex,

Smoked Chicken and Plum Tomato Salad with a Parsley Pesto Dressing

SERVES 4

Smoked chicken has wonderful flavours, and the breasts are luscious and moist, but you can use leg meat as well.

2 smoked chicken breasts

1 tablespoon chopped gherkins

1 shallot, peeled and chopped

salt and freshly ground black pepper

4 plum tomatoes

a handful of mixed salad leaves

1–2 tablespoons olive oil

Pesto

3 tablespoons chopped fresh parsley

1 tablespoon pine kernels

1 garlic clove, peeled

1 tablespoon freshly grated Parmesan

1–2 tablespoons olive oil

Tomato dressing

2 tablespoons chopped seeded plum tomatoes

1 garlic clove, peeled and chopped

1 tablespoon chopped fresh chives

2 tablespoons olive oil

1 tablespoon balsamic vinegar

Cut the chicken breasts into fine dice. Add the chopped gherkin and shallot, mix, season and put to one side. Slice the tomatoes thinly into 6 slices each, lay on a tray and season. Toss the salad leaves with salt, pepper and the olive oil. Divide the dressed leaves between the serving plates.

Use a 5cm (2 in) metal ring. Place 2 slices of tomato in the ring, and spread with an eighth of the chicken mix. Place 2 more slices of tomato on top of this, cover with another eighth of the chicken, and top with another 2 slices of tomato. Carefully balance the prepared salad on top of the leaves and remove the ring. Repeat to make three more 'towers'.

Make the pesto in the food processor, chopping the parsley, pine kernels and garlic well. Stir in the Parmesan, then the oil and some salt and pepper. Drizzle this around the edges of each plate. Make the tomato dressing by mixing all the ingredients together. Season. Pour over the top of the salad, and serve.

which I thought was a mistake, and sure enough Gary came back about a year later, in 1986, for a while before being tempted to the Castle Hotel in Taunton by Kit Chapman. I thought that another mistake, I must admit, but it obviously wasn't, leading him eventually back to the embrace of David Levin at the Greenhouse, to television and book fame, and now his expanding and highly successful restaurant chain in association with Gardner Merchant.

While I was eating out and about, and socialising in the Metro, I also met many of my fellow chefs, some of whom were already well established, some of whom were to achieve fame in later years, such as Tony Tobin, who was actually working for me at the Metro, and who now has several restaurant interests in Surrey and appears regularly on television. One of my favourite places to eat was 192, where Alastair Little cooked before moving to his own eponymous restaurant in Soho in 1985. I also enjoyed Lampwick's in Queenstown Road, whose chef-patron Alan Bennett was to befriend and employ the young Marco Pierre White (he had popped into my office once at the Capital asking for a job, as did Bruno Loubet when he left Gastronome One). The nearby Nico's was expensive, although I managed to eat there a few times; Nico was very talented, but we never quite managed to hit it off together. I regularly now went to the Boulestin to enjoy my friend Kevin Kennedy's fabulous cooking, and I still remained loyal to Foxtrot Oscar. I used to go to Foxtrot Oscar after lunchtime service to have a hamburger and talk about the industry, the personalities and their (and our) love lives, just like girls do – in fact we called it the 'Girls' Club'! My fellow gossips regularly included Patrick Gwynn Jones, Michael Proudlock, Steven Clarke from Laurent Perrier, Dan Whitehead from Dan's, Dai Llewellyn and Nigel Dempster.

The wine merchants, Sichel, used to give lunches which lauded chefs who had won a Michelin star (rather than the owners or proprietors). That widened my outlook, meeting and being recognised by my peers. Up until then, I suppose I had been rather inward-looking so far as *people* in the business were concerned. I met Murdo MacSween at one of the Sichel lunches (now transformed into dinners sponsored by Mumm Champagne), when he had just won a star at Walton's in Walton Street. For a while after he started there, his menu still had an echo or two of the hand of my old mentor, Michael Smith. I also met Stephen Bull, who was cooking at Lichfield's in Richmond at the time (he now has a couple of restaurants in the centre of London called Stephen Bull). He was typical of a new breed of chefs reminiscent of the enthusiastic amateurs who had inspired us years before: he had been in another business – in his case, advertising – before changing tack to go into cooking. Many others were not professionally trained either, and they included many of the most famous names of the time: Raymond Blanc, Nico Ladenis, Alastair Little, Rowley Leigh and Simon Hopkinson.

Raymond Blanc used to come to the Capital when he was in London, probably because it was calmer, more of an oasis than most restaurants – but for the quality of the food, too, I hope! I remember that he was very envious of my ability to sell offal (we were offering a couple of brain dishes at the time); he said no one in the country wanted to eat such delights. A little later I refereed a football match between the Manoir aux Quat'Saisons' brigade and a brigade from the Roux brothers' Waterside Inn: I was obliged to send off Marco Pierre White, then working for Blanc. Pierre Martin (Le Suquet, La Croisette and Quai St Pierre), Lou Siegel (Frederick's) and Gunter Schlender (Carrier's) I also met occasionally, and astonishingly, Lou has just celebrated thirty years in his establishment in Islington.

The major friendship begun in the early 1980s was that with Antony Worrall Thompson. *Food and Drink* wasn't the catalyst, it actually was a chance meeting in the Brasserie St Quentin, *the* in-place of the moment, owned by Lord Hugh O'Neill, Quentin Crewe's cousin. I was dining with David Levin, celebrating a nice piece in the *Evening Standard* the night before, when this cocky, impossibly blond youth came over and said, 'Hi, I'm Antony Worrall Thompson, we were together in the paper last night.' Antony then ran Ménage à Trois (yes, it had been mentioned in the *Standard*), which served only starters and puddings, a restaurant designed for thin ladies who lunched. Michael Mills and his cohorts also ate at Ménage occasionally, and I'd heard good reports from them. Antony had a reputation as the '*enfant terrible*' of the chefs' world, and had risen to the top of his chosen profession in a very short space of time. He also came into the Metro regularly to eat, and once said, kindly, that I had put 'professionalism into wine-bar food'. Cocky he might have been, and he admitted it himself in an article in 1985, but he was great fun, and soon became a much appreciated Fifth Musketeer.

My great friend Antony Worrall Thompson is always causing havoc in the kitchen, and ingredients tend to go flying, this time during a 'specialised chefs' course demonstration at Bournemouth and Poole College in 1989. At least it looks as if he's cleaning me down.

Other very useful means of meeting my fellow chefs were the chef organisations which became popular in the early 1980s. The Académie Culinaire de France was founded in 1883 by Joseph Favre, a foodie Swiss chemist living in Paris. In 1980, Michel Bourdin and Albert Roux were the principals behind an affiliated organisation in Britain, which actually developed from the Club Nine mentioned earlier. Its aims were to encourage talk about the business, about food, about how to train youngsters, how to keep the industry alive. There were twenty-five founder members, among them Richard Shepherd, who became the first chairman of the British group, probably the first non-Frenchman to be chairman of any Académie Culinaire (there are now about forty throughout the world). I didn't join at first, as I and a few others had become

Michel Bourdin and Albert Roux were behind the establishment of the Académie Culinaire de France in this country in 1980. I became executive chairman of the British association in 1993, now rechristened the Academy of Culinary Arts.

members of an American organisation, Master Chefs, which was masterminded by an American publisher, Sandy Lesburg. The Académie quickly decided that no one could be a member of both, thinking that the Americans were usurping the power and prestige of the French. I objected to this non-democratic approach and indeed still believe that the aims and principles of the two organisations were and are completely different and do not clash. However, they managed to persuade me to become the thirty-fifth member in that first year (the French said thirty-five was the permitted number in Britain), and I have held the office of executive chairman since 1993, when Richard Shepherd stepped down (he is still the president).

We had a few arguments over the years with the French-based Académie, as we were much more proactive and hard-working. We actually initiated new annual awards and training courses, and brought in *maître sommeliers* and restaurant managers as important members of the industry, representing *Les Arts de la Table* (the French membership was limited to head chefs only). We also organised an affiliate group of young bloods who wanted eventually to become academicians. The disagreements became so intense that the French organisation severed connections with the British round about the time we anglicised our name to the Academy of Culinary Arts. Happily, thanks to the good work by Richard Shepherd, Michel Bourdin and myself, along with the newly appointed chairman of the French Académie, Gérard Dupont, and his colleagues, we are now enjoying a bigger and better relationship, one which is stronger than ever. A four-yearly award for culinary excellence (which had been awarded by the French Government since 1923) was known first as MOGB, *Meilleur Ouvrier de Grande Bretagne*. We plan to transform this to MCA, Master of Culinary Arts (which could and should be accorded degree status) at the end of the year 2000. It's the culinary equivalent of a Hollywood Oscar, and Antony Worrall Thompson was one of the first three to be awarded the lifelong title at our first MOGB ceremony in 1987 (the others were Michael Aldridge, then of the Connaught, and Michel Perraud, then of the Waterside Inn). Tony was over the moon, and likened his achievement to 'the village football team winning the FA Cup'!

The Academy now boasts about two hundred members, and includes the majority of the most talented and influential chefs and other members of the industry. Some three months after our change of name, the Prince of Wales became our patron, which was and is a great honour. The Academy now goes from strength to strength, one of our major schemes being 'Adopt-a-School', a long-term project begun in the first year of my chairmanship. A chef will go into the classroom two or three times a year, helping the children to recognise the four principal tastes, and teaching them how to analyse and appreciate what is on a plate. There is a similar scheme in France, but it has vast financial backing from the government and industry. Here our resources are much more limited, but we are no less committed. If we can teach our children to eat well and cook good food as part of everyday life, we'll have given them an invaluable gift. The scheme has been enormously popular, but sadly we have many more schools asking to be 'adopted' than we have academicians!

Another important social and professional connection came about through Sandy Lesburg of Master Chefs. He had connections in Bermuda (then famous as a tax haven), and he suggested in the early 1980s that I go there for a fortnight to teach. I was rather dubious at first, as I'd never cooked in that way before, although of course I was an 'experienced' teacher. I talked to David Levin, attempting to persuade him that it would be good publicity for the Capital, encouraging wealthy islanders to come to the hotel. He was a little dismissive – 'Bermudans don't come to London any more' – but allowed me to go, saying I might benefit from the holiday.

I was staying in the Belmont Hotel, where I would demonstrate and teach in the morning. In the evening, I would ship across Hamilton Sound to the Bermudiana Hotel where paying guests would eat a dinner I had created. Most of the dishes I chose were stalwarts from the Capital menu, but there were a few teething troubles. I can never understand why it's so impossible to get fresh fish on an island, but it is and was, and we had to make do with frozen coho salmon flown in from the States. The morning classes were full in the first week, and my pupils numbered about sixteen, among them Janet Lines, Margaret Collis and other Bermudan high-society ladies. They were interested in cooking and enjoyed it, although one of them admitted she'd never actually been in a kitchen before (as her father had owned a major South American railway system, there probably was no necessity for her to do so). Other essential differences in view-point were inevitably brought home to me. One of our first tasks was to make

The Académie often contributed to worthy causes. Here four of us had cooked at the Banqueting House, Whitehall, on 22 May 1984, on behalf of the Greater London Fund for the Blind. From the left, Bernard Gaume, myself, Anton Mosimann and Peter Kromberg.

some mayonnaise. 'Make mayonnaise, Chef? But it comes in jars, you don't make it.' We had good fun, cooking everything in the morning, then eating it together at lunchtime with a bottle of wine. I was in my element surrounded by those ladies!

Because the second week hadn't any bookings, the same ladies decided to come again, which meant I hastily had to write a different course. During that second week, I heard that my ladies' husbands – all apparently interested cooks – were beginning to slightly resent the implication that they were doing things all wrong: 'That's not the way Chef Brian does it...' and 'Chef Brian says you should do this...' The upshot was that I met David Lines (very senior in Coopers & Lybrand) and agreed to run a day of demonstration and teaching for Bermudan men on the Saturday before I went home. I laid down some conditions: they all had to wear aprons, get involved, and pay due deference to the chef, and I also wanted to choose the wines as we were preparing a gastronomic dinner. David agreed, but added his own proviso, that I should sit down and eat with them in the evening.

So at the Lines' island house, ten male guests and I cooked, drank and laughed all day. The ten included some of the most senior financial and political figures on the island, including the prime minister, the Honourable Sir John Swann, as well as Charles Collis, Chet Butterfield and Paul Leseur. All had given the whole day over to be involved in my cookery class. Every so often the telephone would ring, and there would be a little huddle in one corner as a sudden political or financial crisis needed to be defused, but all the personnel involved were still, as per my agreed condition, wearing their aprons! During the meal that evening, I mentioned David Levin's diffidence about my trip. John Swann said, 'I suggest you challenge Mr Levin to get as many members of the Cabinet and British Parliament round one table as you have here today!' And indeed many of the friends made in those two weeks have appeared at the Capital and Turner's, and still appear today some fifteen years on. I count them as regular customers, and I have been back to Bermuda some three times since. So much for the theory that Bermudans don't come to London! I like to think of myself as an unofficial roving ambassador for the island. It is a serene and beautiful place, very close to my heart.

Itchy Feet

After the opening of the Metro in 1983, it seemed as if I had the world at my feet. I was in a job that I loved – running and cooking in three different types of establishment – I was trusted and respected, I was happily married with two wonderful sons, I had a house (albeit on a mortgage) and a Volvo. What more could a Yorkshire lad want? But, a couple of years later, I began to have itchy feet. The Metro experience, which I was so enjoying, made me realise how important the ambience of a bar or restaurant was. Recognising how a restaurant manager or chef-patron could transform a room and an eating experience by sheer personality alone made me determine to find a place in which I could express myself in that same way. I was still an employee although I was allowed a huge amount of leeway, but suddenly it didn't seem to be enough. I wanted to have a *share* in the success I was helping to create.

I knew from 'Girls' Club' conversations that most people equated true success with going solo, so I had to make this quantum leap and establish my own place. My preference was for a small hotel with twelve apartments upstairs, ideally with a central door, to the right a quality restaurant, to the left a wine bar, with kitchens out at the back (very much on the Capital model). I didn't have much of a clue about how I should go about it, so spoke to Michael Mills and Stephen Greene, who were both in finance. They said I should find a place first, then think about money, so in my spare moments I used to tramp around London looking for properties. Victoria and Kensington were my favoured areas, but in retrospect, I didn't really know what I was doing. If someone had said, 'Here's a suitable site,' I wouldn't have had enough business sense to recognise whether it was a fair proposition or not. Good cook perhaps, but no businessman...

Which, of course, is what led me into trouble. At the Metro, the Four (and occasionally Five) Musketeers used to mix with a nice group of beautiful young ladies. One of these was Susie Wood-Roberts, a model who worked for a top dress designer. In several of our conversations, I must have mentioned my ambitions, and she in turn mentioned them to the guy who supervised her boss's business. Thus I was introduced to Martin Davis, who sponsored and financially backed people who could be successful in a particular area, become stars even, but who just needed a little helping hand.

Martin Davis was a businessman, specialising in property, who operated mainly from his Bentley or Porsche, armed with mobile phone and filofax. He was short, bearded, trendy, Jewish, wore black all the time (with no socks), and I was very impressed. He talked me through my ideas, and mentioned several aspects I hadn't even considered. People like me – and that probably includes most chefs – need someone to guide them through the business and financial side of things, and despite some claims to the contrary, many of the top chefs of today have been backed in their ventures by advisors not actually in the trade. Martin Davis, with his energy, enthusiasm and apparent financial acumen, seemed to me like my own personal knight in shining armour. Michael Mills and others at the Metro, and friends at Foxtrot Oscar, all said I should slow down, take legal advice, find out more before I became too involved, but Martin was helping me achieve my dream.

It was Martin who eventually found the freehold property in Walton Street. It had been a restaurant called Bewick's, and was owned by a Julian Sacher. Bewick's was popular with the Chelsea in-set, and was dark green in colour inside and out. It was so murky (sorry, romantic) that to my mind it was the kind of place you went to if you didn't want to see who you were dining with, or you didn't want to be seen at all! Anyway, Martin and I agreed to go into business together fifty-fifty (a mistake, as one person should always have controlling interest). My part of the deal was to raise £50,000, which I did by remortgaging my house in Stanmore (and thereby going into immediate debt). I did this without my wife's knowledge and consent, but not because I wished to hide the facts from her intentionally. I just thought one person in the family worrying about money was enough. Martin was to raise the same amount of money, and the remainder was to come as a loan from the Royal Bank of Scotland. On 4 July 1986, we signed the contract, and a council-estate cook from Yorkshire became part-owner of a three-storey freehold building in Chelsea's fashionable Walton Street.

To this day I do not know precisely what deal Martin Davis struck with Julian Sacher, and never bothered to find out. I now can't quite believe my naïvety, but I was only a cook, and I happily signed what was put in front of me, without asking any pertinent questions. We probably paid about £600,000 for the property – Martin said the price was a steal – and if all had worked as it should, I would have been a very happy and rich man now, with a property worth in the region of two million pounds.

I handed in my notice at the Capital fairly soon after we signed the contract for Walton Street, and was due to leave in August. We planned to open the new restaurant in October, and the next few months were frantically busy. We had to revamp and restyle the restaurant, and plan menus and our approach. Although a lot of it was very enjoyable, the pressures were considerable. I was still running three restaurants after all, and I had many sleepless nights worrying about the financial implications. Martin employed the services of David Franklin and Lynn Jordan, architect and interior designer respectively. He had worked with them before and all three had good ideas to contribute. We took the bottom of the restaurant out, and changed the doorway and bar inside. The route to the kitchen used to be behind the bar, but we put fridges in there. The architectural plans posited a seventy-five seat restaurant, but no one outside the trade ever knows what is really needed. The tables drawn to scale were far too small and close together, so we had to cut the numbers down to sixty (now about fifty-five). I know that those seventy-five seats were part of Martin's financial strategy, but it couldn't be

Here we're putting a few finishing touches to the façade of Turner's in Walton Street (net curtains and all).

done. Those arguments about finance were very useful to me, however, enlightening me about budgeting and expenditure, showing me how sales and the split in sales worked, how we'd take out money and how we would make a profit – for we had to make a profit to service the huge bank loan.

It was also great fun listening to the designer talking about table sizes and shapes, about cutlery, crockery and napery, things I'd only had a residual hand in before, primarily when planning the Metro. They came up with most of the design ideas, but they always ran them by me first. One of the things I fought long and hard over was the initial idea of the colours being powder blue and oatmeal (a lot lighter than the colours of the restaurant today). Martin wanted chairs all the same shape and he wanted them blue, but he thought it would be interesting to have them upholstered with different patterned fabrics. I resisted that idea as well.

During all this – meetings at the restaurant, at various people's houses, at any and all times of the day, whenever I could get away – I was also still supervising my three kitchens and helping David Levin find a replacement for myself. (I wasn't taking anyone with me from the Capital, except for Pam Vincent who had managed the Greenhouse before coming to the Metro.) I came up with a distinguished shortlist: Marco who was at Lampwick's, Bruce Sangster at Rothbury Hall in Leicestershire, Peter Chandler at The Paris House in Woburn, and John Elliott, who was now my second at the Capital. We went to each of the restaurants to eat and talk to the chefs, all of whom were very strong possibilities so far as I was concerned, but in the end Levin plumped for John Elliott. He had started with us, then gone to the Connaught followed by France, before returning to us. He didn't last long after I left (he went to the Goring Hotel, and now runs a sandwich bar), so Levin brought in Philip Britten, previously at Nico's and Dan's.

So my fifteen-year association with the Capital Hotel and David Levin was coming to an end. I did feel some pangs of regret, but excitement was the primary emotion (if tempered by financial nervousness). Those years had been hugely significant, both in my own life and career, and in the history of gastronomy in Britain. The opening of the Capital was in fact a monumental step, both because of its being in the vanguard of the London small hotel movement, and in its boasting a top-class French restaurant. The Capital was the first small hotel restaurant to gain a Michelin star – and with English chefs. The Capital years mirrored the growth of interest in food and cooking in Britain, both from the point of view of practitioner and consumer. The principal influence was still French – the great chefs of the time were either French by birth or their style was French classical cuisine – but they were employing young British people in their kitchens, and thereby infecting them with the 'bug'. Richard Shepherd and I, both English, were at the forefront of the new British enthusiasm for French cooking and cooking in general, and many of the best-known British names in the business today started at around that time. The Capital years saw the emergence of the chef from kitchen obscurity to public prominence, thereby anticipating the chef as 'star' in both books and television, a view which has so characterised the years since. Primarily, though, my time at the Capital had consolidated my skills, my ambitions and my belief in myself, and I couldn't wait for the next phase.

When I left in the middle of August, I got my holiday money and that was all, but I was escaping, and freedom and independence beckoned. Well, that's what I thought!

part four

Turner's

Opening Turner's was the fulfilment of a lifetime ambition for me, as I had long been hankering after somewhere I could truly call my own, where I could be totally in charge, and where I could be myself, both as cook and as social animal. I'd always thought that many fine-dining restaurants were too serious and too imposing to really enable people to enjoy themselves. My principal desire was to offer the same fine quality of food, but simultaneously to make the atmosphere much more enjoyable. When you go out to a restaurant you go to eat and have fun, not to sit in reverence or worship at a shrine. I wanted my restaurant to be the sort of place where people could relax, take their jackets off, tell a few stories and have a good laugh. Enjoying life and enjoying good food were and are not incompatible, as I'd learned at the Metro; they should be and are complementary.

In the narrow kitchen at Turner's, with Jon Jon Lucas, who was my first apprentice and is now the head chef.

Brandade of Sole
SERVES 4

A *brandade* is usually made with salt cod. My version uses sole instead, and cream and garlic along with the potato.

115g (4 oz) floury potatoes (King Edward or Maris Piper), washed

4 Dover sole fillets

150ml (¼ pint) milk

1 bunch spring onions, chopped

3 garlic cloves, peeled and sliced

2 gelatine leaves, soaked in water to soften

salt and freshly ground black pepper

freshly grated nutmeg

4 tablespoons olive oil

150ml (¼ pint) double cream

225g (8 oz) green beans, trimmed and cooked

about 16 green olives, pitted and chopped

40g (1½ oz) shallots, peeled and chopped

4 plum tomatoes, seeded and diced

fresh chervil

Cook the potatoes in their skins – from 15–30 minutes, depending on size – but do not *over*cook. Drain and leave to cool.

Poach the sole fillets in the milk with the spring onions and garlic for 7 minutes. Strain off the milk into another small pan, and simmer to reduce by half. Remove from the heat and add the drained gelatine. Allow the gelatine to dissolve, then put to one side to cool.

Skin the potatoes carefully, and put the flesh into a bowl. Add the poached garlic and sole, and beat until smooth. If necessary, pass through a sieve, then add the gelatine mix. Season with salt and pepper, fresh nutmeg and 2 tablespoons of the olive oil. Mix well.

Whip the cream and then fold carefully into the sole and potato mixture. Check the seasoning and chill until nearly setting, but not quite.

To serve, mix the cold green beans with most of the olives and all the shallots. Season and mix with 1 tablespoon of the remaining olive oil. Using a small ring shape, put the beans in the middle of the plate and push down well. Remove the ring. Shape some sole and potato mixture using 2 dessertspoons and place this oval carefully on top. Mix the tomato dice with the remaining olives and olive oil, and season. Dot around the edges of the plates with tiny sprigs of chervil, and serve.

As it took shape through the summer of 1986, that cool oatmeal and blue room in Walton Street started to resemble my dream. When I left the Capital in August, I spent quite a lot of my time there, urging people on, and making a nuisance of myself. Builders always seem to be working to a different agenda – sitting about waiting for something to happen or some equipment to arrive – and I felt I was paying for that inactivity. I got so difficult that I was actually banned from the site for a week or so. We planned to open in October, but I refused to let us set a specific date, as we seemed to be running behind. In fact, it's something I find very irritating now, all this PR bumph about a new restaurant opening at such and such a time on such and such a date. I've never yet known one make the date that has been fixed.

At some point during the early autumn, Martin Davis decided that the restaurant should be called Turner's. I was never of the opinion that my name was big enough for anything like that, so was reluctant at first. Not many restaurants in Britain were named after chef-patrons: among them were Nico, Chris Oakes, Alastair Little, Sally Clarke and, although not quite the same, as Peter wasn't the chef, Langan's. I think the name Turner opens a few doors now, but I'd love to have called it something else. (I actually now quite like Turner's of Walton Street, which is what I call myself and my company.) Perhaps it was a false sense of modesty, but Martin and I fought long and hard about it, until eventually I gave in.

The next most important discussion concerned the kitchen and the menu. Martin had some input, but not much, as I insisted that I was the expert in that particular area. I'd given way often enough during the planning of the design and décor, but when it came to running the restaurant, I said that they knew nothing. My first decision was to employ Mark Clayton as my second. He had worked for me briefly at the Capital (he was the one who'd trained with Gary Rhodes), had gone to L'Ortolan in Reading with Nico, then come back to London when Nico did. In the kitchen with us were to be Richard Coates, Anne Cremonesi, plus Pam Vincent (from the Greenhouse and Metro) as manageress and David as our wine man, who was as camp as Butlins (I'd met him at Quintet, a restaurant I'd consulted for briefly in Camden Town).

We wanted to have a small menu, so we only offered up to ten first courses, ten main courses and ten puddings. Sally Clarke was starting around this time,

Carpaccio of Wild Rabbit with Pickled Vegetables

SERVES 4

I've loved rabbit for years, especially in casseroles, but I think that wild rabbit can be used in many different ways, including 'raw' as here. You've all eaten beef carpaccio, and this dish, which is very modern and adventurous, is similar, but uniquely tender and flavourful. If you have a friendly butcher who will bone out the saddle to give you two nice fillets, all the better. If not, change your butcher.

4 rabbit fillets, from 2 saddles of wild rabbit

1 teaspoon truffle oil

25ml (1 fl oz) balsamic vinegar

½ teaspoon Worcestershire sauce

olive oil from the vegetables (see below)

salt and freshly ground black pepper

300g (10½ oz) mixed salad leaves

25g (1 oz) shallots, peeled and chopped

15g (½ oz) fresh chives, chopped

Pickled vegetables

100ml (3½ fl oz) each of white wine and white wine vinegar

12 coriander seeds

1 small sprig fresh thyme

12 x 2.5cm (1 in) pieces of carrot, turned

12 small cauliflower florets

8 asparagus spears, trimmed

8 x 2.5cm (1 in) pieces of courgette, turned

100ml (3½ fl oz) olive oil

For the vegetables, bring the wine and vinegar up to the boil in a large saucepan with the coriander and thyme. Add the carrots and cook for 4 minutes. Add the cauliflower and cook for a further 2 minutes. Add the asparagus and courgettes and cook for a final 2 minutes. Strain the vegetables from the liquor, and leave to cool. Season with salt and pepper, and cover with the olive oil. When ready to serve, drain off the olive oil and use it with the rabbit.

Cut each rabbit fillet into 4 pieces. Lightly tap out between pieces of clingfilm into large round discs. Mix together the truffle oil, balsamic vinegar, Worcestershire sauce and 50ml (2 fl oz) of the olive oil, and season with salt and pepper. Place the rabbit pieces into this marinade and leave for 5 minutes.

Arrange the salad leaves and pickled vegetables on serving plates, and place the drained rabbit pieces on top. Mix the shallots, chives and a further 25ml (1 fl oz) of the olive oil together and drizzle around the rabbit. Season and serve.

and she was offering a set daily menu. I would love to have had the courage to do that, but it wasn't our style, and we felt people would like a choice. So we had an *à la carte* menu at first. The average bill started at around £18, I seem to remember, for two courses, about £23.50 for three courses (for food only). It included a few stalwarts and favourite ingredients with which we were familiar. As I was known as Brian Turner of the Capital Hotel, what I served at Turner's was always going to be very similar in style. I didn't want to radically change and become somebody else, but neither did I want to just repeat the Capital menu. In no way did I want to be accused of any sort of plagiarism, nor did I like the idea that David Levin might feel I was trying to transfer people's allegiances from one restaurant to another. So those stalwarts had to be slightly different. For instance, the rack of lamb was obviously roasted in a very similar way, but we changed the sauce. At the Capital we served it with a *jus*; at Turner's we do a creamy garlic and rosemary sauce, which is superb. We made similar changes to other dishes.

Everything was to have its accompanying sauce, which I still firmly believed from my training days with Eric Scamman contributed greatly to the success of a dish. A good sauce, I believe, demonstrates a skilful kitchen, and we worked very hard at our sauce bases, the stocks. (A couple of years later José, our kitchen porter, joined us from the Capital, and he took over the stock-making until his retirement in January 2000.) My strengths at that time, as I analyse them now, were a) simplicity, b) fine produce and c) fine sauces. Simplicity had always been my watchword and good sauces remained a major part of my style. Good produce depended on good suppliers and at Turner's in the early days, I used the same people I'd had latterly at the Capital. Ivor Robbins brought us our fruit and vegetables, and John Davey from Wilson's in Sloane Street our meat (he had come to my rescue at the Capital, through Kevin Kennedy, when my own meat man went bust unexpectedly). For some reason fish – because more perishable? – was always difficult, and over the years I've used a number of suppliers, including William Black (whom I introduced to the fish market at Rungis in Paris – and he was entranced!).

I wanted every piece of meat or fish not only to have a sauce, but a good flavourful garnish as well, and a little separate dish of vegetables. This latter wasn't a half-moon such as you might find in posh hotel dining rooms, but a

Tartare de St Jacques aux Petits Cornichons
SERVES 4

The essence of this dish is the freshness of the scallops. If you can buy them on the shell on the day of eating, then that is the best. The secret lies in the seasoning, it's so simple and effective, but just be careful.

16 scallops, roe removed

25g (1 oz) shallots, peeled and finely chopped

juice of ½ lemon

2 tablespoons olive oil

salt and freshly ground black pepper

300g (10½ oz) mixed salad leaves

12 baby gherkins, cut into strips

Dressing

3 tablespoons olive oil

1 teaspoon Dijon mustard

1 tablespoon white wine vinegar

Cut the scallops into very fine dice. Add the shallot, lemon juice, olive oil, salt and pepper, and mix.

Make the dressing by mixing the ingredients together. Dress the salad leaves, then arrange them on individual plates. Spoon the scallop tartare on top of the salad leaves, and garnish with the gherkins.

little eared round dish with a mixture of root and green vegetables, all seasonal and plainly cooked, but all tasting of themselves, with no frills. I also decided that I would give canapés before every meal, no matter what price customers paid – tasty little morsels such as tiny Welsh rarebits, mushroom vol-au-vents or warm cheese straws. We hadn't done this at the Capital, but I had seen it in my travels around restaurants in both London and France, and thought it a top-class idea. I also offered petits-fours after the meal, so for the set price of two or three courses, people were getting two extra little courses for nothing, which I thought was great value for money. That set price also included free bottled water, service and VAT. The water and service were mistakes, as it turned out, and I have reversed them now, but I firmly believed then and still do that it would be wonderful to go into a restaurant and be confident that the price you see is the price you pay – a great rarity in the business.

Apart from the rack of lamb, we would be offering grilled rib of beef for two on the bone, offal such as kidneys or sweetbreads, and some good fish. One of the dishes which took off was a tartare of St Jacques, raw scallops, as a starter, which was fairly adventurous for those days, as was a carpaccio of *lapereau*, rabbit (one of our more inventive moments). *Quenelles de brochet*, or pike, featured occasionally (although they are difficult to get just right), and we had a version of the famous *Mousseline de St Jacques*: we made it into a timbale, and served it warm. If the scallop tartare became a sort of signature dish, so too did the *brandade* of sole. I'd seen the Mediterranean *brandade de morue*, or salt cod, and thought it a lovely dish, but using sole would be far less peasant in feel, and have much more finesse. The mixture of sole, garlic, potato and a touch of gelatine, served in a quenelle shape on a bed of seasoned haricots verts, with shallots, olive oil and chopped tomato, makes for an excellent dish, described in one review as 'ethereal'.

The menu would be written in French, with English beneath as a concession. OK, I was an Englishman, but I was French trained, and my food was classic French. I was as insistent about the wines. I worked with Giles Townsend on the list, who later became wine buyer for the Savoy Hotel. It was to be printed on either side of the menu, and the whole folded into three, so that customers only had one piece of paper to negotiate. I decided to offer nothing but French wines. Although I was becoming interested in the subject, I still didn't know very much, but the wines I *did* know were French, and I thought the variety available from France should be enough to satisfy anyone's taste. I also took the view in the long term that I would only deal with wine companies whose managing director I could talk to as a friend: we would set up the deal at first, and then his and my staff could take over the daily necessities once the system had been worked out. Over the years, we've met some wonderful suppliers and had some wonderful tastings at Turner's when looking for new additions to the list.

Once Mark and I had got the menu together, and the wines had been chosen, rather than have one formal restaurant opening, I held three 'testing' parties. I was impatient to try out the food ideas, so I organised the parties before the restaurant was completely finished. One end of the room was wallpapered but the other was probably just lined, there was no carpet, and I still had quite a few dustsheets hanging around. I invited in about twenty people at a time − mainly friends rather than Press − and asked them to choose whatever they wanted from the menu. I chose the wines, and I charged them something like £25 per couple. The fact that they were willing to put up with the unfinished room, slightly disorganised service, pay for it (although at a huge discount), and *still* enjoy themselves, was wonderful to me. My friends are great sports! Those parties helped to iron out a few little problems, I'm glad to say. When we actually opened, on 1 October 1986, we did so very quietly, but nevertheless, probably because of those same loyal friends, we started fairly quickly to do pretty good business.

Ironically, some ten days or so after we opened Turner's, I had to go back and cook a dinner at the Capital. Michel Roux was president of an august body of 'diner-outers', composed of gastronomes, restaurateurs, chefs and wine merchants, called the Benedicts. I had negotiated and organised a dinner for him to be held in October, long before I had handed in my notice. But when he and Leonard Dennis (one of the first Masters of Wine in this country) heard I would no longer be there in October, they threatened to cancel the booking. So I was persuaded back for that one night. Michel Roux had tasted my scallop tartare earlier, when I was experimenting with the idea, and thought it would be suitable for the Benedicts' dinner . He gently suggested a little more salt, a little more lemon juice. So my scallop tartare today is in essence a Turner dish, with a pinch of Roux!

I've learned a lot from the Roux Brothers, especially Michel, over the years. Here I'm at a reception (Shepherd nearby as usual) with Albert.

Mark and I did everything together in the kitchen in those early days. We more or less had to, as the kitchen was so small, and there was only one working stove! Shepherd and I had worked well as a team at the Capital, and we'd also had fun. Mark and I recreated both that proficiency and relaxed atmosphere. For a start we were cooking what we wanted to cook, we'd chosen and written the menu, and we felt that these dishes were the right ones to have on the menu, showing our cooking talents at their best. We found we were favouring warm rather than cold dishes; I think this was purely and simply because we had to employ other people to do any cold dishes, and we didn't feel confident that they could keep up to our standards. It meant much more

*In 1988, the Académie launched the British
Meilleur Ouvrier de Grande Bretagne. Nine
of the senior judges were photographed outside
the Roux Brothers' Le Gavroche. Albert Roux
is in the centre front, and from the left front
round to the right front are Peter Kromberg,
Steven Doherty, Pierre Koffmann, Richard
Shepherd, myself, Bernard Gaume, John Huber
and Michel Bourdin.*

work for us, of course, not least in balancing the menu, and it became very much a case of us cooking virtually all the time. But we made a good team.

We had a system during the day concerning deliveries. The quality of our produce was and still is paramount, so we would check everything that came in, and we did so continuously. When the goods arrived, someone had to check that the quality and quantity were correct, then the invoice was signed. The product then went to the section and it was trimmed as appropriate (usually excess fat off meat, bones chined and cleaned; we wouldn't peel vegetables, say, at this stage). Then it went to the cold room upstairs (we'd built a walk-in fridge on the first-floor roof) before being brought down again for the third check. Meat which was semi-prepared and chilled might now have its last layer of fat removed. The food was then checked while it was being cooked, and as it went on to the plate. Very few caterpillars could get through that protective system, and not much extraneous fat. There are too many checks for accidents to happen.

Quite early on, because this was a part of the business with which I wasn't entirely familiar, I needed to work out how to run a manual tab – the system governing the breakdown of the bills. I went to the Roux brothers' restaurant, the Waterside Inn, and sat with their receptionist/cashier for a day to see how she did it. (Michel Roux and Robyn, his wife, were and are still great friends of mine.) We have a manual tab at Turner's to this day: we record each bill on a ledger, and we split it into table number, name, number of covers, food spend, spend on wine from the bottle and spirits from the bar, the type of card used, and its number. This became a daily record sheet, for lunch and dinner, and although required by law (for VAT), it became extremely useful to us in that we could see at a glance where people were spending. If the manual tab lesson was invaluable, another 'acquisition' was even more so: I met a French pastry cook there, Dominic, who not long after came to us at Turner's and helped us plan the desserts for the menu. He was actually responsible for our very special *Marquise de Chocolat Blanc*, another signature dish. It's basically a white chocolate mousse, made with boiled sugar, whipped cream, egg yolks and white chocolate, and it's absolutely orgasmic. At first we made it into a block, which was nice and easy to carve. We later developed it, though, making it in little moulds with a thin lining of chocolate *genoise*, and then putting the two – the dark sponge and the white mousse – together into a shape with a piped chocolate 'T' on top.

I might have mastered the manual tab, but Sylvia, Mark's wife, found it a little harder. She came to work for us as receptionist/cashier, and at first she worked in the passage beside the front door (supplies came in this way). This proved far too draughty, so her desk was moved into the restaurant, where it remains to this day. There actually wasn't enough accounting work for her to do, so she had to help in the kitchen and room occasionally. But come the end of the night in those early days, she could rarely get the accounts exactly right (a manual tab is *very* complicated), and many was the time Mark, she and I would be up until the early hours trying to find an errant penny or two.

There was the odd review in the Press, but because I wasn't exactly a 'new kid on the block', I think Turner's wasn't seen as 'good copy' or the 'flavour of the month'. Neither did I ever court the attentions of critics, being unused to it: David Levin had been responsible for that at the Capital. A *Telegraph* piece, I remember, relished my opening as an opportunity to assess the true state of cooking in Britain: here was a chef who had been working for other people, but who now had the confidence to go out on his own. A sour note came from

Loyd Grossman, then writing for *Harpers & Queen*. I could put up with justifiable criticism, but as he and a few others had eaten at Turner's, without charge, just two weeks after I'd opened, it irritated me. I still do not court restaurant critics, although I am friendly with many. I find it distasteful that, say, the columnist Victor Lewis-Smith can write what he likes about someone like me – and he's done so, very unpleasantly, on several occasions – yet I do not have any right of reply. A letter to his newspaper, the London *Evening Standard*, would not have any effect, probably wouldn't even get published, and I once offered in vain to debate on radio one of the topics in question: chefs who run restaurants and also appear on television (a pet hate of his).

However, on the whole, I was enjoying myself, which was the object of the exercise. I had my own restaurant, I had creative control, we were working hard, but still had time (not much, admittedly) to relax. My role had gelled in my mind. I saw myself with my simple menu as taking the difficulty out of ordering and eating, as moving away from the pretentiousness of *nouvelle cuisine*. All the culinary experiences in my life so far had coalesced into what I thought was an attractive eating experience. There was an element of what I'd learned in my dad's transport café; it may not have served deluxe food, but you got what you wanted, and were never under pressure. Lessons from further up the scale, in the fine-dining places where I'd worked, had also been absorbed, as had those of the slightly cheaper, value-for-money places. The Metro had shown me that I enjoyed talking to and meeting people, and that people enjoyed talking to me, so I developed the persona of the accessible chef, rather than one to be worshipped. I was always happy to talk formally about food, but was as happy to sit down at the table and have an informal drink and chat with people whose only connection with me was that they were sitting in my restaurant. I wanted Turner's to be a restaurant that would be internationally known, visited by an international community, but I also wanted it to be a much-loved local restaurant. Some thirteen years later, in the year 2000, I think we have succeeded on both counts. We had started with the idea of 'serious' food, taken from the French, but we had added the friendliness and ambience. I always say, even now, that my restaurant is somewhere you could take your shoes off, and that no one would notice or mind if you did.

After a couple of years, during which the menu remained quite stable, we

White Chocolate Marquise

SERVES 6

Elegant, sophisticated, gooey and rich, what more can one say? The recipe is rated by friend and colleague Sara Jayne-Stanes who makes chocolates, has written the definitive book on chocolate, and is the Director of the Academy of Culinary Arts.

Chocolate sponge

2 medium eggs

40g (1½ oz) caster sugar

10g (¼ oz) cocoa powder

25g (1 oz) plain flour

2–3 teaspoons Kirsch liqueur

Mousse

50ml (2 fl oz) water

a pinch of salt

50ml (2 fl oz) liquid glucose

1½ gelatine leaves, soaked in water to soften

350g (12 oz) best white chocolate, broken into small pieces

3 medium egg yolks

300ml (½ pint) double cream, whipped

Coffee sauce

600ml (1 pint) milk

1 vanilla pod or 1 teaspoon vanilla essence

6 medium egg yolks

115g (4 oz) caster sugar

1 tablespoon strong coffee or 2 teaspoons coffee essence

To decorate

icing sugar

6 sprigs fresh mint

Preheat the oven to 180°C/350°F/Gas 4. Grease and line a baking tray of 20cm (8 in) square.

To make the chocolate sponge, place the eggs and sugar in a heatproof bowl over a pan of hot water, and whisk until the mixture has reached the ribbon stage (when the lifted whisk leaves a trail in the mixture) and is pale in colour. Sift the cocoa and flour into the mixture and carefully fold in, taking care to lose as little air as possible. Pour the mixture into the prepared tray and bake in the preheated oven for 10 minutes. Leave to cool, then remove the sponge carefully from the tray.

Meanwhile, to make the mousse, in a double saucepan, bring the measured water, salt and glucose to the boil over a gentle heat. Remove from the heat, add the soaked gelatine and stir until dissolved. Pour over the chocolate in a bowl. Stir to melt the chocolate, then allow to cool. When the chocolate mixture is cold, beat in the egg yolks and then fold in the whipped cream very carefully so as not to dispel any air. Set aside.

Sprinkle the chocolate sponge with the Kirsch and then cut the sponge into thin strips. Use most of these strips to line a semi-circular tube mould carefully and tightly. Then fill to the top with the chocolate mousse, and cover the top with the remaining strips of chocolate sponge. Cover with clingfilm or foil and place in the fridge for 24 hours to set.

To start the coffee sauce, bring the milk to the boil, add the split vanilla pod or vanilla essence, and leave to infuse for 10 minutes off the heat. Whisk the egg

yolks with the sugar until pale and creamy. Pour the strained hot milk on to the mixture, whisking continuously. Place in a clean saucepan over a gentle heat and, stirring all the time, gradually bring up to just below boiling point – do not allow to boil. The consistency should be like a custard sauce. Pass through a fine sieve, then add the coffee or essence to flavour. Cool.

To serve, turn the pudding out of the mould. Using a warm knife, cut two thin slices per portion, and serve with the cold coffee sauce. Sprinkle with icing sugar and add a sprig of mint.

started to experiment a bit. The dishes were French still, but a few little British overtones began to creep in – a touch of black pudding here, or another 'twist' somewhere else, usually in the sauce or garnish. We also at one point roasted a joint every now and again, which we'd never been able to do at the Capital. We had good free-range roast chickens, and some good British roast meat, but kept pink in the more classical French way. Then towards the end of the decade, we introduced a *menu du jour*, which changed daily – a choice of, say, two starters, main courses and puddings – with a set price for two and three courses. We also had a daily, no-choice, set dinner menu. I felt we were ready for that: we still wanted people to choose from the *à la carte* menu, but locals and regulars would like the variety of a daily menu, and it would pull them in. Cooking new dishes was also a good testing-ground for the *à la carte* menu, which we revamped about five times a year. It also kept the boys in the kitchen interested, as they could so easily get bored cooking endless racks of lamb.

We've had quite a bit of criticism over the years concerning the fact that the *à la carte* menu did not change all that much or all that often. But once we got the daily menus going, I didn't worry too much about that. At the same time, however, I do think the stability of the menu, which has always got a little bit of excitement at the edges, has actually worked in its favour. Thirteen years later it's still basically the same, although it has changed in minor ways, but despite that, the restaurant is still going strong. To me that's a strong indication that we must have been doing *something* right!

However, on the financial front, it transpired that things weren't quite so rosy. With hindsight, it was obvious that we were heading for trouble. Martin was stretching his wings, in the way businessmen do, generating money from here to finance something else there. This sort of negotiation was very much the tool of the modern businessman of that era. It reminded me strongly of home when I was a boy: my mum would have five jam-jars in the kitchen, in which she kept money, one for the rent, one for the gas, electricity, coal etc. We didn't struggle badly in our house, but the coinage in the jam-jars jumped around quite a bit to cover one emergency or other. Eventually, though, these things have a habit of catching up with you and can make life very difficult. But for a time we were expanding.

The next venture which Martin and I bought was a restaurant once called

Timbale de Ris de Veau aux Champignons
SERVES 6

This dish dates from the earliest of our menus at Turner's. Sweetbreads are not to everyone's taste, but to those of us who are fans, they are marvellous. I guarantee you will impress everyone with this dish, but one tip – just don't tell them what it is until they have completely cleared their plates...

300g (10½ oz) calves' sweetbreads, blanched and peeled

15g (½ oz) unsalted butter

100g (3½ oz) small button mushrooms, quartered

150g (5½ oz) skinned and boned chicken breast

2 medium egg whites

200ml (7 fl oz) double cream

2 tablespoons chopped fresh parsley

Sauce

25g (1 oz) shallots, peeled and chopped

125g (4½ oz) unsalted butter

55g (2 oz) button mushrooms, sliced

100ml (3½ fl oz) dry sherry

200ml (7 fl oz) double cream

Cut the sweetbreads into 2cm (¾ in) dice and quickly pan-fry in the butter. Add the quartered mushrooms, pan-fry for few a minutes more, then leave the mixture to cool.

Roughly chop the chicken breast then purée in a food processor. Beat in the egg whites slowly (see page 119), and then the cream. Pass through a fine sieve into a bowl. Into this mousse, mix the sweetbreads, quartered mushrooms and parsley. Line 6 timbale moulds with clingfilm. Spoon the mixture into the timbale moulds, and place in the top part of a steamer, or in a colander on top of a saucepan holding simmering water. Cover with a lid and steam for 15–20 minutes.

For the sauce, sauté the shallot in a little of the butter together with the sliced mushrooms. Add the sherry and simmer to reduce by half, then add the cream and reduce further; the sauce should be the consistency of thick double cream. Whisk in the remaining butter in small cubes.

Unmould the timbales and remove the clingfilm. Place each timbale in the centre of a plate, and pour the sauce around.

Mini Yorkshire Puddings with Mediterranean Vegetables on a Bubble and Squeak Cake
SERVES 10

This is a good dish for a party, and we served it at the Headline sales conference to the company's representatives and a few all-important booksellers. I have a baby frying pan in which I make bubble and squeak, but you could make the mixture up into balls, flatten them and then fry three or four at the same time.

2 x Yorkshire Pudding recipe (see page 224)	3 tablespoons balsamic vinegar
Mediterranean vegetable stew	salt and freshly ground black pepper
1 medium onion, peeled	*Bubble and squeak cakes*
2 courgettes, trimmed	675g (1½ lb) floury potatoes, washed
1 aubergine, trimmed	115g (4 oz) white cabbage, shredded
1 red pepper, seeded	115g (4 oz) green cabbage, shredded
1 green pepper, seeded	115g (4 oz) *Clarified Butter* (see page 239)
2 tablespoons olive oil	1 tablespoon groundnut oil
2 garlic cloves, peeled and crushed	1 medium onion, peeled and finely diced
280g (10 oz) tinned plum tomatoes	salt and freshly ground black pepper
55g (2 oz) caster sugar	freshly grated nutmeg

Make the Yorkshire pudding batter as described on page 224. Preheat the oven to 220°C/425°F/Gas 7. Bake the puddings in mini muffin tins, making about 30. Keep warm.

To make the stew, cut all the vegetables into small 5mm (¼ in) dice. Heat the oil gently in a large pan and sweat the vegetables carefully for 5 minutes. Do not allow them to colour. Add the crushed garlic. Meanwhile, drain the tinned tomatoes, keeping the juice. Remove and discard the seeds of each tomato, and chop up the flesh. Add the flesh to the vegetables, along with the tomato juices from the tin, and cook for about 20 minutes. Boil the sugar and balsamic vinegar together until a thick syrup forms. Add this to the stew, season, and put to one side.

Preheat the oven to 180°C/350°F/Gas 4.

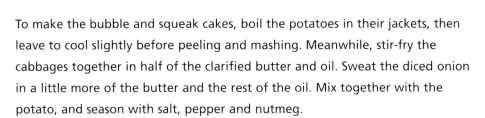

To make the bubble and squeak cakes, boil the potatoes in their jackets, then leave to cool slightly before peeling and mashing. Meanwhile, stir-fry the cabbages together in half of the clarified butter and oil. Sweat the diced onion in a little more of the butter and the rest of the oil. Mix together with the potato, and season with salt, pepper and nutmeg.

Heat a mini frying pan with some of the remaining clarified butter. Add enough potato mixture to the pan to form into a pan-sized cake, about 1cm (½ in) thick. Fry to colour lightly on both sides. Make 9 more cakes in the same way. Put the cakes into the preheated oven until golden brown, about 10 minutes. Keep warm if necessary, but they are best served fresh.

To serve, put a bubble and squeak cake on each plate. Fill 3 mini Yorkshires with vegetable stew, then place on top of the bubble and squeak.

Restaurant Mes Amis, then Willows, just behind Harrods (as one reviewer put it, in 'SW twee'). We rechristened it Sud-Ouest, and we chose to specialise in the cuisine of the south-west of France, including the Basque country. I brought in Nigel Davis as chef, the man who had been at the Greenhouse when I was executive chef at the Capital. He had gone to France to work for Garcia, the chef I'd met on my first Bordeaux trip, at Le Clavel. Garcia was a Spaniard from the Pays Basque, who had chosen to live and work in Bordeaux, and was doing very well for himself. His influence on Nigel was very pertinent to what we planned to do at Sud-Ouest. The restaurant served good, honest, brasserie-type food, hearty servings at reasonable prices – at one point *bavette* (a steak) and chips was under a fiver. It did well, and got some good notices.

Not long afterwards, Martin met the one-time pop-singer and actor, John Leyton ('Johnny, remember me...'), who had the Meridiana Italian restaurant in the Fulham Road. Like so many other amateurs in the business, he was in trouble. One of Leyton's backers was Carlo Colombotti, an Italian society solicitor, and they had organised a BES, a business expansion scheme, at the Meridiana. I didn't know or understand the ins and outs of it, but Martin managed to persuade Colombotti, Leyton and the other people in the partnership, that Venturite, the company that actually owned Turner's, should take over their shares in the BES, and have a major interest in the Meridiana. So now I was the co-owner of Turner's, and part-owner of two other restaurants, Sud-Ouest and the Meridiana. For a while I rather revelled in this. After service at Turner's I'd have dinner in the Meridiana, often with Michael Mills, Richard Shepherd or Kevin Kennedy. The boys there cooked very well, and I enjoyed being a 'prince among men', walking round from a restaurant in which I worked to another in which I would eat – and both of them mine! This was the life, I thought.

Things began to look rather less encouraging on the financial front. At some point I agreed to sign something which meant that the freehold of Turner's no longer belonged to us. The freehold was sold to a landlord, on what is called 'sale and lease-back'. Money had changed hands, and Venturite and Turner's became a leaseholder, paying rent every quarter to the new owner of the freehold. The money raised by that sale helped reduce the loan from the Royal Bank of Scotland – over half a million pounds – so for a while the bank was one of our lesser concerns. I was finding it difficult to pay bills, and I was really worried about VAT and the Inland Revenue.

When Martin met Aziz Suleiman, the driving energy behind Stocks Club in the Kings Road (the old dell'Aretusa and Wedgies), we bought a major interest. Once again we had become the owners of a business that was failing, but one which boasted a property worth millions. I was quite keen for a while, as a nightclub suited me down to the ground. I could look after the restaurants in the evening, then concentrate on the club afterwards – and enjoy myself – into the early hours. I've never needed much sleep, and I think I'm a great party animal!

So here I was in 1990, with a burgeoning empire. I had a fine-dining restaurant with a red M in the *Michelin Guide*, and good ratings in the *Good Food Guide*, the *Egon Ronay* and *Ackermann* guides. We had a brasserie-style restaurant, an Italian restaurant and a nightclub, and all this had come about within four years or so. I didn't know precisely what kind of financial state we were in.

The bank was constantly on to us to supply detailed accounts and at some point we had to get rid of the Meridiana. When Martin suggested making an offer for the Electric Cinema in Portobello Road (he had some wonderful ideas, but we never got them off the ground), I decided I'd had enough. My creative resources were being stretched too far, and I was beginning to feel I couldn't cope. Owning an empire, despite the undoubted pleasures of some aspects of it, was not something about which I felt confident. I'd been on the crest of a wave, happy to go in the direction it took me, but I now realised that it was taking me somewhere I didn't want to go. The prospect of earning a lot of money was tantalising, but I decided I needed to disassociate myself. All I wanted to keep was Turner's; I didn't want anything to do with any of the other businesses. On advice from Michael Mills *inter alia* (there were a lot of lawyers' consultations), I had Turner's valued, in order to negotiate some sort of deal with Martin. Because property prices were now falling after the boom of the mid 1980s, it was valued at around £900,000. Because of the cash we still owed, though, the value was more like £600,000. If I could lay my half of that down, then Turner's could be mine.

Happily, the negotiations weren't too protracted or too difficult, and in the end I got Turner's for the price of half a Mercedes car, even though I had recently had an accident in it, to the tune of £11,000 worth of damage. I gave him the car and my share of its worth, about £13,000, and we parted company in 1991.

Richard Shepherd remained a stalwart friend and supporter throughout those dark days when money was tight and I thought I might lose Turner's. He still is, as this 1999 photograph proves!

It's just as well really, as a recession was fast approaching. Later Martin was to go bankrupt, costing the poor Royal Bank of Scotland a lot of money. However, before letting the partnership be dissolved, the bank – which has been very good to me over recent years – insisted that I raise £100,000 to invest in the company. This would lessen the overdraft, and the remainder the bank would convert to a loan which had to be repaid. I didn't have two pennies to rub together and as I'd already remortgaged my house to buy Turner's in the first place I had to go to friends, colleagues and family, cap in hand, to ask for cash to help me out. Many people were extremely kind, and I will 'owe' them in gratitude forever. They'll get their money back, too, even if they won't make anything from their 'investment'.

Just thinking about that time makes me feel rather ill all over again. For at least a year before that, I hadn't been opening my mail – it was all bills, and I couldn't pay them. At one time, I actually had to try and stop Denise opening letters. She'd seen one by accident and realised that I wasn't paying the mortgage. In fact, on three occasions the building society threatened to come and repossess the house. All in all, it looked as if I could be about to lose, in no particular order, my business, my house and my wife. Now it seemed even worse, but I was determined to pay back all my debts. I had to go to the VAT people and sort things out there. We actually used to have visits from the VAT people almost on a monthly basis: they'd say they wanted some money, I'd say we hadn't got it, and they'd take an inventory of goods to the value of what I owed. The wines were counted regularly, and in fact they did more stock-takes on the contents of my wine cellar than I did! Someone suggested that the best thing might be to go bankrupt, but that was giving up, not something this Yorkshire lad was prepared to do.

It was a horrendous time, probably the darkest weeks and months of my life. Not only was I personally struggling, but outside factors – the growing recession, the Gulf War, snow in May, and the Irish bombing of Downing Street – were having a huge knock-on effect. Locals didn't come in so much any more – eating out is one of the first luxuries to be cut back in a recession – and the Americans and other international customers just weren't coming to London because of war and the IRA. The restaurant was virtually empty on some nights, and I had to cut my staff right down. A restaurant is a business which deals in perishables, so we had to be extraordinarily careful about what we ordered. Richard Shepherd would come across from Langan's and talk to me, listen to me, wipe my tears, and in general try to bolster my confidence. Without his support and the loyalty of family and other friends, I don't know what I would have done. However, help was at hand, and from a most surprising source...

First Flirtations with Television

You'd think that the vision of a man being sick over the side of a naval destroyer would put people off, wouldn't you? Well, it didn't, and one such sequence was to launch a second career for me, on television. In those last few years before Martin and I went our separate ways, and in the couple of years of struggle

Artichoke Hearts Filled with an Avocado and Green Bean Salad
SERVES 4

One of our most successful dishes at the Capital was a stuffed artichoke, so over the years I have taken the idea further. This 'summery' salad is one that will appeal to meat-eaters and vegetarians alike.

4 large artichokes, trimmed

juice of 1 lemon

a sprig of fresh thyme

1 large bay leaf

3 tablespoons olive oil

salt and freshly ground black pepper

175g (6 oz) green beans, trimmed

1 avocado pear, not too ripe

1 teaspoon balsamic vinegar

½ teaspoon crushed garlic

300g (10½ oz) mixed salad leaves

Dressing

a touch of Meaux mustard

1 tablespoon white wine vinegar

3 tablespoons olive oil

2 tablespoons tomato *concassé* (skinned, seeded and diced tomato)

1 tablespoon chopped sun-dried tomatoes in oil

1 tablespoon chopped shallot

1 tablespoon chopped fresh chives

In a saucepan cover the artichokes with water, and add the lemon juice, herbs, 1 tablespoon of the olive oil and some salt and pepper. Cook until tender, about 30 minutes, depending on size. Cool, then remove the leaves and choke, and trim the hearts.

Cook the green beans until nearly tender, then drain well and leave to cool. Cut the beans into baton size, and put into a bowl. Peel and stone the avocado – which must not be too ripe, not too hard, just ready enough to eat, but not too mushy. Chop it into pieces about the same size as the beans. Add the remaining oil, the balsamic vinegar, garlic, salt and pepper and mix well.

For the dressing, mix the mustard, vinegar and oil, then season. Add the tomato *concassé* and sun-dried tomato, shallot and chives. Stir together.

Arrange the salad leaves in the centre of each plate. Pile the bean and avocado mixture into the concave side of each artichoke heart, and place carefully on top of the salad leaves. Sprinkle a little dressing over the top.

thereafter, the 'escape' from my troubles that television offered – and the money, of course! – was invaluable.

I had briefly flirted with the box before, though. Over the years I had kept in touch with Michael Smith, and indeed we became neighbours in Walton Street when I opened Turner's in 1986, his restaurant, Walton's, being just up from mine. I used to see him at Christmas particularly and we'd sing carols around the piano. He had a cookery slot on Pebble Mill in Birmingham called *Posh Nosh*, and I guested a couple of times on that in the late 1980s. I found it a little nerve-wracking, but soon learned to forget about the cameras rolling and the millions of people watching. I was cooking and talking about food, and that's always been easy for me.

And then in 1989, Antony Worrall Thompson hired a rather distinguished public relations consultant, Hilary Laidlaw Thompson, to represent him. The BBC's *Food and Drink* programme had been in existence for a couple of years, there were several other food programmes or food 'slots' popping up here and there on the box, and Antony decided he wanted to get in on the act. Hilary spoke to Peter Bazalgette, the creator and producer of *Food and Drink*, and Antony was duly commissioned to appear on a *Food and Drink* special. He was to go on to a British Navy destroyer, and cook for the troops at the end of the year. He admitted to being a bit nervous – it was his first sortie into television, after all – and asked if he could have someone with him to back him up. I was chosen, so Antony Worrall Thompson was directly instrumental in launching my television career.

We were flown to Gibraltar to join the *SS Birmingham*, in company with the director, Wilfred Emmanuel-Jones, a cameraman, a sound man and a sparks. The *Birmingham* had been in the Gulf – it was just after the end of the Gulf War – and was returning via the Indian Ocean and a furlough in the Seychelles. As she hadn't reached Gibraltar yet, we stayed that first night on the docks, and Antony and I soon realised what we were up against. Wilfred was young, black, handsome, supremely self-confident and rather arrogant, and insisted that he – not one of us 'celebrity chefs' (and this was as early as 1989!) – was in charge (I must add that, over the years, I've come to respect and admire him). There was some altercation as to how we would get up early in the morning to shoot, with no phones, radios or alarm clocks. I thought Wilfred said that he would wake us. He didn't, we were late, and Antony was furious. He and Wilfred

Tower of Scallops and Smoked Haddock in a Smoked Haddock Butter Sauce
SERVES 4

The marriage of scallops with their sweetness and the smokiness of the haddock is pure heaven, which is why I love this dish so much.

8 scallops	*Sauce*
175g (6 oz) smoked haddock	2 shallots, peeled and chopped
1 garlic clove, peeled and crushed	85ml (3 fl oz) white wine
1 tablespoon olive oil	85ml (3 fl oz) champagne
salt and freshly ground black pepper	1 tablespoon white wine vinegar
	300ml (½ pint) *Fish Stock* (see page 242)
	150ml (¼ pint) double cream
	175g (6 oz) unsalted butter, diced
	55g (2 oz) smoked haddock, diced

Clean the scallops, and remove the roe. Make sure there are no bones in the haddock. Cut both scallops and haddock into thin slices.

Have ready 4 metal cooking rings of about 5cm (2 in) in diameter. Mix together the garlic and olive oil. Lay slices of haddock in the base of the cooking rings, season, add a little of the garlic oil, then top with slices of scallop. Repeat the layers, finishing with a layer of scallop. Fill all the cooking rings in this way.

To make the sauce, place the shallots in a pan, add the wine and champagne, and reduce by half. Add the vinegar and stock, and reduce the liquid by half again. Add the cream and reduce by one-third. Slowly beat in the butter cubes, and season to taste. Add the diced haddock, and leave to infuse.

Cut out 4 squares of greaseproof paper or foil, and sit each cooking ring on these in the top part of a steamer or in a colander on top of a saucepan with a little simmering water in the base. Place the lid on the steamer, and steam the scallop and haddock rings for about 6 minutes.

Dry the rings off, then unmould the towers into hot serving bowls. Pour the sauce over and serve immediately – nice with some new chived potatoes and a topping of warm tomato *concassé* and shallots.

sniped at each other all day like two fighting cocks, and that rather set the tone for the whole shoot.

What, however, was to be rather more influential was the power of the sea. Once the *Birmingham* had arrived and we'd got on board with our supplies, she set sail out of the Mediterranean into the Bay of Biscay. A force eight gale hit us, and on the second day, of the 350 or so sailors on board, 120 never stirred from their bunks because of seasickness. I'm afraid I was suffering, too, but as we only had three or four days in which to make two films, I was obliged to work. I was really ill, though, only able to do pieces in single sentences virtually, before I had to rush from the kitchen – down near the engine-room – up three or four flights to the deck. The sound man never left his bunk the entire time we were at sea, Wilfred also looked a little white (if that were possible), but Antony was happy as a sandboy, very galling. He likes to highlight any misfortune, does our Antony, and he would bring the camera down to my bunk, saying to it confidentially and rather gleefully, 'Brian's not very well', and 'Would you like some pie and chips?' It was probably at his instigation that the camera recorded one of my dashes for the side of the ship...

Those days at sea were a nightmare from one point of view, but great fun from another. It was a privilege to be on such a splendid craft, and I thought the captain, Roy Clare – he had trained the Prince of Wales in his Navy days – was a wizard. I'll also never forget the sight that met our eyes in the junior officers' wardroom on the first day. The large central table, covered loosely by a sheet of green baize, would be mounted by one young man at a time. The baize was being pulled from side to side by his friends, and he would sway to and fro to the strains of 'Surfing USA' by the Beach Boys! All good clean fun, but they were on their way back from a war. I also got my own back on Antony. In one of the shipboard pubs as we approached England, Antony leaned back against the double door with a pint in his hand, the door flew open, and Antony fell through it, drenching himself. I think that made for a much funnier TV moment than my ashen seasickness on deck...

However, to give Wilfred his due credit, the two films that he managed to squeeze from such unlikely material were hugely successful when shown in December of that year. It was the start of a new way of life for both Antony and myself, and Antony's television success has gone along in tandem with mine

(I've also worked since with Wilfred). Not long afterwards I had a call from a lady called Paula Trafford. She was a producer on the Granada TV programme, *This Morning*, which starred the husband and wife team, Judy Finnegan and Richard Madeley. Apparently, despite the sickness and white-faced misery of those two *Food and Drink* programmes, she had spotted what she defined as 'amazing talent'! Actually this was all flattery, because she was asking Antony as well, along with the doyenne of cookery writers, Marguerite Patten, to help them celebrate their 999th show, which fell at the end of their season. We were to cook a three-course meal, me the first course, Antony the main course, and Marguerite the cake. Antony and I worked together and he, ever helpful, kept splashing my sauce so that it burned and sent smoke billowing everywhere. Otherwise it went well, and in the car home after a jolly good party, Antony said that he hadn't spilt the sauce on purpose. 'Antony,' said I, 'I know that, you know that, but unfortunately everyone else will think you did, because that's the kind of guy you are.' Whether that had anything to do with it or not, only Marguerite and I were asked back to the 1000th show in the autumn, when *This Morning* was celebrating yet again.

At some point during these first shows, they asked me if I'd like to do an occasional slot which they called *Sunday Best*. The idea was to devise and cook on camera a three-course meal for four which would cost less than £10. I went on a couple of times, and that should have been it, but Richard Madeley, bless his socks, played a major part in making me become very much more regular. At the end of virtually every programme I was on, he would say something like, 'We *do* like your food, what are you going to cook for us next week?' I would never know, of course, because I hadn't been booked to cook, but would blag my way through – 'Whatever it is, it'll taste delicious, and I'll be here!' I could just imagine the fury and dismay of the producers upstairs who had probably already commissioned someone else. So I never really got asked to do a regular slot, I just sort of fell into it!

I enjoyed my stints on *This Morning* despite the hundreds of miles and hours involved in getting up to Liverpool once a week. I could relax to a certain extent about the restaurant, because I knew I had a good team in there, and the television money was proving very useful. We were also just beginning to notice that my being on television seemed to be bringing people into the restaurant,

Terrine of Gravadlax and Asparagus with a Lemon Vinaigrette

SERVES 15

This is a dish for a party, and it's not too difficult if you concentrate. As you have to make it the day before at least it takes away from last-minute pressures. Quite often people seem a little confused about gelatine, but provided that you follow the instructions on the packet, all will be well.

You'll need to buy a 3.6kg (8 lb) salmon which, when the head is cut off, and you've boned and gutted it, will leave you with about 1.8-2kg (4-4½ lb) salmon. Use one side of this for the terrine; the remainder you can poach or bake.

1 side fresh salmon (see above), filleted, skin on, pin-boned

1 bunch fresh dill, chopped

125g (4½ oz) table salt

250g (9 oz) caster sugar

50ml (2 fl oz) brandy

200ml (7 fl oz) *Fish Stock* (see page 242)

juice of 1 lemon

5 gelatine leaves, soaked in a little water to soften

2 bunches asparagus

55g (2 oz) shallots, peeled and finely chopped

300g (10½ oz) mixed salad leaves

Lemon Vinaigrette

finely grated rind of 1 lemon

½ teaspoon made English mustard

2 tablespoons lemon juice

6 tablespoons olive oil

Place the salmon on a large piece of clingfilm on top of a large piece of foil. Mix the dill, salt, sugar and brandy together. Pack on to the salmon, then wrap up in the clingfilm, then the foil. Place on a platter and leave to marinate overnight, in the fridge or a cool larder.

The next day, simmer the stock and lemon juice together to reduce by half. Stir in the drained gelatine. Allow to cool a little and start to become thick. Peel and trim the asparagus, and blanch in boiling water for 4–5 minutes. Drain, and leave to become cold. Brush the seasonings and herbs off the marinated salmon, then cut the fish into long slices.

Line a terrine mould with clingfilm. Use larger slices of salmon to line the terrine, leaving enough to fold over the top. Once lined, chop the rest of the salmon and mix with the shallot.

Place a layer of salmon and shallot in the terrine, followed by a layer of the asparagus, arranged lengthways. Pour in a little of the reduced liquid. Continue filling the terrine with salmon, asparagus and reduced liquid until it is full. Fold the salmon slices over the top, then cover with clingfilm, place a weight on top, and leave to set in the fridge for 4–6 hours.

To make the vinaigrette, simply put the lemon rind, mustard and lemon juice in a bowl and mix well. Add the olive oil, salt and pepper, and stir.

To serve, remove the terrine carefully from the terrine mould and the clingfilm, and cut into thin slices using a sharp, warm, wet knife. Arrange on plates, and garnish with the dressed salad leaves. Scatter a little vinaigrette around the edges of the plate.

which was nothing but good! I used to get driven to Liverpool by Neil, who worked for Granada. He'd come down to London on the Thursday night, pick me up at about 4.30 in the morning of Friday from the restaurant, and once I'd familiarised him with how to get out of London on to the M1 and M6, I'd fall asleep. Once I woke up to find a lorry scraping and screeching along the side of our car, just inches from my head. Neil used to enjoy his London trips, I think. I took him to the casino a couple of times, and card-playing with my mates. He ate well, too!

The researchers used to despair when I'd turn up at the Liverpool studio, dressed in jeans, unshaven, having been up all night. But I have great powers of recuperation, and a quick shower and change of clothes would transform me. When I first started on *This Morning*, I used to have production meetings in the morning after the show, then get the 12.45 train from Lime Street back to London. After a while, though, I thought up a much better solution. There's nothing quite like eating together to bring people together, and as I didn't have to be back at my restaurant until 7.30 in the evening, I organised a lunch each week on Friday for all the people involved in the programme. At Est Est Est next to the studio, we'd have long, drunken and extremely creative meals, with the crew and the producers, occasionally a guest or Richard and Judy themselves. I'd then sleep on the train before starting to cook in the evening.

I've got lots of good memories of many of the people I worked with, particularly Anne Stirk, a brilliant home economist (we're working together still), and the talented Susan Brookes, who worked alongside me on the same regular basis, but as a domestic cook rather than professional chef. For a while, they brought in celebrities to sparkle in the kitchen with myself or Susan. This was a foretaste of *Celebrity Ready Steady Cook*, and very good training, as I had to learn how to continue cooking and talking, while coping with a battery of questions, witticisms and interruptions from whoever was trying to hog the limelight on that particular day. I had to stand on the comedian Frank Carson's foot at one point to shut him up. Leslie Nielsen, the American actor from the *Airplane* and *Naked Gun* films, and Lily Savage were wonderful to work with, but you had to remain so focused, and not allow yourself to be distracted by such fantastic and spontaneous wit. The most challenging comic was Rowan Atkinson who, face characteristically deadpan, told the researcher, in the third person, what Mr Bean was going to do, not what he was going to make Mr Bean do. What Mr Bean in fact did was very appropriate: he showed me how to cook baked beans on toast! My role was to try and keep up with all of them, a sort of unrehearsed stooge, while preparing food that could actually be eaten.

It was quite hard work, but I revelled in it, all the time aware that my face was becoming better known. After Tony Blair appeared on the programme – *before* he became prime minister – even my father acknowledged what I was doing. As he walked through Morley, passers-by would say to my father, 'Hello, Len, all right? Good to see your lad on the other night with the future prime minister.' Morley was a staunchly Labour area then, and I went up considerably in the estimation of people at home thereafter.

That was a very pleasurable part of my life, but it came to an end in 1996, when Richard and Judy and the programme moved to London. Perhaps because I'd become too familiar a face, or perhaps they just didn't like me any more, but I got the chop, and John Torode, then at the Mezzo, took over as resident chef on *This Morning*.

However, now we have to go back a bit. Michael Smith had been presenting a programme on BBC TV's *Daytime Live*, called *Campaign for Great British Food*. Always a champion of British food through his writing and broadcasting, Michael had done more than almost anyone else through the years to promote a pride in our national dishes. I believe Michael is the true starting-point of the renaissance in and current passion for British food. The aim of the *Campaign for Great British Food* was to find the best, most mouth-watering viewers' recipes for some of our traditional British dishes. There were seven in that first series – steak and kidney pie, fruit cake, brown bread, fish pie, apple pie, stew and dumplings and trifle. The viewers' response was overwhelming, and Michael and his team found it very difficult to choose twenty-one finalists, three in each category.

I made a couple of brief appearances on that first series in 1988, and the show was recommissioned, but sadly Michael died, tragically early, not too long before it reached the final stages. I got a phone call from Norma, a friend of Michael's, who worked at the BBC. 'Brian, we are already a good way down the road on this series, and we need a presenter. We think you, another Yorkshire lad, would be ideal for it.' It was to be filmed in Birmingham, at Pebble Mill, and the

Daytime Live presenters were Alan Titchmarsh and Judy Spiers. Norma very kindly arranged for me to have a couple of hours of media training – how to stand in front of a camera, essential basics like that! – as I'd only done a couple of TV studio appearances before (not including that shipboard *Food and Drink* debacle). Remember, I was to have a ten-minute slot in which I had to learn lines, introduce competitors, talk intelligently, cook, describe what I was doing and generally keep it all going. *Quite* different from what I'd done before.

That first programme was terrifying, and it was live, not pre-recorded as most programmes were then. I have this philosophy that if you're nervous (as I usually am, still), you breathe deeply and get lots of oxygen to your brain to help you think clearly. How I got my timing wrong on the introductory sentences I'll never know, but the first shot of me on that particular *Daytime Live* was of an obviously terminally nervous man taking in a great deep breath! I was cooking something meaty – can't remember what now – and asked Judy Spiers to taste it. 'I can't, I'm a vegetarian,' was the disconcerting answer, which knocked my socks off.

The series was transmitted over a period of about seven to eight weeks, then we had the grand final. The dishes concerned were shepherd's pie, Lancashire hotpot, home-made pickles and chutneys, bread and butter pudding, scones (I remember learning how to make these at school, with Elsie Bibby, as had Michael Smith!), and chocolate cake. By the time I reached that final stage, I had gained some confidence, enough to enable me to keep talking when all around were trying to interrupt. No less an expert than Derek Cooper told me at around this time that he thought what I was doing was nightmarish, in that it was very potentially accident-prone because live; everything he did (and that was for *radio*) was pre-recorded. However, on that last day, there was a bit of a blip. Normally a floor manager will count you out at the end with his fingers, so you know you've got five minutes, then four minutes and so on. At the end of the final, there were grins all round, and Alan and I had said our goodbyes. We'd been counted out, then, horror, there had been a mistake and the floor manager held up two fingers. Now two minutes in televisual terms is a very long time indeed, especially when you've nothing to say! Alan was brilliant though, he's a great professional, and immediately said something like, 'It's been right good, lad, having you on the show, we've really enjoyed it.' I agreed, and muttered a few compliments in return, then he went on, 'We've just seen examples of really Great British food. Now tell us what kind of British dishes you have on the menu of your restaurant, Turner's in Walton Street.' Oh dear...but I couldn't lie, and had to admit that, 'Well, um, actually Alan, it's French cuisine in my restaurant.'!

During those first years of the 1990s, I was appearing quite regularly on television, and I also started demonstrating at the BBC *Good Food* Show in 1990, in Birmingham, something I've done every year since. I must admit that I was rather preoccupied with firstly what was happening between Martin and me, and then with financial worries. But when the recession started to ease, and terrorist threats diminished, people began to return to the restaurant, and things got better. In 1992 our finances were so improved that I actually refurbished the restaurant, employing a Walton Street habitué, Robin Anderson. The walls became bright yellow with some wonderful light-reflecting mirrors; the chairs and banquettes were reupholstered in mellow blues and golds. The team at the restaurant had changed, but were still superb: I could rely on them absolutely when I left to go to various television studios around the country, and I had it written into most of my contracts that I had to be back at my restaurant every evening whenever humanly possible. Mark Clayton had left (he and his wife went to Australia), and Peter Brennan took over as head chef from 1990. (He was followed by Alan Thompson from 1993, Jonathan Bibbings from 1994, and Charles Curran from 1996. Jon Jon Lucas has been with me since 1989, having spent about three years away, but coming back to me in 1998 when he took over as head chef.)

I was on a couple of *Food and Drink* Christmas Quizzes, cooking against Michael Barry. On one, I seem to remember, I cooked the unlikely combination of sun-dried and fresh tomato sandwich, 'pang pang' chicken dip and 'spomlette'! In one Special, directed by Wilfred, my father appeared with me, which was fantastic. We took part in a challenge set for Leeds City Council's catering division, Crown Point Foods, to see if the organisation which cooked 65,000 meals a day could prepare something that I might cook in my own kitchen. I did a stuffed chicken dish. We had to measure everything out very carefully, as if cooking for a few, and then multiply it up for the thousands necessary. Trying to weigh a minuscule amount of salt, my father's hand shook so much that he kept getting the weight wrong. After several unsuccessful attempts, he eventually got it right, and I was so chuffed that I kissed him! The editor kept it in, and that turned out to be my first screen kiss... And in 1995 I made two films with Antony Worrall Thompson and Sally Clarke, when we went to cook for the British Army on Salisbury Plain, surrounded by NATO troops from Europe. It was serious war games, our lads against the invaders from across the Channel, and in the pitch-black night, Sally clinging to my coat, we lost our protective sergeant. A moment later we were held up at gunpoint by the enemy, at which I declared bravely, 'Don't shoot, we're with *Food and Drink*'!

Ready Steady Cook *and After*

But 1994 also marked the beginning of a new phenomenon on British television, what has been described as the 'leisure-based game show'. The multi-talented Peter Bazalgette had come up with the concept, and the first 'child' of his imagination was *Ready Steady Cook* (the title thought up by executive producer, Linda Clifford). The idea was that two teams, each composed of a chef and a viewer, would compete to make a couple of dishes each in twenty minutes using a £5 bag of shopping selected by the contestant (although actually bought by the production staff). The chefs would not know what was in the bag of shopping, and the only concession was that they were allowed two to three minutes before the show continued, off air, to enable them to think about what they should cook and to assemble their equipment. (I often think they tried to take as much of that thinking time away as possible, always aware of the studio costs...) The chefs also had access to a number of larder, fridge and fresh stock items, such as herbs, milk, cream, butter, oil etc. Three pilots were made by the production company to find the right presenter, and eventually the delectable Fern Britton was chosen. Peter wanted someone who was 'mumsy', approachable, friendly, and who would ask the right sorts of questions throughout the countdown. By repute, Fern was famously unable to cook, so her rather basic questions might reflect those of a majority of viewers.

I appeared on the pilot of *Ready Steady Cook* that was shown in October 1994. The concept immediately took off, quickly becoming the most popular show

Ready Steady Cook *began in October 1994, and I was in the pilot show with Fern Britton.*
Here we are working at the BBC Good Food *Show, both of us looking very characteristic, I think*
– she full of fun and joie de vivre, *me rather confrontational…*

on daytime television. It was screened on three afternoons a week at first, but was extended in early 1995 to five days. It regularly pulls in up to four million viewers now, not much in comparison with the fifteen million, say, for *EastEnders*, but that is *every* afternoon throughout the week. I must admit that I didn't recognise its potential at first. Linda Clifford insisted I include here the remark I made after the first programme: 'This won't last long, there's only very little cooking you can do in twenty minutes.' I also cooked on the very first *Celebrity Ready Steady Cook* in 1997, when my fellow chef was Antony, and the celebrities were June Whitfield (with me) and Rory Bremner. A year later, ratings showing the top twenty daytime programmes revealed *Ready Steady Cook* at number two, and *This Morning* (I was still appearing) at number eleven. I didn't seem to be doing badly for myself! Antony Worrall Thompson and I wrote the first *Ready*

Chicken Breast Stuffed with Chestnuts
SERVES 4

I've been cooking dishes like this in foil for quite a while now, and find that stuffed chicken works the best. All kinds of filling are possible – butter, herbs and garlic, mushroom duxelles (see page 238) and ham, sweetbreads and parsley.

5 boneless chicken breasts

4 tablespoons double cream

225g (8 oz) shelled cooked chestnuts, broken up into large pieces

2 tablespoons chopped fresh parsley

salt and freshly ground black pepper

25g (1 oz) unsalted butter, plus extra for greasing

350g (12 oz) button Brussels sprouts, trimmed and finely shredded

1 garlic clove, peeled and chopped

Parsley sauce

600ml (1 pint) *White Chicken Stock* (see page 243)

300ml (½ pint) double cream

115g (4 oz) unsalted butter, chilled and chopped

salt and freshly ground black pepper

juice of ¼ lemon

3 tablespoons chopped fresh parsley

Chop 1 of the chicken breasts roughly, having removed the skin. Put in the food processor and blitz until smooth. Add the double cream and then put into a bowl. Mix in the chestnuts with the parsley, salt and pepper.

Open up the remaining 4 breasts, skin side down. Stuff the breasts with the chestnut mixture. Place each on a piece of buttered seasoned foil. Roll up tightly like a Christmas cracker in the foil, and leave to rest for about 30 minutes.

Preheat the oven to 200°C/400°F/Gas 6. Cook the foil packages in the hot oven, turning regularly, for about 12 minutes. Leave to rest for 5 minutes.

Meanwhile, make the sauce. Reduce the stock by half. Add the cream and again reduce by half. Remove from the heat, and beat in the chopped butter. Add seasoning and reheat very gently. Add the lemon juice and parsley just before serving.

To cook the sprouts, melt the butter and add the chopped garlic and sprouts. Stir-fry for 4 minutes, and season well. Put the sprouts in the middle of 4 plates. Slice the chicken breasts in half and arrange on top. Serve with the sauce poured around.

Steady Cook book together; it was published in 1996 (the year I reached the grand old age of fifty), and it stayed at the top of the best-selling paperback non-fiction list for quite a few months.

The reasons for the popularity of the show (and others like it) have been debated endlessly. Baz's own theory was quoted in a *Telegraph* article: 'Research shows that some people, who tend to be the A, B and Cls, feel guilty about having the telly on during the day when they should be doing something else. If you put together a programme package that has some benefit for them, they are more likely to watch.' The article also recorded his delight at the results of a *Big Breakfast* poll: that *Ready Steady Cook* was the number one programme among students.

I heartily agree with the idea that something like *Ready Steady Cook* benefits and 'teaches'. I and my chef colleagues on the programme are not trying to show people how to cook a gourmet, three-star meal: we're showing how to make something edible with what's available, and if that process also turns out to be entertaining, then I think that's absolutely fine. It's much the same with the chefs' cookery books appearing virtually weekly in this country now. Most of the recipes may be beyond the skills of the average domestic cook, but if they just give one or two ideas which are delicious, helpful or inspiring, then I think the book is of value to the purchaser.

Ready Steady Cook has been accused of being in the vanguard of a 'dumbing-down' of television, let alone of food and cooking. It is an extremely derogatory term, and I think it unjustified. But at the same time, in a sense it is just a stage further on from what I was trying to achieve when I opened Turner's. I wanted to get away from the breathless reverence attached at one time to food and fine-dining restaurants, and put some enjoyment and relaxation back into the eating-out experience. *Ready Steady Cook* is doing much the same, putting fun into eating and cooking, albeit at a slightly lower level. It all now seems to have come full circle. I was a judge at the 1999 Chef of the Year competition, and if you cast your mind back to the 'rules' of *Ready Steady Cook*, here's how the competition was arranged in that year, for the first time in front of an audience. Ten finalists were competing against each other, and were given a predetermined selection of food items, plus access to larder and stock items. They were given an hour to study (only five minutes on television), then three and a half hours

Gratin de Jabron
SERVES 6

At Turner's we cook these potatoes in a rectangular tray and then press them overnight with a weight. The next day we cut them with a round cutter into 4cm (1½ in) circles and reheat them individually. They look nicer than spoonfuls, but taste just the same.

> 900g (2 lb) King Edward or Maris Piper potatoes, scrubbed
>
> 115g (4 oz) unsalted butter
>
> 4 garlic cloves, peeled and crushed
>
> salt and freshly ground black pepper
>
> 300ml (½ pint) double cream
>
> 150ml (¼ pint) milk
>
> 115g (4 oz) Gruyère cheese, grated
>
> 55g (2 oz) Parmesan, grated

Gently boil the potatoes in their jackets until almost cooked – i.e. insert a knife and if it slips in fairly easily, but with some resistance, the potatoes are ready. Drain and cool, then skin and cut into 5mm (¼ in) slices.

Preheat the oven to 190°C/375°F/Gas 5.

Melt the butter in a frying pan and add the crushed garlic. Gently toss the sliced potatoes in this, just to coat with the butter, not to colour. Season with salt and pepper, and put in layers in a suitable ovenproof dish (or individual dishes).

Boil the cream and milk together, pour over the potatoes, and cook in the preheated oven for 20 minutes. Sprinkle the cheeses on top of the potatoes, increase the oven temperature to 200°C/400°F/Gas 6 and cook for a further 25 minutes. Serve straight from the oven and the dish.

(as opposed to twenty minutes) to cook and prepare a set meal for four. This was deemed the best way of revealing their skill and expertise at cooking... I think this alleged 'dumbing-down' of food is actually contributing to how classical technique is being taught. And producing edible food on *Ready Steady Cook* within twenty minutes cannot be criticised: it's a minor miracle of timing, delegation, skills and expertise, with a large pinch of humour thrown in for good measure!

The same applies to criticisms aimed at myself, and other restaurant chefs such as Antony Worrall Thompson, Paul Rankin and Nick Nairn. How could I, critics ask, being classically trained, allow my skills and experience to be so debased, especially when I *lose* on *Ready Steady Cook*? Isn't that letting myself and my restaurant down? To be honest, I don't think my skills are being debased, I think they're being utilised in a very constructive and entertaining way. If I still cook the sort of food my customers want in the restaurant, then I'm satisfying a much larger audience, I'm bridging a huge gap. At the end of the day, after all, food is only fuel for the body, it's maintenance, whether it's pie and chips or a *mousseline* of scallops. And, I must be honest, I've relished the commercial benefits that my television career, not just *Ready Steady Cook*, has brought. I *am* a classically trained chef, and I like being associated in people's minds with the Krombergs, Mosimanns, Bourdins and Gaumes of this world. But if you ask people in the street who Bourdin or Gaume are, a lot won't know, but they know *me*. Perhaps I once hankered after a Michelin star, such as I'd held at the Capital, but to achieve that would involve a single-minded and perhaps even blinkered dedication that I don't feel comfortable with now. It may sound naïve, but I have a fame which I can't deny I enjoy, I still love cooking, eating and drinking, I earn nice fees from my TV appearances, and I have happy customers and a full restaurant virtually every night. 'Dumbing-down' has not hurt me in any way, and in fact has lifted my profile rather than the reverse.

And *Ready Steady Cook* has contributed positively to my life. I've made some great mates and I've had some of the greatest laughs! One of the most memorable programmes involved rather a lot of double cream. With Antony Worrall Thompson as my rival, I had made a fruit crumble which included a chopped Milky Way chocolate bar from the shopping bag. I wanted to put some whipped cream on at the end, so got my helper to put one of two nozzles into a piping bag. I whipped the cream, spooned it into the bag, and as the final seconds ticked away, I squeezed the bag to pipe the cream on to the hot crumble. But in vain – not realising that my lady had put *both* nozzles in the bag, thus effectively stopping up the hole. Nothing came out, and I squeezed harder, encouraging an intense pressure to build up. The bag burst and cream shot out. It splattered on to my face, all over my moustache, then bounced off and hit Fern in the eye. She started laughing, I started laughing, and then she began to cry, cream and mascara running down her face. She turned to me and stage-whispered, 'Keep going, nobody's noticed!' At that I couldn't contain myself, and the whole place fell apart in uproar. Why the producer didn't call 'Cut' I don't know, but they were apparently all in hysterics upstairs as well. Because the cameras were still rolling, we had to do the judging of the dishes with cream still all over our faces. I won, and Antony claimed it was a sympathy vote, that I'd done it on purpose (no way, not possible). We were still laughing after cleaning up and coming on to do the next show in front of a fresh audience (we filmed three, back to back). In fact it took us a full half hour before we were ready to start again! That episode stuck in people's minds – the classic banana-skin mentality – and I believe it's been seen twice already on *It'll Be All Right on the Night*.

But there are more serious sides to my life in television. I did a piece in Nottingham once about the homeless – trying to help them help themselves – which I found emotionally disturbing. I had had to fend for myself from the age of seventeen, and had managed against all the odds, but here I met a group who, for various reasons, were *not* coping, and it moved me. At the beginning of 1996, for *Food and Drink*, we introduced a group of Kent schoolchildren to ingredients they might not have seen or tried before, and taught them how to cook them. Teaching children to cook and to be confident in the kitchen is something that is very close to my heart. A month later, we took the same children to Paris to look at a market and to eat some French food *in situ*. Astonishingly, most of them loved frogs' legs, but they were full of trepidation about snails, and yes, I'm afraid humour does always seem to creep into all my stories... At lunch in a huge brasserie in the centre of the city, I was demonstrating how to remove the flesh from the shells with pincers, and I decided one particular small boy, who was rather chubby, would be my guinea pig. Much against his will, he took a snail in his mouth, but it immediately shot out as he gagged, and the snail hit the camera lens squarely in the middle!

In November 1996, I went to Louisiana for the BBC's Food and Drink – *and shot an alligator. I'm looking quite relaxed, only because I know it's dead, and I've had quite a few whiskies…*

And some of the programmes are not laughable at the time, although they might perhaps raise a laugh later. I for one most certainly don't think it funny when my life is under threat! In the autumn of that same year, again for *Food and Drink*, I went to the deep south of America to find out about Tabasco sauce. That was fascinating, but some local hunters asked me if I'd like to shoot alligator. The hunting season (more like the culling season, in fact) only lasts for one month of the year, and they obviously thought it a great honour for me to be included. However, I'm neither 'hunter' nor 'shooter', and I have a healthy respect for (no, a healthy *fear of*) alligators. After an afternoon negotiating a flat-bottomed boat around the bayous, camera and sound in the boat behind, we did eventually find an alligator of the right size, not too small, although it looked frighteningly large to me. It seemed to be sleeping on the bank, and they tried to encourage me to touch it. Well, after much mockery of my cowardice, I gingerly touched its tail, one foot still in the boat, and the animal reared round,

Pea and Mint Soup
SERVES 4

Only occasionally do professional chefs prefer frozen products to fresh, but when making pea soup, frozen peas are a must. Everyone likes to have soup as a choice in the restaurant every now and again; this is perfect for that very reason. The soup reminds me of the day when I picked peas on Bird's Eye fields near Lowestoft for TV. They assured me that the time between harvesting the first pea and freezing the last was less than ninety minutes. That's some feat, I tell you.

900g (2 lb) frozen peas, thawed

1 large onion, peeled

1 garlic clove, peeled

85g (3 oz) unsalted butter

55g (2 oz) plain flour

4 tablespoons finely chopped fresh mint, plus 4 sprigs for garnish

1.2 litres (2 pints) *White Chicken* or *Vegetable Stock* (see page 243)

150ml (¼ pint) double cream

salt and freshly ground black pepper

2 slices white bread, crusts off, cut into small cubes

Blanch the peas in boiling water for 2 minutes. Strain. Chop the onion and garlic, and sauté gently in 55g (2 oz) of the butter for 5 minutes until soft but not brown. Add the peas, and stir in the flour, the chopped mint and the stock. Bring slowly to the boil, then reduce the heat and simmer for 10 minutes. Ladle off any excess scum.

Turn the soup into a food processor and blend until smooth. Return to the pan and heat very gently. Stir the cream in well, and season with salt and pepper.

Meanwhile, for the croûtons, fry the bread cubes in the remaining butter until golden on both sides. Drain well and keep hot.

Serve the soup hot in individual bowls, garnished with croûtons and a sprig of mint.

In September 1996, the Carlton Food Network, a new cable channel devoted entirely to food, was launched. TV presenter, Anthea Turner, tasted some of the dishes prepared by Aldo Zilli, myself and Antony Worrall Thompson.

ferocious snout agape, not having been asleep at all. Heart thudding, I held the rope now attached to the alligator while they tried to disentangle the rope from a tree. I noticed that one of the hunters was missing an index finger and inquired why: 'Was holdin' a 'gator on a rope, just like you, when it started goin' and pulled ma finger off...' Anyway, once the alligator was back in the water, I was able to shoot it, and then we had to haul it into the boat. Unconvinced that it was dead, I nervously and determinedly kept a beady eye on the body all the way back to shore. At this little hut on the bayou, they were going to show me how to cook an alligator stew which, not surprisingly, was very similar to any other stew, with onion, garlic, loads of tomatoes and at least four hours' slow cooking. 'What do we do for four hours?' I asked. 'Drink whiskey,' came the reply. That was fine by me, so one of the hunters and I retired to the verandah where we sat on rocking-chairs and drank. When I was woken up a few hours later to be filmed eating the stew, I learned that my companion didn't in fact drink, so I had consumed an entire bottle of corn liquor on my own. Nice sleep, nice stew!

That year television cookery went into overdrive. Well established already were *Food and Drink* and the two versions of *Ready Steady Cook*. *Can't Cook, Won't Cook* had been around for a while, while *Who'll Do the Pudding?* had just started, as had *Quisine*, ITV's new cookery quiz. The Carlton Food Network launched in August – I did a brief series, *Chef on a Shoestring*, for them at the end of the year – and Granada's Food and Wine Channel on Sky a month later.

Perhaps to acknowledge my elder statesman role in the television cookery field, Anglia asked me to do a one-man series for them, *Out to Lunch with Brian Turner*. What Paul Freeman, the producer, wanted me to do was travel

Out to Lunch with Brian Turner, *for Anglia Television, was my first solo series. Here I'm cooking away on my table-top burner, for once in good weather!*

around the Anglia region, talk to local food people, farmers, suppliers and cooks, and go to places associated with foods, food production or good eating. I'd never thought of doing my own series, having always worked with other people, but it was a challenge, and great fun, not least because I insisted on working with Anne Stirk again, the amazing researcher and home economist from *This Morning*. We ultimately did four series in all, the last in 1999, and I saw some wonderful places, ate some delicious food, and met so many astoundingly dedicated people. I particularly remember Cedric Sutherland who took us unerringly, at Brancaster Staithes, to the spot where grey mullet shoaled. I could have talked to him for a week, his knowledge of the sea and the area was so wide and fascinating. The camera crew stranded on a sandbank raised a few laughs that day, as did my later trying to cook those squeaky fresh mullet on shore. Throughout the whole series, all the equipment I had when cooking outside was a trestle table and a portable, single-ring gas burner (yes, you have to suffer for your art). That day the burners kept blowing out as a thunderstorm approached, and the sky got darker and darker. We managed, however, to finish just before the rain started to fall, and I was dying for a cup of tea. Cedric returned about five minutes later with daughter and teapot, having slipped home in response to my need.

Nor will I ever forget mussel collecting with John Green at his mussel farm. I had such trouble getting into the chest-high waders with braces – they were virtually strangling me – that Steve Abson, the sound man, had to come in on camera to help me. Then I had to stand in the middle of the creek where the mussels were, and use a whim – a forked net on the end of a six- to eight-foot-long pole – to gather them. How John Green manages to do it for four hours or so at a time, I'll never know. And I couldn't possibly gather watercress professionally like the Samson brothers from near Hitchin. My back was aching after bending down to cut the cress for just thirty minutes. They have done it for forty years, and can pick for eight hours at a time! They are the third generation on the farm, and told me how their grandfather used to take the watercress up to London by horse and cart. I also visited Richard Davies and his wife in their shop, and saw them catch, steam and dress the famous Cromer crabs. Later I cooked in their backyard, in glorious sunshine, but somehow put too much cayenne pepper in the crab. Richard and I gamely tasted it on camera,

For the BBC Out and About *programme in 1997, I went back to Yorkshire to play with the Brighouse and Rastrick brass band during the Whit Friday march contests. The band is based between Morley and Elland, so were my childhood heroes. They let me play 'Royal Trophy' on the street march, but not in the contest proper (I was a bit – twenty-five years – out of practice!).*

declaring heroically, while choking back tears, that it was wonderful! I loved making *Out to Lunch*, and hope to be working soon again with Paul Freeman and Anne Stirk. Another series would be a nice idea too...

If television has allowed me to travel all around England, finding out about food, it has also taken me as far afield as Hong Kong. Bruce Burgess, an independent producer, and I went out there in 1998 for Carlton Food Network to make a thirteen-part series called *Turner's Tour of Hong Kong*. Cable television always has less cash to spend, and we economised as much as possible, cutting back on expenses including, I'm sorry to say, pre-planning and research. We made those thirteen programmes on a wing and a prayer, organising venues the night or day before, and cooking in temperatures of up to 38 degrees on the roof of the Mandarin Oriental Hotel (organised by my friend Peter Lowe, who is now the general manager). It was so hot that I had to go and change my shirt about every fifteen minutes. We filmed all the 'links' – 'And today, we were going to

Red Mullet in a Rich Saffron Mussel Stew
SERVES 4

The delicately textured flesh of mullet is so good to eat, and has a wonderful flavour as well. Add this to mussels with a bit of saffron, and you have a dish that I think even Rick Stein would appreciate!

60 large mussels

1 medium onion, peeled and diced

175ml (6 fl oz) dry white wine

150ml (¼ pint) *Fish Stock* (see page 242)

2 potatoes, peeled and cut into 1cm (½ in) dice

4 baby leeks, white parts cut into diamond or lozenge shapes

50ml (2 fl oz) double cream

a pinch of saffron strands, infused in 1 tablespoon white wine

2 tablespoons olive oil

4 large red mullet fillets

salt and freshly ground black pepper

4 sprigs fresh chervil

Put the mussels, diced onion, white wine and fish stock into a large pot, cover with the lid, and cook to steam open all the mussels, about 8 minutes. Remove the mussels and put aside. Strain off the stock, then return to the pan. Add the diced potato, and simmer gently for 10 minutes. Add the leek shapes and simmer until tender, about 10 minutes. When just cooked, remove the vegetables using a slotted spoon, and place in a large bowl.

Meanwhile, shell the mussels. Put about 40 into the bowl with the vegetables, and keep them warm and moist. Add the rest of the mussels to the stock with the cream, and simmer to reduce the liquor by about one-third. Put the liquor and mussels into the food processor, blitz to a purée, and then return to the pan. Add the vegetables and whole mussels and reheat gently. Warm the saffron and wine, then put into the stew and leave to colour up.

Heat half the oil in a frying pan and fry the red mullet skin side down for 3 minutes. Turn and cook for a further 2 minutes. Do not overcook. Season with salt and pepper, and check the seasoning of the stew.

To serve, put the vegetables and mussels in the middle of soup bowls, and pour the liquor over and around. Carefully lay a fillet of red mullet on top. Drizzle with the remaining olive oil, garnish with chervil and serve.

I'll never forget my evening at the East Ocean Seafood Restaurant in August 1998, during Turner's Tour of Hong Kong *for Carlton – the food, the drink, the singing. Here I'm photographed with, from the left, Chow Yung Kwai, Tommy Tam, Cheung Chi Choi, Paul Chung and Stephen Yeung.*

show you...' – on a tram in one fell swoop, writing the words as we went along, and with me again changing shirts all the time to represent a different day and programme. It was a prime example of budget programme-making.

One evening, we had planned to visit three restaurants to see which would be most suitable to film, but we didn't get beyond the first. The East Ocean Seafood Restaurant had prepared a fifteen-course banquet for us, the prospect of which was very persuasive. But when I asked for a drink – something cold and white for preference – and got a glass of red wine, my mind was made up: we had to stay, and we promptly cancelled the other two restaurants. The wine was wonderful, obviously a Margaux, and in fact I seem to remember it was a Lascombes 1973! It was a spectacular evening, twelve of us in a private room. The owner, Paul Chung, had imported some local luminaries, including a Chinese actor who sang in musicals. Despite the presence of such talent, I apparently took over and sang the whole of 'Nessun Dorma' – curious since I know I cannot sing, and I didn't think I knew the words.

Samphire and Asparagus Salad
SERVES 4

I first encountered this sea vegetable – not strictly speaking a seaweed, but nearly – when I was making the *Out to Lunch* series with Anglia Television. Samphire grows in bright green tufts in marshy shallows and salty mudflats all along the shorelines of Norfolk and elsewhere on that east coast – but, increasingly, you will also find it in your local fishmongers. It makes a delicious salad, or can be served as a starter, much as you would asparagus – just boiled until tender, then dipped in melted butter and eaten in the fingers. It also makes a delicious vegetable accompaniment to fish, whether by itself or in a salad as here. Never salt the cooking water, as samphire has lots of natural salt.

225g (8 oz) samphire

16 asparagus spears, trimmed and peeled

salt and freshly ground black pepper

125ml (4 fl oz) olive oil

25ml (1 fl oz) white wine vinegar

2 level teaspoons French mustard

4 tomatoes, skinned, seeded and diced

1 bunch fresh chives, finely chopped

2 tablespoons chopped fresh chervil (or flat-leaf parsley)

Wash the samphire in plenty of cold water, then drain well. Bring a large pan of water to the boil. Add the samphire and boil until tender, a few minutes only. Drain well and refresh in cold water to retain some colour. Drain and cool.

Bring a fresh pot of water to the boil and add some salt. Add the trimmed asparagus, and boil for 2–3 minutes. Drain and cool.

Make the dressing by whisking together the olive oil, vinegar and mustard. Season with salt and pepper. Add the tomatoes and herbs to the dressing.

Place the cold asparagus and samphire in a bowl. Pour the dressing over and toss well. Serve with seafood and chunks of French bread.

Yorkshire Pudding with Foie Gras and Onion Gravy

SERVES 6

Grandma Riley used to make her Yorkshires with malt vinegar, so that's what I do too. For a slightly different taste, add 2 tablespoons chopped fresh herbs (tarragon, parsley, chives) to the batter along with 1 teaspoon white wine vinegar instead of the malt.

18 x 25g (1 oz) pieces foie gras

55g (2 oz) duck or goose fat

2 tablespoons chopped fresh chives

Yorkshire pudding batter (use a 250ml/9 fl oz cup)

2 cups plain flour

2 cups eggs

2 cups milk/water, half and half

2 pinches salt

2 teaspoons malt vinegar

Onion gravy

225g (8 oz) onions, peeled and thinly sliced

25g (1 oz) duck or goose fat

85ml (3 fl oz) Madeira

85ml (3 fl oz) ruby port

600ml (1 pint) *Veal Stock* (see page 240)

salt and freshly ground black pepper

Make the Yorkshire pudding batter by mixing all the ingredients together. Beat until the mixture is smooth, with the consistency of double cream.

Make the gravy by slowly frying the onion in the duck or goose fat until golden brown. Drain off the fat from the onion – keep it and add to the fat for the puds – then add the Madeira and port to the pan. Simmer to reduce by two-thirds, then add the stock. Simmer to reduce again if necessary, then check the seasoning.

Preheat the oven to 220°C/425°F/Gas 7, and put a little duck or goose fat into the bottom of 18 individual bun tins. Place in the oven until the fat smokes. Remove the tins from the oven and pour batter mixture in up to the top of each bun tin. Replace in the oven, and cook for about 20 minutes. *Do not open* the oven door during this time, or the puddings will collapse. Open the oven door, and carefully put a piece of foie gras into the 'hole' in each pudding. Return to the oven for 3–5 minutes to allow the foie gras to heat up. Do not overcook. Allow 3 puddings per serving, pouring a little hot sauce around them.

The most recent new television venture for me was a BBC programme called *Anything You Can Cook*. The concept was very simple. A contestant would come into the studio and tell us what their favourite dish was, one they cooked and ate often, list the ingredients and then cook it on camera. I, not knowing what the chosen dish was, had to use the same ingredients, with some help from the store-cupboard, to make another dish on the spur of the moment. Thereafter, volunteers from the audience, who had been secreted elsewhere, had to taste both dishes to see which was best in terms of smell, taste, presentation, etc. There were two disasters in the filming of twenty-seven shows. One show featured a lady who got so nervous on camera that she refused to identify her dish – and this was the whole point of the programme! 'Guest, what is this dish you think you can cook? Anything you can cook, I can cook.' 'I'm not going to tell you.' This happened about four times, with me sweating and wondering what to do – had I missed a trick? – before the director called 'Cut!' And 'cut' was the operative word in another show, when I nearly chopped one of my fingers off. I tried to staunch the blood flow off camera, while Merrilees, my assistant, took over, but the finger just would not stop bleeding. The filming actually had to be stopped while I recovered myself – I get faint when I see blood, always have – and was bandaged and cleaned up. As studio time is horrendously expensive, that particular 'cut' was very unwelcome. The first-aid chap swore it was all due to the garlic I used in my cooking, which prevented my blood from clotting. Well, it certainly wasn't the alcohol...

Out of twenty-seven programmes, I lost seven, which wasn't bad, although the BBC wanted me to lose more to encourage the viewers and potential participants. Making the series was good fun and we had high hopes for the concept, but sadly it hasn't been recommissioned. Because I chose to make *Anything You Can Cook* rather than stay on *This Morning* (yes, I'd been invited back), sadly I haven't got my slot back on *This Morning* either. However, something will turn up, I have no doubt. Television has been very good to me over the last ten or so years, but if my face didn't fit any more, I'd be quite happy concentrating solely on my restaurant, cooking, drinking, socialising and talking. That's enough to keep this Yorkshire lad contented.

Today and Tomorrow

Who would have thought that a chef – once the backroom boy of the hospitality industry – would be a television star, super salesman, singer, stripper, after-dinner speaker and all-round entertainer? Well, I and many of my fellow chefs have become all that in the last ten years or so, and it's astounding.

Chefs, food and cooking are the new rock and roll, so they say, and it's interesting to speculate on how this came about. When I was at catering college in Leeds, my mother seemed nervous of admitting what I was doing, training to be a chef. The profession then was slightly looked down upon, and it was somewhat of a last-ditch solution for (mainly lower-class) people who didn't qualify for something more practical or academic. Now, however, to be a chef, at whatever level, carries some considerable kudos, parents quite happily boast their children are in the food business, and every fashionable restaurant is staffed by kids, cooking and waiting, who sound as if they've been educated at the best and most expensive schools. The whole social ethos has changed. Television

In February 1999, I went back to Morley to cook with present-day pupils for a dinner to celebrate the opening of a new Morley High School building. There's actually a plaque on the wall with my name on it to commemorate this momentous occasion!

and the sheer in-your-face omnipresence of food and cooking have played a considerable part in this, but that's not the whole answer.

I think there are several reasons for our present-day passion for cooking. One, I believe, is our lack, after the war, of a 'gastro culture' in Britain. Other European countries had long-established food traditions, but we had little in a culinary sense to fall back on. After the post-war years of rationing and food shortages, we had much more 'room' than other cultures in which to grow and develop, and this we started to do very rapidly. When travelling abroad on holiday began to be popular in the 1950s and 1960s, we encountered many food influences, brought them back, and absorbed them into our new burgeoning style. Because we had so far to go, we had to catch up quickly, and in some cases I think we've overtaken some of our neighbours. London is now considered by some to be the gastronomic centre of Europe, although personally I don't believe this is the case. It's more to do with that rapid catching up in so short a time.

In tandem with this, chefs began to be more visible. Although I've emphasised elsewhere how much myself and Richard Shepherd were in the vanguard in this respect, I think it was really Silvano Trompetto at the Savoy who began the 'socialisation' of chefs. Escoffier and Carême, and later chefs like Käufeler and Virot, were all names to conjure with, but they remained firmly in their kitchens. Trompetto, however, used to walk round the Grill and River Rooms, in his whites and tall chef's hat, occasionally stopping to talk. He would only stay for a brief time, and it was all very formal, but it was a start, a move towards transforming the perceived role of a chef from tradesman, or 'skivvy' even, to professional. The enthusiastic 'amateurs' mentioned before – the George Perry-Smiths and John Toveys – took the idea further, talking to and moving among the tables, making food and eating out more customer-friendly. The open kitchens of places like the Capital contributed another facet, and in a huge majority of new restaurants opening today you can see and watch the brigade at work. And I think the advent of plate service – where the chef dictates how the food will look on the plate (one of the more valuable legacies of *nouvelle cuisine*) – was influential as well. The chef was now an artist, having come full circle from a lowly role in a subterranean kitchen. I suppose I could be characterised as the end result of that evolution, a chef-patron who cooks, walks round and sits down to chat and drink. In fact, quite often nowadays I leave the cooking in the very capable hands of Jon Jon, and work the room with the restaurant manager, currently the invaluable Louise-Anne Hewitt. I pride myself on going to the door, hanging coats up, answering the telephone, taking orders, then serving. It's very satisfying to be involved in the *whole* business of a restaurant, particularly when it's small, and it's mine!

The BBC *Good Food* Show could be classified as both cause and effect of the new passion for food and cooking. I've demonstrated there for the ten years of its existence, and it has become an amazing phenomenon, now pulling in over 100,000 people in only five days. The BBC, of course, who make programmes with and publish books by chefs and food writers, could see which way the tide was flowing, and it was in their interest to go with it. But entrepreneurs and businessmen played a part, too. Recognising that the culture of gastronomy was about to take off in this country, and helped along by the Press, they have been instrumental in hyping up individual chefs, individual food products and the forums in which both can be combined, such as the Birmingham show. The more popular the chef, the more products associated with him or her can be sold. The crowds are enormous there these days, and I and my peers virtually have to have bodyguards to get round the show. In fact the adulation that we see now is extraordinary. I run the Tesco theatre at the Show, and always have a question and answer session when I interview someone like Gary Rhodes, say, after his cookery slot. In a 150–200-seat theatre, I've seen 600 people, squashed into the aisles, and they queue patiently for hours just to get an autograph or exchange a word with their hero. It's almost like Beatlemania all over again.

Television is inevitably the prime mover in all this, and oddly enough television has actually created some of the more startling personalities involved. Gary Rhodes and Ainsley Harriott are both known for their extravagant deliveries on screen. In real life, though, both are rather restrained, serious men – well, Ainsley can *occasionally* be serious. Once they're on stage, though, they change into something different, becoming 'chef as showman'. But that ability to come across well on screen or on stage is the mark of a particular type of personality, and a chef who doesn't look or sound right will never make it on television, however highly regarded his cooking might be. It's the young people of today who worry me. A lot of the catering students I meet are interested only in the business because they foresee stardom and a glittering career in television. I can't

At the height of the BSE scare and beef ban, I was photographed with the Deputy Agriculture Minister, Joyce Quin. Via Eurostar from Waterloo, I was taking a platter of British beef to a lunch hosted in Brussels by the Meat and Livestock Commission.

count the number of times I've reiterated that not only do you need the right sort of personality and looks, you also need the skills and the knowledge. There are of course very young lads who have recently made it big – James Martin and Jamie Oliver among them – but in general there's nothing quite like experience to carry you through any crisis, whether in the kitchen, in front of a camera, or in life itself.

I've recently become chairman of the UK Hospitality Skills Board, taking over from Prue Leith, and I think it is a very important and vital institution. A tenth of our workforce in the UK is in the hospitality industry, but we live in a time when people are being de-skilled. Restaurants are opening in their hundreds every month, and yet ludicrously the business is in a downward spiral as far as training is concerned. It's essential that students are taught properly, are encouraged and instilled with confidence about their skills.

It's that experience, too, as well as the stardom, that has led chefs to fulfil even more worthwhile roles. I believe that so-called 'personality' chefs and food writers are having a very great influence on farmers, suppliers, food producers and retailers. Because of our greater visibility, the people who actually grow, produce and import our food are listening to what chefs have to say, and to what they're looking for. People like us, who know so much about food, can only bring positive benefits. Thus the trend for chefs and food writers to be consultants and advisors to supermarkets has grown – among them Delia with Sainsbury's; myself, Rick Stein, Anton Edelmann of the Savoy and Paul Gayler of the Lanesborough, all with Tesco.

Chefs have also become great ambassadors for this country, and for its culture and lifestyle. Television has contributed to this again, but many chefs are actually travelling to other parts of the world to demonstrate how and what we are cooking in Britain. John Tovey used to do this in the 1970s and 1980s, well ahead of the rest of us, but I, too, have been all over the world in the last few years. I've cooked in hotels doing promotions for Turner's, British Airways, Food from Britain and also for the hotels themselves, among them the Mandarin Orientals in Hong Kong and Jakarta, the Hotel Saint-Geran in Mauritius, the Peach Tree Club in Atlanta, and those hotels in Bermuda. I've cooked in the British Embassy in Berlin, and on the QE2, and this year I'm off again to Mauritius, South Africa and back to Yorkshire. Travelling is another of the great benefits cooking and 'fame' have brought me.

My own first priority, however, is still the teaching of young people through my meetings with catering students and the school project, Adopt-a-School, run

Turner attempts to teach schoolchildren all about taste at an Adopt-a-School session, with Michael Coaker of the Mayfair Intercontinental in attendance.

Fillet of Beef on Roasted Vegetables with Fondant Potatoes and Madeira Sauce

SERVES 4

This recipe offers a complete meal in itself, serving the best beef in the world – British, of course – with good old-fashioned root vegetables and a classic Madeira sauce. If you tend to be a well-done meat person, just try the beef a little under-done. I'm sure you will be pleasantly surprised.

4 x 140g (5 oz) beef fillet steaks

1 tablespoon olive oil

225g (8 oz) carrots, peeled

115g (4 oz) each of parsnips, swede and celeriac, peeled

12 button onions, peeled

450g (1 lb) duck fat

2 heads garlic, cut in half

1 sprig fresh thyme

salt and freshly ground black pepper

4 sprigs fresh chervil

Fondant potatoes

1 large baking potato, peeled

115g (4 oz) *Clarified Butter (see page 239)*

To serve

425ml (¾ pint) *Madeira Sauce (see page 152)*

4 tablespoons *Beurre Blanc (see page 239)*

Preheat the oven to 150°C/300°F/Gas 2. Pour the oil over the fillet steaks, turn them over and leave while you prepare and cook the vegetables.

Cut the carrots, parsnips, swede and celeriac into 1cm (½ in) dice, and the button onions in half. Melt the duck fat in a deep roasting tray, and add the halves of garlic head, the thyme and all the vegetables. Roast in the preheated oven for 45 minutes.

Meanwhile, prepare the fondant potatoes. Cut 4 slices 1cm (½ in) thick from the potato to make ovals roughly the same shape as the steaks. Trim with a sharp knife to bevel the edges. Put into a small ovenproof dish with enough clarified butter to come halfway up the potato.

Remove the vegetables from the oven, strain through a colander, and leave to rest in the colander. Remove the garlic and thyme. Turn the oven up to 200–220°C/400–425°F/Gas 6–7.

Bake the fondant potatoes in the hot oven for about 30–40 minutes, or until golden. Remove from the oven and drain carefully. When the vegetables have rested, drain their fat off carefully. (If you pass the duck fat and clarified butter separately through fine sieves, they can be used again.)

Reduce the oven to the lower temperature again. Put both potatoes and vegetables into the low oven to keep warm. Check the seasoning. Preheat the grill or ridged cast-iron griddle pan.

Place the steaks on the preheated griddle or under the grill, and cook them on both sides until done as you like them. Put to one side to rest for a few minutes.

To serve, place a 7.5cm (3 in) metal ring in the middle of each hot plate (or use it in turn). Pile the reheated vegetables in the middle of the ring, then lay a potato slice on top. Squeeze down to hold the shape, then carefully remove the ring. Season the steaks quickly, and arrange on top of the circle of vegetables. Pour Madeira sauce around each little tower, and decorate with the *beurre blanc*.

by the Academy of Culinary Arts. I was also Chief Examiner for the City and Guilds Advanced Cookery Kitchen and Larder diplomas for three years. I think that with all this publicity and exposure, chefs should be a good example to youngsters, to help ensure the future of the industry and the credibility of the British cooking scene. Lately, bullying and viciousness in some professional kitchens have been exposed and highlighted in the Press and on television. This reflects badly on the industry, perhaps even discouraging some potential recruits, which is a great shame. Professional kitchens are indeed places of great stress, the hours are incredibly long, and tempers can flare, but really bad behaviour is rare. Most kitchens – although far from calm – are run on teamwork, and a bully would find it difficult to create and maintain that team ethos. I think it's important, when you're in the public eye, that you are very careful about what you do and say. You can have fun and express your personality, but there are certain barriers you must not pass.

However, that said, I must admit to passing a few personal barriers I never dreamed I would or could. This year I ran in the London Marathon in aid of The Food Chain (a registered charity in the Greater London area, which delivers specially prepared, nutritionally balanced meals to people with HIV and AIDS, their carers and dependants, every Sunday). If you'd said ten years ago that I'd be running twenty-six miles, I'd have laughed at you. (Actually, even a year ago would have brought a dis-believing guffaw.) But I'd have laughed even more if you had suggested I was going to sing in front of seventeen million viewers, and then three years later do a full strip on television! It was

I went to the Canaries for a few days to train for the London Marathon. Here I look quite fit, I think.

all to do with Children in Need, and the annual television marathon to raise money. People at the charity came up with the idea that four chefs, known as the Four Chops, would sing a Four Tops number, 'I can't help myself...' Gary, Antony, Ainsley and I dressed up in red sequin suits, with red shoes and white socks, slicked our hair back, and sang and danced to a tape we'd pre-recorded. There were about 500 people in the audience, but there was also that enormous number watching at home. It was terrifying, but Barry Manilow, who was also on the bill, said we had stolen the show. We did it once again at the BBC *Good Food* Show a few weeks later, again for charity, and this time in front of a live audience of 3,000!

If you thought we couldn't top that, well you'd be mistaken. Fern Britton mentioned to the producer of the Children in Need programme the idea of a '*Full Monty*' striptease. Five of us this time – myself, Antony, Ainsley, James Martin and Tony Tobin – agreed to reveal our all for the cause. We rehearsed all afternoon, helped by Nikki, the choreographer who'd advised the Four Chops as well. When it was time to actually perform live, it was just like another

The chefs of yesteryear would turn in their graves, as the chefs of today – from left, Ainsley Harriott, James Martin, myself, Tony Tobin and Antony Worrall Thompson – take their clothes off in a burlesque Full Monty. *It was in aid of charity, though, for Children in Need.*

rehearsal, and it was over in minutes. We came off set so excited, so high – I now understand how pop singers feel, pumped up with adrenaline – that we went straight up to the bar and performed our striptease three more times! The publicity people had hyped the act up so well that they received more telephone pledges in an hour than ever before or since, and raised a spectacular amount of money (and they showed the film of it again on the programme the next year).

Then, as before, we decided we'd take the '*Full Monty*' to the BBC *Good Food* Show. We had to rehearse again, this time taking into consideration the fact that there were no cameras to pan in and show what's what, we had to do it for real, and rely on lights being dimmed at the most opportune moment. That was OK, but when we ran 'naked' off stage to collect our dressing-gowns, four of them had been stolen and we couldn't take a proper bow. It was great fun, but I think that's it for me now. Quit when you're ahead…

Or so I thought. As I wrote these last words, a press release headed 'CELEBRITY CHEF KIDNAPPED' came in from Beefeater, the restaurant chain I work with. 'Women all over the country are sneaking celebrity chef, Brian Turner, into their bedrooms. But this is no ordinary Brian Turner. Life-sized cut-outs of Brian which are being used in Beefeater restaurants have been disappearing as fast as they are being put up. In excess of seventy of the cut-outs have been stolen from the 256 branches nationwide. The highest percentage of disappearances have come from restaurants in the Yorkshire area, presumably because people there feel closer to Brian as he is a Yorkshireman himself.' They're apparently offering an amnesty on the return of kidnapped Brians, but who would have thought that being a chef would have turned me into a sex symbol! It's actually very flattering to think that so many women trust my advice that they want to take me home as well…

Cooking over these thirty-five years or so has given me an opportunity to do many wonderful things (not including taking my clothes off in public). The down-side of all this is that, despite being married for over twenty-five years and having two wonderful sons, I haven't seen my family as much as I would have liked. But I've travelled, I've met many new friends, and been enabled to keep in touch with old friends, and I've become very familiar with the medium of television. I'm now being asked to do after-dinner speaking (the money is fantastic), and because I don't think I'm very good at it, I'm hoping to take lessons from Lance Percival and another friend. As people at grand dinners sup their port and light their cigars, I'm going to tell them some of the stories I've written here. In fact, I'm going to be a very boring old man, telling and retelling the same stories (and a few which I'll save for another time). I've come a long way in those three to four decades – not bad for a Yorkshire lad!

I've done it! Contrary to all expectations, I ran my twenty-six miles in the 2000 London Marathon, and was one of thirty-four runners raising money for The Food Chain, an HIV and Aids charity.

basic recipes

Wild Mushroom Duxelles
MAKES ABOUT 350G (12 OZ)

This flavourful mixture can be used in a Beef Wellington, and for stuffing artichoke hearts. If let down with white wine and cream it makes a good sauce; if let down with stock and cream it makes a good soup. The method is exactly the same for ordinary mushrooms: use 450g (1 lb) white button mushrooms instead of the wild mushrooms. I often add 55g (2 oz) diced ham to the latter mixture to use as a stuffing for meat dishes.

> 55g (2 oz) unsalted butter
>
> 115g (4 oz) shallots, peeled and finely chopped
>
> 450g (1 lb) wild mushrooms (we use shiitake, oyster, trompettes and morels in no particular ratio)
>
> 1 tablespoon lemon juice
>
> 1 tablespoon chopped fresh parsley
>
> salt and freshly ground black pepper

Melt the butter in a large pan, and sweat the chopped shallot for 2 minutes. Do not colour.

Finely chop the mushrooms or pass through a food processor. Add to the butter and shallot, along with the lemon juice. Cook the mushrooms until all the liquor has evaporated, stirring regularly. When the mushroom mixture is dry, add the parsley, season with salt and pepper, and remove to a bowl to cool.

Beurre Blanc

MAKES 300ML (½ PINT)

A tasty and rich butter and cream emulsion that can be used to dress vegetables served as an accompaniment, or as a decoration on dishes served with a brown sauce (see page 233).

2 shallots, peeled and finely chopped

175g (6 oz) unsalted butter, cut into cubes

50ml (2 fl oz) *White Chicken Stock* (see page 243)

75ml (2½ fl oz) dry white wine

1 tablespoon white wine vinegar

50ml (2 fl oz) double cream

salt and freshly ground black pepper

juice of ½ lemon

Sweat the shallot in 25g (1 oz) of the butter to soften, but not to colour. Add the chicken stock, wine and wine vinegar, and simmer to reduce by half. Add the double cream, and boil until thickened. Remove from the heat.

Whip in the remaining butter cubes quickly but carefully. Bring back to the boil, season and add lemon juice. Strain and use.

Clarified Butter

Cut 450g (1 lb) of butter, preferably unsalted, into cubes and put into a heavy-based pan. Bring to the boil, turn down the heat and simmer for 3 minutes to melt. Leave to settle and cool for 10 minutes. Strain through muslin, taking care to leave behind the sediment at the bottom of the pan. This will leave a golden clear liquid which will cook at a higher temperature than normal butter.

Meat Stocks
MAKES ABOUT 4.5 LITRES (8 PINTS)

Throughout my cooking career from the Savoy until today, I have fervently believed that stock-making and sauce-making are the essential building blocks of great cooking. Today this may not seem to be quite so important, but I still have my views and stick to them quite strictly. All the cooks and chefs that have passed through my hands have been fed the same philosophy, so I hope my ideas have stood the test of time.

It is imperative that a stockpot is seen as a producer of the finest flavours from the freshest meats, vegetables, herbs and spices possible. It should not be a receptacle for goods that are on their way out, using the stockpot rather like a dustbin (although we do use the skins and seeds of tomatoes chopped for *concassé*). If you use fresh vegetables and bones you can, with love, care and attention, end up with a delicately flavoured stock that will eventually give body and character to your final dish without either masking or destroying it. With this in mind I have written here exactly how we at Turner's make basic stocks, some of which take us over three days (well, we don't *cook* them for that time, but we don't end up with the product we need until three days later). This need not be the way you approach stock, but I urge you to have a go. Especially in autumn and winter, may I suggest that you keep bones in the freezer until you have enough to make a stock.

Once made and cooked, store the stock in small plastic cups, preferably with lids, and then freeze for use as and when. (If you run out of containers, decant the frozen block into a freezer bag, releasing the container for further use.)

A veal stock is the cornerstone of every professional kitchen, and that is the one I would usually choose, but the same principle applies to dark stocks of beef, lamb and pork, which are made in exactly the same way. If all this is really too impractical for you, just reconstitute the relevant stock cube (vegetable, chicken, fish etc.) in water, add some wine, garlic, tomatoes and fresh vegetables, and allow to simmer gently for about an hour. Strain and use. It's good, but not quite the real McCoy.

Stage 1	Stage 2	Stage 3
4.5kg (10 lb) raw meat bones, chopped	900g (2 lb) raw meat bones	2 carrots, peeled and minced
15 litres (26 pints) water	a little groundnut oil	4 shallots, peeled and minced
1 leek, trimmed	1 onion, peeled and chopped	1 bunch fresh rosemary
2 carrots, peeled	1 leek, trimmed and chopped	
2 onions, peeled	1 carrot, trimmed and chopped	
1 x 400g (14 oz) tin plum tomatoes	1 head garlic, halved	
½ bunch fresh thyme	55g (2 oz) tomato purée	
	1 litre (1¾ pints) white wine	

For the basic meat stock, stage 1, put the bones into a stockpot, cover with the water, and bring up to the boil. Skim off all the scum, then add the vegetables, tomatoes and thyme. Bring back to the boil, then simmer for 3 hours, skimming regularly. Sieve, cool, then refrigerate. Remove any solid fat.

To enrich the flavour of the basic stock, stage 2, brown the meat bones in a little oil in the stockpot. Add the vegetables and garlic, and colour lightly. Add the tomato purée, stir in and cook for 3–4 minutes. Pour in the white wine and the basic meat stock, and simmer for 2½ hours, skimming regularly. Sieve, cool and refrigerate. Remove any solid fat.

To intensify the flavour of the stock, stage 3, bring it back to the boil, add the minced carrots and shallots and the rosemary, and simmer for about an hour. Pass through a sieve, and allow to cool, or continue boiling to reduce to the taste and flavour you want and need. The stock will also acquire a good rich dark colour.

Thickened Stock

Where a recipe calls for a thickened stock, I recommend the use of potato flour or fécule, which you should be able to find in good supermarkets. (If not, use cornflour.) Slake (mix) 1 dessertspoon flour in 25ml (1 fl oz) white wine per 600ml (1 pint) stock needed in a recipe.

Fish Stock

MAKES 2.25 LITRES (4 PINTS)

1.8kg (4 lb) fish bones (sole, turbot, brill and halibut)

1 medium onion, peeled

3 celery stalks, trimmed

1 whole leek, trimmed

55g (2 oz) unsalted butter

1 bay leaf

3 parsley stalks

6 black peppercorns

175ml (6 fl oz) white wine

4.5 litres (8 pints) water

juice of ½ lemon

Clean and wash the fish bones, removing any blood and roes, and drain them well. Chop them. Chop the vegetables into small rough dice.

Melt the butter in a heavy-based pan, add the vegetables, herbs and peppercorns, and sweat slowly for 5 minutes. Do not colour. Add the chopped fish bones and sweat for 5 minutes. Pour in the white wine and cold water, bring up to the boil, then skim off any scum. Add the lemon juice, and simmer for 25 minutes.

Strain through muslin, and reduce by boiling to the required flavour.

Vegetable Stock
MAKES ABOUT 2.25 LITRES (4 PINTS)

2 large onions, peeled

4 carrots, trimmed

2 leeks, trimmed

1 head celery

6 black peppercorns

½ teaspoon salt

1 bay leaf

1 bunch parsley stalks

4.5 litres (8 pints) water

Cut the cleaned vegetables into large and rough shapes. Put into a large saucepan with the rest of the ingredients. Bring to the boil and simmer for 1½ hours.

Strain, check for seasoning and taste. Reduce further if needed to concentrate flavours. Cool and use.

White Chicken Stock
MAKES ABOUT 2.25 LITRES (4 PINTS)

3 raw chicken carcasses

2 onions, peeled

2 leeks, trimmed

4 celery stalks

4.5 litres (8 pints) water

6 black peppercorns

1 bay leaf

6 parsley stalks

Chop the carcasses and put into a large saucepan. Chop the onions, leeks and celery and add to the pan. Cover with the water and bring up to the boil. Skim off the scum, add the peppercorns and herbs and simmer for 1½ hours. Strain and leave to cool. Remove the excess fat from the top. If the taste is not as strong as you wish, reduce over heat until more concentrated.

Brown Chicken Stock

Sauté the carcasses and vegetables in a little groundnut oil to colour first, then proceed as for the white chicken stock.

index